P9-ECV-070

NICOLAS BERDYAEV:

Captive of Freedom

NICOLAS BERDYAEV: *Captive of Freedom*

MATTHEW SPINKA
Waldo Professor of Church History
The Hartford Theological Seminary

Philadelphia
THE WESTMINSTER PRESS

PRINTED IN THE UNITED STATES OF AMERICA

Contents

Preface

I OWE to Nicolas Alexandrovich Berdyaev a great debt of gratitude. For almost thirty years I have read his writings with increasing interest and profit as they appeared from the presses in Prague, Berlin, and Paris. In course of time I also secured his earlier works published in Russia. I was drawn to him by the attractiveness and force of his thought, for he "spoke to my condition." He taught me much: among other things, the nature of our civilization, the liberating character of the philosophy of personalism, and the value of mysticism as mediated by the great masters of both East and West. Without accepting all his views, I bear testimony that he has helped me to understand the significance of human destiny—the greatest service any human being can render to his fellows.

The book is an attempt to pay the debt I owe; but it was written also in the hope that the synthesis of his thought and its interpretation might render the same service to the reader that Berdyaev had rendered to me.

I have tried to be critical as well as appreciative. My aim has been to present in as brief a form as I could the main points of Berdyaev's total world view. Since he was primarily a religious philosopher, it seemed necessary to set forth his existentialism. Although my treatment of this subject, written in as nontechnical terms as possible, is by no means exhaustive, I trust that it is nevertheless adequate. But my chief concern has been to expound Berdyaev's basic faith, the faith he lived by. I believe this to be the first such attempt that takes into consideration his entire literary activity extending over nearly half a century.

Furthermore, although Berdyaev never claimed to be an exponent of the official Russian Orthodoxy, yet in the West he has become the best-known representative of the Russian religious renascence. Therefore, he deserves to be better known and understood, not only for the intrinsic importance of his thought, but also for the value that such knowledge may have for the growing Christian ecumenicity. Moreover, in view of our Western preoccupation with natural science and technology, it is exactly the intuitive, existential emphasis that our rationalistic, mechanistic, secularized culture needs.

Berdyaev wrote almost exclusively in Russian. Although practically all his major works published after his exile are available in translation, those published prior to 1922 are not. I have purposely quoted extensively from the nontranslated works in order to make such passages available. Moreover, I have likewise used the original text by preference even when translations were at hand. Among all Berdyaev's books, his "philosophical autobiography," which was published in Paris during the summer of 1949, proved of the greatest value for the understanding of his personality as well as of his thought. For that reason I have made an extensive use of it.

In this connection I gratefully acknowledge the kindness of the Y. M. C. A. Press in Paris, which since 1922 has published practically all Berdyaev's major works in Russian, in granting me the permission to quote from these writings. Furthermore, I am glad to make a similar acknowledgment of permissions to quote from the translations of Berdyaev's works, or from other publications, accorded me by the following American firms: Charles Scribner's Sons; Sheed & Ward, Inc.; Morehouse-Gorham Company, Inc.; Harper & Brothers; The Devin-Adair Company; Random House, Inc.; The Macmillan Company; The International Council of Religious Education; The Westminster Press; and the English publishing house of Geoffrey Bles, Ltd., and the International Review of Missions. All quoted materials are fully identified in the Notes and Bibliography of this book.

Moreover, it gives me great pleasure to extend my thanks for the active interest he has shown in my undertaking to Professor David E. Roberts, of Union Theological Seminary, and for the help rendered me by Professor George P. Fedotov, of St. Vladimir Orthodox Theological Seminary, as well as for the encouragement and aid I received from my erstwhile colleague, Professor Karl Löwith, at present of The New School for Social Research. Furthermore, I express my sincere appreciation to Professor Ford Lewis Battles for his most valuable stylistic improvements which he rendered in the final revision of the text.

MATTHEW SPINKA

The Hartford Theological Seminary,
October 8, 1949

PART ONE

THE WORLD BERDYAEV REVOLTED AGAINST

1

Up from Marxism

Our age lacks a sense of awe and mystery; therefore, it is in revolt against God and his order. For the first time in history this revolt is, at least in some measure, aggressive and militant. It is not quite correct to call it neopagan except with an apology to the genuine pagan antiquity. For, after all, pagans believed in gods. In fact, they accused the early Christians of atheism—for not believing in enough gods. Therefore, if the modern revolt against God be paganism, it is for the first time an atheistic paganism. Our age is disintegrating because of its inner sterility. During the Renaissance man asserted himself only to discover the truth which Dostoevsky knew so well, that to assert oneself is to destroy oneself. The modern autonomous man, in his revolt against God, is destroying himself. For he has failed to learn the truth proclaimed by One greater than Dostoevsky, that to lose one's life for His sake is to find it. Man has repudiated this axiom, and has sought to find his life in an autonomy which, at the worst, has resulted in the loss of his personality, and at the best, in a romantic humanism which is but secularized Christian ethic. The whole proud culture of the Renaissance, particularly its systems of economics and politics, was founded on the shifting sands of individual self-assertion, in the fatuous belief that the sum total of individual selfishness would somehow add up to common good. As the men of the mythical past aspired to build a tower that would reach the very heaven, but found themselves dispersed because of confusion of tongues, so the men of today, having built a tower infinitely greater than that of Babel, see the proud structure crashing to the ground. Their tongues

too became confused, so that there is no co
among them. There is no unity of culture,
loyalty which would provide cohesion to t
sand of which our modern society is built. I
upon itself and has become antihumanis
Chronos, it is devouring its own children.
the modern world" is antithetical to the fier
tion of freedom with which the age began
veritable slave to his class, to the leviatha
talitarian state, and to the technology whi
ingly developed mechanical skill has create
nority really desire freedom and are willin
vast majority of men prefer security. The
creation of Dostoevsky's brain — the Grand
quered: men will gladly live by bread alon
for them is hunger. They prefer "short
economic, political, and cultural schemes
than the spiritual transformation of themsel
their leader any megalomaniac who will pr
things will I give thee if thou wilt fall dow
The age of individualism appears to have c
end; we perhaps stand on the threshold of a
tic collectivism.

It is against this dark background that th
Berdyaev must be understood. The decad
world, which he saw with uncanny clarity
scribed with stark realism, called forth his r
in revolt against the world in revolt agai
ever felt himself a stranger in this seculari
longed for a transformed world. Like Goeth
it would cost him his soul were he to say to
longer! thou art fair!" Just because he learn
radical movements of our times and analy
man "on the inside" could, he was merci
about them. He arrived, after an intense stru
passionately opposed to modern secularism

1

Up from Marxism

OUR AGE lacks a sense of awe and mystery; therefore, it is in revolt against God and his order. For the first time in history this revolt is, at least in some measure, aggressive and militant. It is not quite correct to call it neopagan except with an apology to the genuine pagan antiquity. For, after all, pagans believed in gods. In fact, they accused the early Christians of atheism—for not believing in enough gods. Therefore, if the modern revolt against God be paganism, it is for the first time an atheistic paganism. Our age is disintegrating because of its inner sterility. During the Renaissance man asserted himself only to discover the truth which Dostoevsky knew so well, that to assert oneself is to destroy oneself. The modern autonomous man, in his revolt against God, is destroying himself. For he has failed to learn the truth proclaimed by One greater than Dostoevsky, that to lose one's life for His sake is to find it. Man has repudiated this axiom, and has sought to find his life in an autonomy which, at the worst, has resulted in the loss of his personality, and at the best, in a romantic humanism which is but secularized Christian ethic. The whole proud culture of the Renaissance, particularly its systems of economics and politics, was founded on the shifting sands of individual self-assertion, in the fatuous belief that the sum total of individual selfishness would somehow add up to common good. As the men of the mythical past aspired to build a tower that would reach the very heaven, but found themselves dispersed because of confusion of tongues, so the men of today, having built a tower infinitely greater than that of Babel, see the proud structure crashing to the ground. Their tongues too became confused, so that there is no common understanding among them. There is no unity of culture, no spiritual center of loyalty which would provide cohesion to the atomistic heap of sand of which our modern society is built. Humanism has turned upon itself and has become antihumanism. Like the ancient Chronos, it is devouring its own children. "The fate of man in the modern world" is antithetical to the fierce and proud affirmation of freedom with which the age began: man has become a veritable slave to his class, to the leviathan of the modern totalitarian state, and to the technology which his own astonishingly developed mechanical skill has created. Today only a minority really desire freedom and are willing to pay its price; the vast majority of men prefer security. The spirit of that greatest creation of Dostoevsky's brain — the Grand Inquisitor — has conquered: men will gladly live by bread alone, for the only reality for them is hunger. They prefer "short cuts to salvation" — economic, political, and cultural schemes of all sorts — rather than the spiritual transformation of themselves; they will hail as their leader any megalomaniac who will promise that "all these things will I give thee if thou wilt fall down and worship me"! The age of individualism appears to have come to its inglorious end; we perhaps stand on the threshold of an era of antihumanistic collectivism.

It is against this dark background that the thought of Nicolas Berdyaev must be understood. The decadence of the modern world, which he saw with uncanny clarity and insight and described with stark realism, called forth his revolt. He was a man in revolt against the world in revolt against God. For he had ever felt himself a stranger in this secularized era; he had ever longed for a transformed world. Like Goethe's Faust, he felt that it would cost him his soul were he to say to any moment: "Stay longer! thou art fair!" Just because he learned to know the most radical movements of our times and analyzed them as only a man "on the inside" could, he was merciless in his judgment about them. He arrived, after an intense struggle, at a world view passionately opposed to modern secularism. This view he identifies with the insights of freely conceived Christianity. He devoted a lifetime to its clarification and exposition.

There is a great deal in his writings and thought that cannot be included within the scope of this work. During almost half a century of an unusually fruitful and productive career, Berdyaev wrote more than thirty books, and countless articles, in which he dealt with a surprisingly wide range of philosophical interests. But I shall restrict myself to his basic tenets, particularly those aspects of his thought which constitute his unique contribution to religious philosophy. Fortunately, these original insights provide the foundation for all else, for he saw the destiny of man and the meaning of the world only in relation to God. Accordingly, the first part of this work deals with Berdyaev's instinctive as well as conscious revolt against the dominant idolatries and slaveries of the era in which he lived; while the second is devoted to his passionate affirmation of freedom and the ways of transforming the world closer to his heart's desire.

Nicolas Alexandrovich Berdyaev came of an aristocratic family.[1] He was born in 1874 in the exclusive suburb of Kiev known as Lipky. On his father's side he was descended from a long line of military men. His grandfather, M. N. Berdyaev, distinguished himself in the Napoleonic wars. According to the family tradition, Lieutenant Berdyaev remained alone in command of his regiment in one of the campaigns of 1814, and his conduct during this engagement is said to have resulted in the defeat of the French Army. He was, of course, lavishly rewarded, and later became the ataman of the Don army. Nicolas' father was an officer in the Imperial Horse Guards—an exclusive, aristocratic regiment. On his mother's side, young Nicolas had a French countess of the ancient family of Choiseul for his grandmother. His mother was a renowned beauty, born Princess Kudasheva. She always remained more than half French; the children were, therefore, brought up in a predominantly French household. Both his father and mother had intimate friends in the court circles of Czar Alexander III. Berdyaev's mother was also related to Polish nobility, the fabulously rich Countess Branicka being her cousin.

Young Nicolas was destined by his family to continue the military tradition of his forebears. He was at first educated in the Corps of Cadets in Kiev, an exclusive school for the training of the future members of the Guards regiment; later he was transferred to the Corps of Pages. But soldiering was distasteful, and even abhorrent, to him. He cordially disliked his fellow cadets, whom he found coarse and stupid. But perhaps his chief reason for leaving the military career was his independent spirit, for he could never submit to formal discipline.

Accordingly, he himself chose his own lifework: he wanted to learn the meaning of life. He really never planned any " career " — least of all an academic career. He had become interested in philosophy unusually early and decided to devote himself to its study. As a child he was not robust (both he and his older brother were subject to nervous disorders) and once he spent a whole year in bed. Under such circumstances much of his education was self-directed or conducted by a private tutor and at all times he was allowed a large amount of freedom. During this time he read philosophy and at the age of fourteen he was reading the works of Schopenhauer, Kant, and Hegel. Among his chief mentors he gratefully acknowledged practically every great mind of the Greek and Western cultures — Plato, Plotinus, Boehme, Kant, Fichte, Schelling, Hegel, Schopenhauer, Nietzsche, Marx, Leontiev, Dostoevsky, Ibsen, Tolstoy, and many others.[2] He particularly stressed the influence of Boehme, Kant, Schopenhauer, Hegel, Marx, Dostoevsky, and Tolstoy. To these great minds he owed much; they all counted at one time or another, but none too much. He never accepted their philosophy wholly, and some of them, like Marx and Tolstoy, he later severely criticized.[3] He never belonged wholly to any party, never wholly identified himself with any " school of thought." He remained aloof all his life, for he could never submit to anyone or anything.

" I never had the experience of living under authority. I did not know it in the family; I did not know authority in school; I did not know it in my philosophical studies; and particularly I did not know authority in religious life. Since my childhood I have decided that I will never enter service and will never subject myself to any authority." [4]

Consequently, throughout his life Berdyaev manifested a marked independence of manners, as well as of thought. In fact, he was not easy to live with. Even his friends discerned a certain aristocratic mien in his conduct which they did not always judge favorably or leniently. He never lost traces of character reminiscent of the feudal seigneur. Despite his repeated emphasis on the spiritual nature of true aristocracy, there remained in his intercourse with others a certain aloofness which set him apart from them.

Along with the majority of his generation, young Berdyaev read the writings of that native revolutionary leader, N. K. Mikhailovsky, who prepared him for the more radical gospel of Karl Marx. In 1904, Berdyaev described this period of awakening social consciousness as follows:

"We belonged to that generation of 1890's that was lifted up by the mighty new wave and engaged in a ceaseless struggle with all the old tendencies. The struggle was waged with the daring and mercilessness of green youth, but with the consciousness of growing strength. We believed implicitly that the future belonged to us. Particularly daringly and hotly have we fought with that veteran of the old orientation and its last mighty representative, N. K. Mikhailovsky. In the heat of polemic we have often been unjust and even rude to that truly remarkable man. . . . [He and] we had but *one* love, although not the same one. [He and] we, like Janus, or the two-headed eagle, looked in different directions but at the same time *our hearts beat as one*. We had but one love — that of freedom; our hearts beat as one — the hearts of the members of the Russian educated classes. And even more than by common love we were bound by a common hate. . . . Later, we left our first teacher [Mikhailovsky] — we outgrew him; but to this day we fight in behalf of the problems raised by him which bring closely together philosophy and life." [5]

Having passed a special examination required for entrance by the University of Kiev, young Berdyaev, after six years of study at the Cadet school, became a student in the department of natural sciences. In the university he came under the sway of Marx (1894), and joined the Social Democratic Party, as the Marxists then chose to call themselves in distinction to the older populist Social Revolutionary Party. He became quite active in the movement, and was invited to read lectures before both the leaders and the rank and file. Because of his precocious philosophical training, he was recognized as being far ahead of his fellow students; moreover, as a " nobleman revolutionary " he enjoyed a certain pre-eminence not accorded to mere plebeians. One is forcibly reminded of the early experiences of so many other great Russian thinkers whose spiritual pilgrimage was similar: Khomyakov, the founder of the native Orthodox theological school, also began his career in the Army, and remained a layman all his life. Tolstoy is another example of a nobleman soldier who later became a philosophical writer; Dostoevsky was originally trained as a military engineer. Vladimir Solovev in his early teens passed through a violent revulsion against religion. Sergius Bulgakov, later Berdyaev's fellow exile in Paris and the head of the Russian Theological Academy there, started his academic career as a Marxist professor of sociology at the Kiev Polytechnic Institute.

But even while under the Marxian influence, Berdyaev adhered to Kantian philosophy and maintained that truth, goodness, beauty, and justice are values independent of outward circumstances; he believed that they determine the revolutionary attitude instead of being determined by it.[6] It was the concern for social justice that won young Berdyaev over to the Marxist camp; under the circumstances in which he found himself in his own aristocratic circle — which he never loved — he rebelled against his own social class and went over to the revolutionaries.[7] He was first arrested, along with many other students, for taking part in a mass demonstration, but the imprisonment lasted only a few days. Later, in 1898, when an older member of the Social Democratic Party, Peter Struve, published a manifesto, Berdyaev was arrested along with one hundred and fifty others, and interned in the Lukyanovsky prison on the outskirts of Kiev. But since the governor general of Kiev, Dragomirov, was a friend of Berdyaev's father, Nicolas was soon transferred to another cell, where he was free to visit other prisoners. He actually presided over some meetings held in the prison court. Within a month he was released, but was forbidden to leave Kiev. However, when the trial was concluded, he was sentenced to deportation for three years. His place of exile was in the northern guberniya of Vologda. Several of his comrades were sent to Siberia. The conditions under which Berdyaev lived in Vologda were not unduly harsh. The governor of the guberniya was a distant relative of Berdyaev's grandfather; accordingly, Nicolas enjoyed a privileged position and treatment. Nevertheless, he was not free.

In his first book, written in exile, *Subjectivism and Individualism in Social Philosophy*,[8] Berdyaev valiantly attempted what so many other "revisionist" Marxists tried to do, namely, to integrate idealistic philosophy into the Marxist system. On the publication of the book Berdyaev was hailed as the leader of the movement to which Bulgakov gave the name "From Marxism to Idealism." Peter Struve, Sergius Bulgakov, and S. L. Frank likewise represented this tendency within Russian Marxism. Struve, in fact, wrote the preface to Berdyaev's work in which he stated his grounds of disagreement with Marx. As the subtitle of the book indicates, and as the author himself asserts in the Foreword, the book is a critique of Mikhailovsky's "subjective sociology." For so young an author (he was only twenty-seven at the time) Berdyaev shows himself exceedingly well versed in all European, particularly German, literature dealing with sociology, psychology, and philosophy. The book gives an impression of having been written by a typical German "*Gelehrte*"; it is as ponderous as a troop of elephants on the march. The author differs from Marx in insisting that only transcendental critical idealism, deriving from Kant, can solve the theoretical aspect of the problem of truth. On the other hand, he sees the greatest contribution of Marx in the idea

"that the relationship of one man to another is determined by his relationship to nature. In other words, it may be said that the social relationships of men are determined by the degrees of their rule over nature. That rule, or ability, we also call productive power. Hence the economic conclusion that the productive power governs all others.

. . . We challenge the enemies of historical materialism to prove not that there is something else in history besides the economic factor — that we ourselves know exceedingly well . . . ; but that the rule of the social man over nature, as the result of his struggle for life, is not the primary source of everything social." [9]

Nevertheless, even during the Marxist period of his life, Berdyaev was not a materialist, nor a positivist. Referring to Auguste Comte in the book mentioned above, he rejected the latter's positivism as a "profoundly reactionary phenomenon," and "as extraordinarily naïve and lacking in all epistemological foundations." In summing up his judgment of Mikhailovsky, Berdyaev claimed that he did "not leave a stone upon a stone" in demolishing Mikhailovsky's system. And yet Berdyaev felt a sense of affinity with the old revolutionary, who defended "in his own way human personality which is dear to us also, thus anticipating in part the point of view of critical philosophy which acknowledges the sanctity of man as an end in himself." [10] In other words, Mikhailovsky defended the philosophy to which Berdyaev himself devoted his entire life.

As a "revisionist Marxist," Berdyaev published several German articles (1899, that is, during the Vologda period) in *Die neue Zeit.* The first of these dealt with "F. A. Lange and the Critical Philosophy in Its Relation to Socialism." This article aroused the interest of the editor of the publication, the veteran German "revisionist," Karl Kautzky. As a result, a correspondence ensued between Kautzky and the young Russian author.

Nevertheless, the inner contradictions of Marxism were not to be overcome by some "revision"; they stubbornly resisted all attempts at harmonization. There can be no freedom without spirit, and dialectical materialism denied the existence of spirit or of any other spiritual realities in their existential sense. Many years later Berdyaev described the struggle he had waged over this contradiction. He wrote:

"That problem disturbed me very much when in my youth, as a Marxist, I wrote my first book, *Subjectivism and Individualism in Social Philosophy*. I even attempted to construct an original proletarian theory of knowledge. I have never been a materialist, and consequently I could not be an orthodox Marxist. I was an idealist in philosophy, and derived my inspiration from Kant and Fichte. Even prior to that period, I had been infatuated with Schopenhauer. For me truth, goodness, beauty, were not relative but positive; they were rooted in the transcendental consciousness. Only the degrees of our comprehension of them were relative. The whole problem consisted in ascertaining what conditions render the psychological apprehension more favorable to the revelation of the transcendental truth. I then thought that the proletariat, as a working and class-conscious group, exploited but at the same time free from the sin of exploitation, possessed the psychological structure that is favorable to the revelation of truth; that in it psychological consciousness, as it were, coincided with the transcendental consciousness. . . . I have since greatly departed from the ideological concepts of my youth." [11]

Even prior to Berdyaev's exile, as well as during that period of strain and stress, Ibsen exerted a decisive influence upon his thinking.[12] For Ibsen taught him to understand personalism. Many years later Berdyaev wrote:

"I cannot reread Ibsen without being moved. He had a tremendous significance for me in the spiritual crisis through which I had passed toward the end of the past century, during the period of my liberation from Marxism. Ibsen intensifies in an extraordinary manner the problem of personality, of creativity, and of spiritual freedom. When one reads Ibsen, one breathes the northern mountain air." [13]

It is fitting to be reminded, in this connection, of the commonplace that Communism is no mere economic theory but an integrated world view, a philosophy of life, a religion. Moreover, Communism is intensely activist, militantly aggressive; the problem for it is not merely to comprehend the world theoretically but to change it. As a doctrinaire religious system it tolerates no "deviations." All modifications, attempts at "revision," no matter how well-meant or how insignificant, are summarily treated as heresies. It has no affinity with the liberal's broad sympathy with divergent viewpoints in religion; rather, it is a rigidly orthodox, literalist, fundamentalist sort of religion. No medieval inquisitor could have had a more sincere horror of heresy than an orthodox Marxist has.

Accordingly, the "heresy-hunting" complex of Berdyaev's orthodox fellow revolutionaries compelled him to part company with them. He saw with grief that there was no more reverence for the dignity of personality among the Marxists than among the most philistine bourgeois. Nor did his fellow Marxists have any more love for freedom of the spirit than the most reactionary procurators of the Russian Holy Governing Synod — even Pobyedonostsev himself, with whom we shall deal later. This growing estrangement became increasingly clear to him even during the Vologda exile, particularly when his article "Struggle for Idealism" (published in *God's World*) was received with marked disapproval on the part of his Marxist comrades. In the end, Berdyaev decided upon one of the most important steps in his spiritual career — upon abandoning that phase of Marxist philosophy which denied the reality and the validity of spiritual values, and hence of personality. Always intrepid and fearless where a principle was involved — and perhaps also not a little contemptuous of "public opinion" — he did not hesitate to break with his erstwhile revolutionary comrades. Henceforth Marx, as an exponent of dialectical materialism, became his lifelong antagonist. He expressed this sentiment in the strongest terms when he dedicated his *Christianity and Class War* "to the memory of the Socialist teacher of my youth, and now my fell enemy, Karl Marx." Not that he repudiated the critique of bourgeois capitalism as essentially formulated by Marx. He continued to regard Marx's diagnosis of social pathology as substantially correct. But he held that Marx prescribed the wrong cure. Of the latter aspect he wrote, "Marxism is, in the last analysis, a lie, because God exists, i.e., a higher power and a source of power exist — a spiritual and not only an economic power." [14] Marxism was right in criticizing the failure of capitalism to realize a just society. But Marxism, in its turn, likewise has failed at that task.

2

From Marxism to Christianity

After his return from the exile in 1901, Berdyaev, then twenty-seven years old, went to Germany. There he entered the University of Heidelberg and during the summer semester attended courses in philosophy under the celebrated neo-Kantian, Professor Wilhelm Windelband. But by that time Berdyaev was no longer a thoroughgoing Kantian. He continued to participate in liberal, revolutionary movements and took part in two congresses at which "The Union of Liberation" party was organized. Members of this liberal political organization were to play an important role in the Provisional Government which held office — although precariously — during the spring and summer of 1917.

Upon his return from Germany, Berdyaev removed, in 1904, to St. Petersburg. It was at about this time or shortly after that he married. For the next two years he edited, in co-operation with Sergius Bulgakov, a review bearing the name *The New Way;* after the demise of this publication, the editors collaborated in another venture in journalism, their new magazine bearing the title *Problems of Life*. The latter periodical represented the viewpoint of the Religious Philosophical Society, which had been organized in that city in 1903. The articles Berdyaev published in this and other journals during the years 1900–1906 enable us to observe the growth of his opinions, religious and philosophical. This was a period of tremendous, indeed fateful, significance for the old czarist Russia, if only men had had eyes to discern the signs of the times. For during this period occurred the First Russian Revolution (1905), the harbinger of the events to come.

The articles published during this time Berdyaev republished in a book entitled *Sub specie aeternitatis.* In them for the first time he turned from idealism to what he called " mystical realism."

> " Idealism was well enough for the initial criticism of Marxism and positivism," he wrote in the above-named book; " but it possessed nothing creative. It is impossible to stop with it. That would be neither realistic nor religious." " I arrive in my articles at God-manhood, the incarnation of the Spirit in society, at the mystical union of love with freedom. From the Marxist pseudo ecumenicity, from the decadent romantic individualism, I arrive at the true ecumenicity of mystical neo-Christianity." [1]

For Berdyaev to arrive at a religious interpretation of life was not the simple matter of accepting the Russian Orthodox Church as his mentor in matters spiritual. What he arrived at was " neo-Christianity." Nor is this surprising. Anyone who knows the condition of the Church during the two centuries prior to the October Revolution, after Peter the Great had made it subservient to his governmental policy, should readily understand that a man of Berdyaev's spirit could not turn to it confidently and unquestioningly. Indeed, he did just the opposite. He denounced the Church as the Government's tool for the subjugation of the people. He asserted that the driving " of the traffickers from God's temple has long been overdue — these traffickers in the shameful trade of religious conscience in the interests of the police." He furthermore passionately charged the Russian Government with responsibility for the religious indifferentism which dominated the educated classes, because the Government had debased religion, " that highest manifestation of spiritual culture, into something repulsive and worthy of rejection." [2]

At a later period, referring to the time of his conversion to " free religion " (rather than to traditional Orthodox Christianity which he, none too justly or critically, identified with the hierarchy), he wrote in terms which one suspects of certain unconscious idealization:

"He who has freely, inwardly, conquered the seductions and temptations of humanism, who has discerned the emptiness of the deification of man, can never, to all the ages of the ages, renounce that freedom which brought him to God; he can never renounce that inward experience which freed him from the devil. The controversy over religious freedom cannot be placed on abstract grounds and be judged statically. I have come to Christ freely, by an inner experience, by the path of freedom. My Christian faith is not a conventional, secondhand faith, inherited traditionally from my forebears. It is a faith wrested by a torturing experience of life, from within, freely. I know no compulsion in my religious life, and have no experience of an authoritarian faith, of an authoritarian religiosity." [3]

Consequently, Berdyaev's spiritual odyssey follows an independent, often devious, and always a lonely path. Yet through all his labyrinthine meanderings there runs, like the saving thread of Ariadne, his basic, surprisingly unfaltering, and constant conviction of man's supreme worth and of his eternal destiny. These convictions appear in his earliest writings and persist, in a developed form, throughout his later works.

During the Petersburg period Berdyaev fell under the bewitching influence of the novelist, D. S. Merezhkovsky, a former Nietzschean, best known in the West by his great historical trilogy, *The Death of the Gods, Leonardo da Vinci,* and *Peter the Great.* But in the end the two men drifted apart to such an extent that Merezhkovsky wrote "coarse articles" about Berdyaev, as the latter bitterly complained. But this was later, in exile. For the time being, Merezhkovsky exerted a potent influence upon Berdyaev, particularly in their common opposition to traditional ascetic Christianity and in the attempt to create a "neo-Christianity." For despite the fact that Berdyaev, in his spiritual autobiography, wrote that "between me on the one hand and Rozanov and Merezhkovsky on the other, there existed an abyss," yet in his own way he too opposed the ascetic, obscurantist type of Orthodoxy.[4] He wanted a Christianity that would synthesize Golgotha with Olympus — religion with culture. "Not only the suffering God who died on the cross calls and draws us, but also the god

Pan, the god of the earthly elements, the god of joyous life, as well as the ancient goddess Aphrodite, the goddess of plastic beauty and of earthly love." Berdyaev held at this stage of his development that the Christianity of the past had revealed only a partial truth. Theologians of the Church were too narrow in their outlook to perceive in the ancient pagan gods "different masks" of the eternal God. To effect the synthesis of the two religious insights was the task of the new religious movement.[5] Historic Christianity exhibited only the negative, ascetic half of the religion of Christ, which was the religion of life abundant, and not of death, as Merezhkovsky thought. It "understood heaven as the rejection of the earth and the spirit as the rejection of the flesh." This dualism has "poisoned life, has turned the world into total sinfulness. And the life of the world goes on its own way, justifying itself with sanctity that is not Christian. The sexual life, the social life, all the brilliance of the world of culture, of art and science, have ranged themselves at the opposite pole, having repudiated the religious interpretation of historic Christianity."[6] The new religious orientation, Berdyaev insisted, desires to bring about "religious sanctification of life, of universal culture, a new holy love, sanctified social life, holy 'flesh,' transformed 'earth.'" "It appears that it is not only possible to love heaven and earth at the same time; it is not possible, according to Christ's teaching, to love them separately."[7]

Nevertheless, Berdyaev resolutely opposed Vasily Rozanov's crude naturalism: he asserted in his autobiography that in Rozanov's conflict with Christianity he — Berdyaev — was on the side of Christianity. For Rozanov, who justified all natural desires of the flesh on the ground that they were natural, may be regarded as the Russian D. H. Lawrence. Berdyaev, who for strictly personal reasons repudiated all sexual functions, could by no stretch of the imagination be classified, in this regard, along with Rozanov. Berdyaev concluded that there is both good and evil in the flesh, or rather that the good and evil categories apply to the ways in which flesh is used. Accordingly, there is need for asceticism: we must conquer the waywardness of the flesh, but cultivate and develop its positive elements. Nevertheless, asceticism in the sense of a complete denial of the flesh is in his view "not our religion: the spirit in which all 'yea' is overcome by a vast 'nay' is in opposition to the new religious consciousness." One does not find it possible to be too hard on Berdyaev at this stage of his development.

In another article, written the following year (1906), Berdyaev still criticized the Russian Church in a way familiar to us Americans, brought up in the nurture and admonition of the "social gospel," for its emphasis upon the otherworldly, ascetic aspects of Christianity, and for its lack of emphasis upon the cultural and social implications of religion. But his tone was already changing; he now definitely chose the path of religious transformation of human personality.

"We do not aim to invent a new religion," he writes, "but to reveal the only eternal religion in new religious creativeness. Christianity alone cannot save us; not because it is a lie but because it is an incomplete truth, not integrating into itself all the fullness of our experience and of our desires, because in it truth is revealed only in part, although it is very important and central, but still only in part. Christianity, considered in its historical relations and limitations, does not yet possess positive social truth, does not comprise in itself all the wealth of culture dear to us. It has the God-man, but not yet Godmanhood. Historical Christianity, ascetic, flesh-denying, is individualistic; it speaks only of individual, otherworldly salvation. One cannot find in it this-worldly truth, salvation for all, transformation of the earth and of the earthly flesh. The religion of Christ is the central point of universal history, and makes possible the apprehension of the meaning of history. But Christianity has remained torn away from this meaning of history — as if everything great in history did not exist for it — all cultural creativity, all dreams of social transformation of the earth. The meaning of the religious crisis which overshadows contemporary humanity — although it has not yet been recognized by many — consists in this: that it is not possible to rest satisfied either with the old, ascetic, flesh-denying, nonsocial and noncultural religion, nor with the new, although already senescent, secular nonreligion. . . . The Comforter Spirit, promised by Christ, has plainly not yet descended upon human society; the body of humanity has not yet become theanthropic — a holy humanity and a holy culture, possessing an endless fullness of being. Christian ascetics have gained salvation for themselves by individual ascetic feats and have prayed for the sins of the world; but we are still awaiting the coming of social, cultural, and universal righteousness.

"We may further raise the question: Has there been up to the present time a true Church in a historic embodiment? Was not religion merely individual in its truth? . . . The sins of the Church against the earthly truth, against culture and freedom, are astounding, almost unbearable. The old Church cannot assimilate new social virtues; a new, living spirit cannot be breathed into her by compelling her to acknowledge the benefits of the Constitution and of the eight-hour working day — that would be mechanical, almost positivistic. A new mysticism, which has long been seeping through from the depths up, must flood the earth, and a new love must flame up in the body of humankind. . . . Our task is to hasten the coming of the organic religious period which will conquer the rationalistic abstractions and atomization, and will unite into a higher unity the torn spirit of humanity." [8]

But this represents only a transitional period in Berdyaev's spiritual career. The influence of the great Russian religious philosophers, Khomyakov, Dostoevsky, and Vladimir Solovev, in the end outweighed that of Merezhkovsky and his coterie. Berdyaev himself asserted that in "his conversion to Christianity, the legend of 'The Grand Inquisitor' of Dostoevsky was of the greatest importance." [9] Ever since childhood he had loved Dostoevsky and had an unrivaled insight into the spirit of the great novelist who used his books as means to express his own understanding of Christianity. In the Foreword of his book on Dostoevsky, Berdyaev confessed:

"Dostoevsky has had a decisive significance for my spiritual life. While I was still a youth, I received a grafting from Dostoevsky. He shook my soul more than any other writer or philosopher has done. I have always divided people into Dostoevskyites and those to whom his spirit is foreign. The very early direction of my consciousness toward philosophical problems is bound up with Dostoevsky's 'cursed questions.' He reveals to me some new aspect of himself every time I read him. The theme of the legend of 'The Grand Inquisitor' fell into my soul in youth with penetrating sharpness. My turning to Jesus Christ for the first time was a turning to the image of Christ in the legend." [10]

Berdyaev's estimate of the influence that Dostoevsky has exercised upon him is by no means exaggerated. His writings bear abundant testimony to it. The legend of " The Grand Inquisitor " is mentioned repeatedly; its conception of Christianity as utter spiritual freedom, to which every form of external compulsion, wielded either by God or man, is foreign, is absolutely basic and axiomatic for Berdyaev's way of thinking. If he became the philosopher of freedom par excellence, it is because he had made Dostoevsky's central concept his own, and had since spent a lifetime in elaborating it by applying it to every aspect of life and thought.

Perhaps the legend is familiar to most readers; if not, it must be read in its proper setting in the novel *The Brothers Karamazov,* or, better still, in the perspective of Dostoevsky's whole thought. I regard it as the most inspired piece of writing in modern literature. Its profundity is almost inexhaustible; its moving quality is not even approached elsewhere. Let us examine it in Dostoevsky's own words.

The locale of the legend is laid in medieval Seville; it opens on a splendid *auto da fé* in the public square in which all the population of the city was gathered. Then suddenly, unobserved, Christ appeared among them. All recognized him and thronged about him, while he extended his hand over them in blessing. He approached the cathedral just as a sad little procession was nearing it: mourners carrying an open white coffin in which lay a seven-year-old girl. The mother, encouraged by the crowd, threw herself at his feet, imploring his help. And he, as of old, again spoke his " Talitha cumi." The little girl opened her eyes, sat up, and wonderingly looked at the flowers in her hand.

The scene had been observed from a distance by the ninety-year-old Grand Inquisitor. He frowned and motioned his guards with an imperious gesture that they should take Him. The crowd, cowed, fell back. The guards took their Prisoner and threw him into the dungeon of the Palace of the Inquisition.

That night the old Inquisitor called upon his Prisoner and spoke, while the latter answered not a word in return:

"Why hast thou come to interfere with us? For thou knowest that thou hast come to interfere with us. But knowest thou what will happen tomorrow? . . . Tomorrow I shall condemn thee and burn thee at the stake as the worst of heretics."

The old man then charged his Prisoner with the folly of rejecting the beneficent offers of "the wise and dread spirit" in the wilderness. The spirit had said on that occasion:

"Thou wouldst go into the world with empty hands, offering men some kind of freedom which they, in their simplicity and natural licentiousness, cannot even comprehend and which they fear and dread — for there has never been anything at any time more insufferable for man and the human society than freedom! But seest thou these stones in the barren wilderness glowing with heat? Turn them into bread and humankind will run after thee like a flock, grateful and obedient, although ever trembling lest thou withdraw thy hand and thy bread cease! But thou didst not desire to deprive man of his freedom, and therefore thou hast rejected the offer; for what kind of freedom is it, thou hast thought to thyself, where the obedience is bought with bread? Thou hast replied that man does not live by bread alone. But knowest thou that in the name of that earthly bread the spirit of the earth shall rise up against thee and shall attack and vanquish thee? And all shall follow him, shouting: 'Who is like unto this beast? for he has given us fire from heaven!' Knowest thou that ages shall pass and mankind shall proclaim by the lips of its wise men and scientists that there is no crime, and consequently no sin; there are only the hungry? They shall write on their banners: 'Feed them, and then expect virtue of them!' . . . We alone shall feed them in thy name, lying that it is in thy name! . . . In the end, they shall lay their freedom at our feet and shall say to us: 'Make us slaves, but feed us!'"

Passing on to the second "temptation," the old Inquisitor continued:

"Thou didst desire man's free love, that he should freely follow thee, being fascinated and captivated by thee. Instead of the rigid, ancient law, man should decide for himself with free heart what is good and what is evil, having only thy image before him as his example. . . . Thou didst hope that man, following thee, would remain satisfied with God alone and need no miracle. But hast thou not known that as soon as man rejects miracle, he rejects at the same time God? For man seeks not so much God as a miracle. . . . We have corrected thy feat, and based it upon *miracle, mystery, and authority*. And men rejoiced that they were again led like a flock and that at last there was lifted from their hearts that terrible gift which had brought them such tortures. . . . Why hast thou come to interfere with us? . . . We are not with thee, but have gone over to *him* — that is our mystery! We have left thee long ago and have gone over to *him* — eight centuries ago!

"Why hast thou rejected the last offer? If thou hadst accepted the third counsel of the mighty spirit, thou wouldst have accomplished everything that man seeks on earth: that is, before whom to bow, to whom to entrust his conscience, and how all may unite, finally, in one peaceful, common, and harmonious ant heap, for the need of universal unity is the third and last torture of men. . . . Hadst thou accepted the world and Caesar's purple, thou wouldst have organized a universal rule and wouldst have brought about universal peace. For who can rule men but he who rules over their consciences and in whose hand is their bread? We have taken over even the sword of Caesar; and in taking it over, we have ultimately rejected thee and have gone over to *him*. I repeat, tomorrow thou shalt see that obedient flock, which at the first motion of my hand shall heap glowing coals at thy stake at which I shall burn thee, because thou hast come to interfere with us. For if anyone has ever deserved our stake more than others, it is thou! Tomorrow I shall burn thee. *Dixi!*" [11]

Such, then, is the conception of Christianity that dominates the thought of Berdyaev. He himself testifies to it when he writes in his spiritual autobiography: "The image of the Christ of 'The Legend of the Grand Inquisitor' has entered into my heart and I have accepted the Christ of the Legend." "To renounce unlimited freedom of the spirit would signify for me the renouncing of Christ and of Christianity and accepting the temptation of the Grand Inquisitor." [12] Accordingly, Berdyaev's is the religion of the few, of the spiritual aristocracy, of free men who have accepted Christ because they have been irresistibly attracted by him, enamored of him. Theirs is the bold, heroic faith, a leap in the dark; a faith that spurns all material or economic rewards, or even physical necessities; an utter, unconditional trust in God without any "proofs"; a repudiation of all outward force which comes from political or economic support. It is a naked spiritual strength which rests upon the power of the spirit — the faith of Jesus in the wilderness, tempted to disbelieve that he is the Son of God, and the faith of all who trust him because to them he is the Son of God. Even in this regard Berdyaev manifests the Russian characteristic of extremism, of an eschatological temper: it is only the noble few who commit themselves to Christ and his cause. These spiritual aristocrats are moved solely by the highest and noblest motives, by the austere sense of freedom from all external slaveries and by the ecstatic response to the divine love. They love God neither for the fear of hell nor for the hope of heaven. It is the Christian Gnostic as Clement of Alexandria conceived him, or the "*homo nobilis*" of Meister Eckhart who interest Berdyaev. The masses of ordinary Christians who, perforce, have to live on a lower level because they are incapable of mystic insight and the ecstatic experience and because their religious motivation falls short of the maximal, interest him far less. He likewise has far less to offer them, for his religious philosophy is not likely to appeal to them. To be sure, he does not go so far as to deny them place in the household of faith, but they fail to reach his ideal of a Christian. Nor is the category of "minimal Christianity" applied solely to the uneducated Christians; it is more likely to prevail among the educated classes. Of the three characteristic aspects of historic Christianity — the institutional, the doctrinal, and the mystical — only the latter two evoke Berdyaev's interest, or even his enthusiasm. His demand for a maximal Christianity is both his strength and his weakness. Nevertheless, it is by this criterion of aristocratic Christianity that all his thinking must be judged and interpreted.

Among the indications of his growing acceptance of the Christian world view must be counted his severe, almost violent, denunciations of the skeptical scientific positivism that prevailed not only among his former Marxist comrades but among the Russian educated classes generally. He was, as could be expected, in his turn shrilly attacked and mercilessly mauled by his former fellow Marxists for his "treason" in abandoning the only true faith. Berdyaev speaks of such attacks often and without much humor. "It is deemed sufficient," he writes in an article, "to show that such and such person has deviated from the 'class' point of view and has openly contradicted Marx, and the unlucky heretic is condemned as a 'bourgeois.'" "The orthodox economic materialists regard as 'barbarians' all who think differently, all who are not sufficiently permeated by 'class' psychology."[13] With the proverbial zeal of the new convert, he assails his former friends with violent diatribes such as the following:

"You count yourselves skeptics and for that reason you reject all things divine, everything which relates to other worlds. But be consistent in your skepticism, consistent and honorable skeptics, and do not trust so blindly all common-sense facts, everything which you ascribe to secular empiricism. . . . I may doubt the reality of God and immortality, and in fact I have had to pass through such doubts; but I likewise have doubted the reality of the material world, the reality of the deterministic and the law-abiding character of the world, the reality of human welfare and of human progress, to the service of which you are constantly exhorting me. For the radicalism of my doubts, the material universe has no preference over the otherworldly. You believe absolutely in everything positive and conduct your life on the basis of that faith. You absolutely doubt everything mystical but do not doubt, but rather believe, that everything mystical is an illusion and an absurdity. Why? Who gave you the right? On whose text do you base such a distinction between faith and doubt? You can appeal only to 'common sense' but behind this 'common sense' there lurks your positivistic character, your *wish* to believe everything positive, secularist, empirico-rationalistic; and your *wish* to reject everything mystical, transcendental, otherworldly. In that character of your will there is nothing objective, nothing deterministic; and your 'common sense,' your shallow rationalism, are only very subjective states of your heart — nothing more. . . .

"Be pleased to tell us which specific science has refuted religious faith, the mystical experience, and the metaphysical knowledge? . . . No science can prove that miracle is not possible in the world, that Christ did not rise from the dead, that divine nature is not revealed in mystical experience: all that is simply outside science, and science has no words wherewith it could express not only anything positive in that realm, but even anything negative. Positive science can only say: According to natural laws, revealed in physical science, chemistry, physiology, and other disciplines, Christ could not rise from the dead. But therein science only corroborates religion, which also asserts that Christ rose from the dead not in accordance with the laws of nature; but by vanquishing natural necessity he conquered the law of decomposition; for his resurrection is a mystery, a mystical act with which we communicate only in religious life. . . .

"Oh, I know, my positivistic gentlemen, that you *wish* there were no miracles, that there were nothing shattering your earthly fortress, sapping your positivistic defenses. You *wish to believe* there exist no such things. At other times, you naïvely believe that, God willing, all these things may be circumvented. Miracles do not exist because you do not want them to exist — only for that reason. . . .

"I have listened as you prayed secretly and surreptitiously: O Lord, arrange it so that thou shouldst not exist, arrange it that there be no miracles, that everything be in accordance with law; otherwise all has perished, all shall come to nought, all our earthly calculations are vain and good for nothing! . . . You want to believe only one miracle, the miracle of the natural law, of the earthly 'little reason' to which you bind your hope of ordering the earth for your well-being. Your hearts are full of repugnance and hate against all interference with your way. . . .

"Why are they so prejudiced as to think that they must believe Mill and Spencer more than Hegel and Schelling? Who has proved that reason has spoken with the lips of the former and folly with the lips of the latter? . . . Do not call upon Kant, whom some of you look up to — for the old gentleman has disclaimed your 'common sense' and the idea of reason is, according to him, suprahuman."[14]

Berdyaev left St. Petersburg in 1907 and spent the winter in Paris, where he studied Catholic modernism and French syndicalism. Upon his return to Russia he did not go back to St. Petersburg because of his break with the circle of Merezhkovsky, but settled in Moscow. The situation at home, both cultural and political, was extremely critical. Black reaction was busily organizing its forces to nullify the pitifully meager gains that the First Revolution had made. The czarist regime, defeated in the Russo-Japanese War of 1905 because of the incredible rottenness and inner decay with which the entire administrative system was permeated, was at first obliged to make concessions to the liberal demands for reforms. Nicholas II granted the *Manifesto* on October 30, 1905, thereby ostensibly converting his autocratic rule into a parliamentary monarchy.

However, this situation changed quickly; hardly four months after the granting of these concessions, the reactionary court circles began plotting measures for the overthrow of the "liberties." The Church was called upon to co-operate in this reaction. In 1906, there was organized, under the auspices of the hierarchy, an intensely reactionary body popularly known as "The Black Hundred." It became notorious for its share in anti-Semitic pogroms and other nefarious acts. During this period all liberal, progressive, democratic forces united in denouncing the Church, particularly the hierarchy, for its reactionary political activity. Those among the educated who had long ago ceased to profess Christianity in any real sense of the word now seized the opportunity to identify all Christianity, and all religion, with the misdeeds and the political subservience of the Russian hierarchy. It is chiefly from this period, as well as from a somewhat later time when the notorious Gregory Rasputin enjoyed the confidence of Czarina Alexandra and through her of Czar Nicholas II, that the almost ineradicable popular impression of the utter corruption of the Russian Church has become imbedded in the consciousness of Western peoples. The Bolsheviks, in their turn, took extremely good care not to do anything that might tend to correct that impression; in fact, they found it ridiculously easy to establish it firmly.

Berdyaev, of course, did not belong to the group of uncritical, indifferent secularists or militant atheists for whom religion had lost all meaning or who regarded it as the chief support of the *status quo,* economically and politically. And yet, just because he felt, with an ever-increasing fervor of conviction, the tragic necessity of a religious revival both in Russia and in the world generally, he could not condone the abject subservience of the hierarchs to the Russian State. It was painfully clear to him that, during the two centuries since Peter the Great had enslaved the Church by imposing upon it the Holy Governing Synod, the Orthodox Church had "reached a condition which Dostoevsky called paralysis: insincerity, self-interest, and conventionality were dominant. The most creative and valuable elements of society had left the Church, and Orthodoxy assumed a wholly governmental character."

Therefore, after his return from Paris, Berdyaev threw himself into an effort to bring the educated classes back to religion. He believed firmly at the time that the world was tending toward a religious awakening.[15] Moreover, he sensed the coming of a revolution far more thoroughgoing and destructive of the old society than the Revolution of 1905 had been; in an article written in 1907 he predicted that the Bolsheviks would emerge victorious from that cataclysm.[16] In order to do all he could to avert the catastrophe, he joined the Moscow Religious Philosophical Society composed of like-minded intellectuals. The initiative in the first meeting of this group had been taken chiefly by Sergius Bulgakov in 1905. Among this group of distinguished cultural leaders — men like M. Gershenzon, Leon Shestov, Vyacheslav Ivanov, A. Byely, G. Rachinsky, and Prince E. Trubetskoy — Berdyaev was regarded as a "modernist," a "leftist." Bulgakov by that time was already close to the traditional Orthodoxy, and enjoyed prominence as "the central figure of the Orthodox revival."[17] Previously, in St. Petersburg, Berdyaev had frequented the meetings of a similar organization, at which Merezhkovsky and his group had arranged discussions with high Church representatives. On one occasion the meeting was presided over by Metropolitan Sergius who later (after the death of Patriarch Tikhon in 1925) became "the keeper of the patriarchal throne," and finally, in 1943, was elected patriarch with Stalin's express approval.

The Moscow group likewise devoted much time to discussions of religion from the cultural point of view. The interest aroused by these discussions was astonishing: the crowds attending them were so great that Berdyaev, who presided at one such gathering, received a warning from the Moscow University authorities that the floor of the assembly room might collapse. It was this group of the ex-Marxists and other "God seekers" which, in March,

1909, published one of the most notable books of the time, entitled *Milestones* (*Vyekhy*). Comprising articles written by intellectuals from many walks of life, the book proclaimed their disillusionment with the humanistic and positivist systems of thought which they had formerly adhered to, and called the intellectuals "back to religion." Among the contributors were S. L. Frank, Peter Struve, M. Gershenzon, as well as Berdyaev. The book caused a sensation. On the one hand, the liberal, positivist press, which identified everything religious with obscurantism and reaction, denounced it unsparingly. Paul N. Milyukov, leader of the liberals, even felt it his duty to make a lecture tour for the purpose of excoriating the "reactionary" movement.[18] On the other hand, it was greeted with enthusiasm by the "God seekers" among the educated classes and by many members of the clergy, particularly those who possessed a liberal education, as the harbinger of a new day in Russia. For it signified, indeed, a milestone in the spiritual life of the country. Here were laymen of the educated classes, hitherto almost without exception alienated from, if not actively and aggressively hostile to, the Church, who publicly professed their return to religion!

Berdyaev himself contributed to *Milestones* an article dealing with the current condition of Russian philosophy, in which he sardonically compared the popularly acclaimed "philosophers," Bogdanov and Lunacharsky (his former comrades during his Marxist period, who later became the official Soviet philosophical luminaries), with the really great Russian philosophers such as Khomyakov, Vladimir Solovev, and Dostoevsky. He sadly pointed out how unappreciated, if not positively despised, these truly great Russian thinkers were.[19]

He took part, among others, in various discussions with the ecclesiastical authorities regarding reforms of the antiquated theological curriculums current in the clerical academies. Many years later he recalled one such occasion when he had advocated the introduction of courses in the history of religion and an increase in philosophical instruction in the Moscow Theological Academy. The rector, Bishop Theodore, however, hotly rejected any such suggestion.[20] In fact, a year later, the curriculum of the academies was changed in the direction of greater conservatism. This was part of the campaign against political and cultural liberalism waged by the Procurator of the Holy Governing Synod, Sabler, notorious as the "creature of Gregory Rasputin."

Berdyaev had written much on the relation of Church and State even prior to this particular period. Thus, for instance, on the occasion of the death of the reactionary Constantine Pobyedonostsev (1907), Berdyaev had given vent to his damning judgment of the Church which was personified in the former Procurator. The latter had been the tutor of Czar Nicholas II, and for many years the Procurator of the Holy Governing Synod. He was so intensely conservative that in 1905 he had resigned his office because he could not countenance the mild reforms granted by the czar as the result of the First Russian Revolution. Berdyaev had lashed out furiously at the subservience of the Church to the State, denouncing the Church leaders for their practical denial of the very essence of the religion of Christ. Pobyedonostsev's chief characteristic, in Berdyaev's estimation, was his "unbelief in the power of good." The former Procurator, Berdyaev wrote, distrusted man, even the religious man, the member of the Church, so much that he relied on the governmental restraint as alone capable of preventing man from destroying himself. Like the Grand Inquisitor, Pobyedonostsev believed in saving men by force, against their will, and dreaded nothing more than the freedom that is in Christ. And like Thomas Hobbes, he *believed* in the leviathan — the State — as being alone capable of preventing men from cutting each other's throats. As Berdyaev put it,

"A nihilistic attitude toward humanity and the world, growing from religious attitude toward God — that is the pathos of Pobyedonostsev, shared by Russian statism, and grounded in the historic Orthodoxy. Pobyedonostsev was a religious personality: he prayed to his God, he engaged in 'saving his soul'; but toward life, toward humanity, toward the world process, his attitude was nonreligious, atheistic. He saw nothing divine in life, no reflection of the divine in man. Only a terrible, yawning abyss of emptiness opened itself before him in the world. The world was not God's creation for him; he never sensed the divinity of the world soul. . . . He was of the number of those who are hypnotized by the Fall, for whom being is hidden, who are cut off from the mystery of God's creation. The devil rules the world and determines the course of universal life; he penetrates to the very roots of man's nature. The good, the divine, has no objective power; one cannot build his life upon its foundations; with the power of good no historic perspectives are bound. Like Mark, Pobyedonostsev looked upon human society as a mechanism.

"Pobyedonostsev is a tragical type — one of those for whom Christianity has killed Christ and the Church has obscured God. Christ made God infinitely near to man, made man a son of the Heavenly Father; the spirit of Pobyedonostsev makes God infinitely distant from man, and turns the son into a slave." [21]

The appearance of *Milestones* was joyfully greeted even by some members of the Russian Orthodox hierarchy, who publicly expressed their approval of the religious earnestness manifested by the writers. Among these, the most important was the Metropolitan Antony (although his identity is somewhat in doubt), of St. Petersburg, who published a letter addressed to the authors of the book. Berdyaev seized the welcome opportunity to reply to the hierarch. This "Open Letter" is characteristic of the author's moral courage; for this bold speaking of truth in love, even to an exalted hierarch of the Church, reveals much of his own intrepid spirit. Since the letter is not available in translation, I shall take the liberty of quoting it extensively:

"By devious and winding paths have I come to the faith of Christ and to the Church of Christ, which I now count as my spiritual mother. Nevertheless, I have not forgotten those obstacles that stood in my way. I cannot forget them because of the fate of those who are unable to overcome those obstacles. The activity of the Church, the abomination of desolation in the holy place, throttles as a heavy incubus those who seek God and his truth. Many, impelled by the love of truth, and by strict claims upon the servants of God, who in words speak the name of Christ but in deeds oppose Christ, doubt the sanctity of the place (i.e., the Church) itself. For all know and all agree that the deeds of Christ are deeds of love. Is it not a stumbling block that the official Christian camp, confessing the true faith and accordingly possessing privileges almost incomparably greater than the others, commits deeds of hate and evil rather than performing deeds of love? Men are weak and their religious will is ruined by offenses and temptations; it is difficult for them to withstand the most terrible offense which turns men from faith — the spiritual downfall and ethical decomposition of the Church in her human, historical, empirical aspects (for in her divine, mystical aspects the Church is unshakable and guards eternal truth). But woe to them through whom such offense comes into the world! . . .

"I have deeply and tortuously experienced the guilt of our atheistic society, and have scrutinized the results of that guilt; accordingly, I have learned the mystery of the offenses. Thus I have earned the right and have assumed the obligation to denounce the lie by which our educated classes live. We, the authors of *Milestones,* have discharged our debt as well as we could, having borne testimony to those educated classes with which we have formerly been identified by sharing their ideas, and for whom we now desire a better future. . . .

"Russian revolution, nihilistic and atheistic in accordance with its basic ideas, has filled Russia with malice, has poisoned the very blood of the Russian people by class and caste hatred and spiritual enmity. But are not the reactionaries breathing even greater malice? Do they not spill blood and force souls with more oppressive power? The 'Union of Russian People'[22] is all malice, all hatred — its deeds are a terrible offense. It supports fratricidal division in the Russian nation and society, and is the chief obstacle to the religious rebirth of our Fatherland."[23]

Berdyaev then asks: Can the hierarchs justify such anti-Christian "politics"? Why do they resort to force rather than deeds of love? "Why do they disbelieve the strength of God's truth, but believe in the governmental, outward strength?" We observe with amazement, he goes on, the union of Church and State in this hateful work. It is this very subservience of the Church to the State that has resulted in the loss of faith on the part of so many people. Our hierarchy habitually trusts in outward force and compulsion, which are the very antitheses of Christianity.

Everywhere the "prince of this world" has won a victory over faith. But is salvation by compulsion possible? Is force in matters of faith and conscience possible? Is not the freedom of Christian conscience a necessary concomitant of Christianity itself, an obligation laid upon us by God, rather than a right as is commonly asserted by those who defend freedom?

The sinful, fallen world cannot exist without restraint, and hence without a government. But that does not apply to the Church which is governed by love. " Where is the voice of the Church, my Lord, the voice of the *ecumenical* Church of Christ to which I submit in everything and in the name of which I shall renounce everything? What has become of the tradition of *sobornost,*[24] which is preserved by our Church? "

It is an error to desire that Christianity shall conquer by force — that is the very spirit of the Grand Inquisitor. This spirit is exhibited by socialism and Marxism. For the official Church, Berdyaev charged, " the truth of Christ is crucified; it is above all 'politics'; for true Christianity is neither reactionary nor revolutionary, neither 'rightist' nor 'leftist'; it is not of this world, but above it — a rule of love and freedom."

A similar critique of the Church and its servile relation to the State had been published by Berdyaev a year earlier. One is amazed at the frankness with which he dared to express himself, as well as at the relative tolerance of the czarist Russia which allowed such scathing criticisms of itself to be published. For the czarist Russia has for long been portrayed as a land of absolutistic suppression of all liberties. The very fact that the author of the bold critique remained unpunished should lead to some revision of the popular thinking on that subject. Certainly no one would be allowed to attack the present Soviet regime with such freedom and with impunity!

To begin with, Berdyaev categorically declared that " there has never been a Christian government, and never shall be."[25] Hitherto, the attempts to realize Christian society have been compromises with paganism. In the West, the attempt assumed the form of papal caesarism; in the East, of caesaropapism. " Thus was organized in the West a pseudo-Christian society with the rule of the pope at the head — the pope as the vicar of Christ on earth; in the Byzantine East no less pseudo-Christian society with the rule of the emperor (czar) at the head — the emperor as the vicar of Christ. But both in papism and czarism, decked in

Christianity, there continued to live the pagan principle of rule, the pagan imperialism." Christianity changed from the persecuted to the persecutor, and Christians ceased to be martyrs in order to become martyr makers. For Berdyaev, every theocratic government embodies the spirit of the Grand Inquisitor. He writes:

"A Christian theocratic government is a lie, because Christian theocracy is a rule of grace, but the State is a rule of law, a pagan rule. Saint Augustine founded the theocracy of the Middle Ages by confusing law with grace. Humanity in the development of its self-consciousness has sensed the lie of a Christian government, the religious falsity of absolutistic papalism and theocratic absolutism, and has become aware of the confusion, which was the great offense of Christian history, one of the temptations of the devil which had been overcome by Christ in the wilderness. The Reformation, and later the progressive disintegration of Christianity and religion in general, were the results of the great collapse of the effort to establish a Christian government, to organize a religious rule over the world. . . . Humanism became victorious over the antihumanistic pseudo theocracy, papal and imperial. In place of the human self-assertion and will-to-power which cloaked themselves in the pretense of divine rule and gained the aura of religious authority, humanism openly and honorably affirmed man and purely human rule. The truth in this instance was on the side of humanism; but only a relative, not an absolute, truth. And even this truth is at present transforming itself into a lie, into a new deceit.

"Unbelief has more and more increased, but the false bond between the Church and the Government has remained as if untouched. This relation has continued to poison the sources of religious life increasingly. Society has become atheistic, and for the greatest part does not know any more who Christ was. In the soul of the nation, the religious sense of the holy has died. The conventional and forcibly imposed lie of the official, governmental religion continues to corrupt human souls. Religion has become a utilitarian tool for the rule of the world. . . .

"All forcible support of the Church and faith by the Government is the result of unbelief in the power of Christ. His faith shall revive only when it again is persecuted, not when it persecutes. . . . The Holy Spirit has never been on the side of the persecutors and of force — but the Spirit of the Great Inquisitor has been!" [26]

But Berdyaev's repudiation of the Government and his severe criticism of the Church on account of its sycophancy did not derive, as was true of many liberal members of the intelligentsia, from a revolutionary attitude. For revolutions do not create new life; they only destroy the old. When the First Russian Revolution broke out, it succeeded merely in revealing the decadence, the rottenness of the old order, but failed to bring health to the Russian soul. Berdyaev gives expression to his disappointment by saying, "All my life have I lived in the hope that one day Russia shall be free." But when that time came (1905), his joy was turned into sorrow. For "hooligan nihilism" conquered the revolutionary struggle, for it had no "sanctuary in the soul." It brought Russia new slavery: having destroyed the old imperialism, it attempted to set up democratic imperialism in its place. Like the czarist regime it too rejected God and spiritual values. The Revolution revealed the depth of nihilism in the soul of all classes, particularly the educated. "God died long ago in their soul; the poison of nihilism has soaked, drop by drop, into the upper as well as the lower classes." "Was it for this that the Westerners had fought the Slavophiles, that Herzen had made himself a permanent exile from Russia, that Belinsky had sorrowfully sought truth, and Leo Tolstoy had challenged the world history?"[27] Interpreting the post-Revolutionary situation with a marvelously penetrating insight, using for the purpose the form of a commentary upon the healing of the Gerasene demoniac, Berdyaev looked upon both the Revolution and the reaction against it as a case of demonic possession:

"The revolutionary demonic madness has ended, the Revolution has failed; it has lost its objective and, according to all signs, there begins a new madness — the madness of reaction. An unsuccessful revolution is always followed by serious consequences: those who have experienced a sense of the loss of their station in life, even for a moment, revenge themselves upon it. Demons have entered the sick body and soul of Russia, for they pass over from reaction to revolution and from revolution to reaction. Nevertheless, they are the very same demons, assuming now a reactionary and then a revolutionary aspect. In the second Duma the 'leftists' raged; in the third Duma the 'rightists' are beginning to rage.

"The vicious circle from reaction to revolution is an incubus upon human life, the reward for the grave sins of the past. Both reaction and revolution are sent from above as a punishment for transgressions — the sins of the Government and the sins of the people. The lightning of revolution strikes the unworthy, sinful Government which has failed in its task; the terrible rain of reaction falls upon the unworthy, sinful society which has failed to be worthy of its responsibility. A healthy, organic growth follows only upon the purity of the people's heart, and upon the crystal-clear consciousness of the difference between good and evil. Once the unclean spirit has found an entry into the body and soul of Russia, the torment of reaction and revolution is inevitable, and with it the harm to the whole nation. For the prevention of the demonic madness of revolution, the Government and the ruling class of society must repent of their sins; for the prevention of the demonic madness of reaction, the educated classes and the society must repent of their sins." [28]

Among the characterizations of the Russian upper society, I can scarcely think of any that would equal, not to say surpass, the apt and terribly truthful delineation of its condition penned by Berdyaev:

"The historic Government committed great crimes: it worshiped the idol of imperialism and served the instincts of the ruling classes; with a few exceptions it was not of the people. The Russian educated society lost the feeling of being Russian citizens and saw their dignity and worth in alienation. The *people,* until now, remained a puzzle. The educated Russian has felt himself a citizen of the planet Mars, in no way a citizen of Russia. . . . In his wholly isolated society, the educated Russian has become accustomed to profess the most extreme socialistic and anarchistic ideals, totally abstract, devoid of historical flesh and blood. An obligatory break with his ancestry, with the whole past, with history, has become the life norm for the educated Russian. The Russian intelligentsia have been alienated, not only in relation to the Government — in that respect they were right — but in relation to Russian literature, Russian philosophical thought, the faith of the people, the feeling of nationality — in which respects they were wrong. Much has been written and spoken among us on the theme of the break between the educated classes and the people, but the writers and speakers have viewed the theme exclusively from the sociological point of view. From that point of view nothing can be understood or solved. The theme goes immeasurably deeper.

"For a century we have been nurturing negative consciousness, strengthening atheistic and nihilistic ideas. The latest conclusions of European culture have been reflected in Russia in their most extreme, radical form. When a Russian became a socialist, he was no mere Western socialist, but the most extreme, fanatical socialist; his socialism was outside time and space; it was his religion. When a Russian became an anarchist, he was the most radical anarchist, plotting against the very first principles of being. When a Russian became a materialist, then for him materialism became theology; when an atheist, his atheism became religion; when a decadent, then he disintegrated into his component parts. Radicalism is our national characteristic, and that characteristic gave birth to much that is bad; but it may also become the source of the greatest good, for it prevents us from being merely bourgeois." [29]

Since Berdyaev could join neither the Revolution nor the reaction, he found himself isolated. Having broken away from the Marxist camp, he could scarcely find a group of like-minded educated Russians with whom he could wholeheartedly co-operate, with the exception of the group with whom he had collaborated in the publication of *Milestones,* and whose voice expressed the anti-Revolutionary mood of the period. Isolation and loneliness became his fate from then on. But it was also his difficult temperament that was responsible for his isolation. In his old age he rather gloried in it, for he felt that he had fought the good fight and had kept the faith. During the period of reaction following the First Revolution, he chose to stand outside both the "left" and the "right" parties. "The extreme rightists as well as the extreme leftists breathe wrath and hate, desire destruction, and deepen the gulf and schism within the national life." [30]

Nor could Berdyaev share the faith of the Constitutional Democrats in their panacea. Nevertheless, he recognized that the "Cadets" (as the Constitutional Democrats were nicknamed) were to be preferred to the other parties; for they were "free from the madness of the 'blacks' as well as that of the 'reds.' But they succumbed to the danger of making for themselves an idol of the 'constitution' just as the revolutionaries had made an idol of the 'Revolution.' A 'constitution,' even the most ideal, was as little sacred as was the 'Revolution,' or the Government, which was the idol of the rightists. . . . The fetish of constitutionalism has been the snare of the Cadets, and their humanism was unable to save them from that snare."[31] Only religion could do that.

Neither did Berdyaev join the "Democrats," since from religious motives he rejected the "national rule," the rule of the majority. For the majority may desire, and very often do desire, their private advantage rather than the good of the whole society — not to speak of the highest good, which is the will of God. Christianity aims to satisfy man's needs, not his desires. Berdyaev was then, and remained henceforth, a believer in the supreme value of human personality. Both the collectivist and the democratic or equalitarian forms of political organization are, in his judgment, unfavorable to personalism. Somewhat in the spirit of a perfectionist, for in this and many other respects Berdyaev is a true Russian, he declares: "Nor do I believe, as do the Constitutional Democrats, in the saving character of abstractly considered politics, political parties, and political struggle, which elevate a tactical lie into a principle. To the ideal of constitutional democracy I can oppose only the organic ideal of free theocracy."[32] Nevertheless, he has enough comprehension of the truth expressed by Bismarck in the aphorism that "politics is the art of the possible" to admit the relative advantages of constitutionalism and democracy; for the rejection of these would be "tantamount to a rejection of history, to the ignoring of the sufferings of evolution."

What, then, is Berdyaev's solution of the tragic problem that confronts the Russian people? Does he shrug his shoulders and irresponsibly, no matter how piously, remark that the world lies in evil and that is the end of it? Indeed not! There is a terrible sensitiveness toward evil in Berdyaev, a tragic sense of responsibility for even one tear of an innocent little child (to use the expression of Ivan Karamazov), which makes the problem of evil ever present to his mind. He feels that Christians must not merely denounce their secularist opponents, or comfortably lay the blame for everything upon them: they must outthink, outlive, and outlove their opponents. They must produce something better. As for Berdyaev's own specific treatment of these weighty questions, we shall deal with them in their proper place.

Suffice it to say here that for Berdyaev the Revolution was not *radical* enough: "We shall be free when we free ourselves from the criteria of leftism and rightism, revolution and reaction, and when we perceive what truth really is. That will be radicalism." [33] Let us revert to his article on "Sick Russia," in which Berdyaev writes:

"Man cannot be free as long as the demon dwells in him; so long he is bound by chains and ropes. The enchanted circle of reaction and revolution binds with fetters and enslaves. From that enchanted circle one cannot escape unless the unclean spirit is driven out, unless one is freed from the demons. Who can be the redeemer; who has the power to command the demons to depart? The reaction does not possess the strength to cast out the demons of reaction. . . . The ruling government does not possess the spiritual strength to conquer the chaotic anarchy; while the revolutionary intelligentsia and the revolutionary masses do not possess the spiritual strength to gain victory over the demonic rage of the reactionary government and the reactionary part of society. Russia tears her bonds, but is driven by the demons into the wilderness of chaotic reaction or chaotic revolution. Only Jesus can command the unclean spirit to depart from the body of Russia! Only Christ can be the Redeemer! But for that it is necessary that there be an inner return to Christ, seeking him for the assuaging of our thirst and for the ending of our tortures. . . . And the unclean spirit shall depart to its proper dwelling place, into the herd of swine!" [34]

This, then, was Berdyaev's ideal of free theocracy. Although reminiscent of Vladimir Solovev's dreams of theocracy, which had led the latter to place an exaggerated trust in the Russian political autocracy and to develop schemes of union with Roman Catholicism, Berdyaev's concept was free from such fantastic misjudgments. He never shared Solovev's crude and childishly naïve conceptions. His was a "free" theocracy, a truly ecumenical Christendom, in which there would be no compulsion of any sort. The rule of God, he held, must be voluntarily accepted by man, for there can be nothing forced in religion. Nevertheless, Berdyaev at this stage of his development believed in the possibility of realizing a free reign of God in the hearts of men such as would usher in the Kingdom of God. One remembers the vogue that similar ideas enjoyed in American liberal circles a quarter of a century ago, and they have not altogether lost their persuasiveness even now. Berdyaev, then, believed in the possibility of the actual realization of the rule of God on earth. In fact, he violently assailed the Russian Orthodox Church for not sharing this belief with him. He formulated his burning convictions in the program of neo-Christianity, which he opposed to the official, historic Russian Church:

> "The new religious consciousness rises against the nihilistic attitude toward the world and humanity. If religious rebirth is possible, it is only on the ground of the revelation of the religious meaning of secular culture and earthly liberation, of the revelation of truth about humanity. For the new religious consciousness, the declaration of the will of God is at the same time the declaration of the rights of man, the revelation of the divine in humanity. We believe in the objective, cosmic power of God's truth, in the possibility of ordering the terrestrial fate of humanity in God's way. . . . Christ cannot have a human vicar in the person of a czar or a high priest. He himself is the Czar and the Chief Priest, and shall rule the world! Thy *Kingdom* come, Thy will be done *on earth* as it is in heaven!" [35]

Alas! These brave words, this burning faith, had to be modified later! The mature Berdyaev could not retain the unshakable confidence of his youth that the Kingdom of God, a "free theocracy," may be realized within the confines of human history. The terrors of the October Revolution coming on the heels of the First World War, and perhaps a more systematic consideration of his own basic axiom of the freedom of personality led him to a more sober conclusion: The Kingdom of God cannot be realized in time, for it transcends human history.

3

The Pre- and Post-Revolutionary Berdyaev

By 1911 a subtle change is discernible in the writings of Berdyaev, although the difference does not amount to a total break with his previous spiritual development. He remained the same and yet was not the same. He had matured. His spiritual perception had become clearer, deeper. His world view had begun to be increasingly molded by mysticism. Whatever of mere intellectualism, rationalism, had lurked in his mind previously was increasingly superseded by what he called mystical realism, which he had learned largely from Jakob Boehme, Angelus Silesius, John Tauler, and perhaps Franz von Baader. These religious mystics, together with the German idealists to a much more qualified degree, now became his guides. In his spiritual autobiography he confesses: "German mysticism has always had a pre-eminent significance for me. After the prophets, The Book of Job, Ecclesiastes, and the Gospels, my favorite spiritual authors were the German mystics, above all, J. Boehme and Angelus Silesius, and partly Tauler." [1] Furthermore, Berdyaev had been powerfully influenced, as we have seen, by Dostoevsky and Vladimir Solovev from his earliest youth, and these Russian thinkers certainly had taught him to view the world through the eyes of mysticism. Nevertheless, there was a change. Perhaps these initial influences had now been powerfully reinforced by the thinking of Boehme and Von Baader. At any rate, they gave his writings a new, more inward, spiritual tone.

One feels this new atmosphere in the work *Philosophy of Freedom,*[2] published in 1911 but containing articles that had appeared previously from 1908 on. Berdyaev himself, however, toward the end of his life did not think favorably of this book, and regarded it as predominantly an expression of his relatively unenlightened past.

A real milestone in Berdyaev's spiritual development was reached in his very important work *The Meaning of Creativity*. This book, which its author regarded as among the most important of his writings and to which he frequently referred throughout his later life, was published in 1916, in the midst of the First World War.[3] It was written partly in Italy, "almost in a state of ecstasy," during the year 1912. Berdyaev's own judgment of the book was that "although it is not the best written of my productions, it is the most inspired."[4] He propounded in it one of the most original themes of his thought, namely, man's creative role in the transformation of the world. This concept ultimately brought him to an "eschatological metaphysics" in which he thought of man's creative role as his co-operation with God in the bringing about of the "end of time," thus ushering in a new aeon. For these daring concepts Berdyaev was severely criticized even by his friends. For example, Sergius Bulgakov wrote that Berdyaev's concept of creativity bears "a demonic, titanic character."[5]

Furthermore, although Berdyaev was not yet wholly free from ontological presuppositions, he already affirmed the essentially existential insight that creativity is derived from freedom, is "creation out of nothing." This aspect of his thought must also be counted among his most important contributions.

The eschatological note introduced in *The Meaning of Creativity* lays stress on the idea that the realization of the Christian ideal is in the far distant future. This idea is lacking in Berdyaev's earlier writings. The stress there fell on the imminent realization of the "neo-Christianity" — on a buoyant hope of a speedy transformation of the world into the Kingdom of God. But although the realization of the Kingdom receded into the future, it was still to take place on the earth. Nevertheless, "the earth is metaphysical, not only physical, and belongs also to another world, to eternity."[6] But in that case, does not the surprising transformation of the concept of the earth already foreshadow the author's mature judgment that the Kingdom of God shall be realized only "beyond space and time," namely, in eternity? It is difficult to escape such a conclusion.

How, then, shall the New City be brought about? Revolutions do not create it. "All revolutions, political and social, are directed toward a mechanical, outward destruction of law and redemption, i.e., of the Government and the Church. In such revolutions there is no real revolution of the spirit; they are not creative but reactionary, turned backward rather than forward. . . . In the revolutionary psychology there is an unhealthy hysteria. . . . People of creative spirit are never revolutionaries in the social-mechanical sense of the word. Their revolution is different, incomparably more radical, fundamental, organic."[7]

Both imperialism and anarchism, and the bourgeois capitalism and socialism, are opposed to Christian principles. Christianity requires voluntary inner asceticism in relation to worldly goods, possessing them as if one possessed them not. It repudiates the bourgeois values and renounces the kingdom of this world. Moreover, the latter pair, the bourgeois capitalism and socialism, instead of being irreconcilably opposed to each other, forming an absolute antithesis to each other, are essentially one and the same in principle. "Socialism is flesh of the flesh and blood of the blood of the *bourgeoisie*. The socialist ideals are bourgeois ideals. Socialism accepts wholly the bourgeois values of the goods of this world and desires only to develop them farther and distribute them differently, to make them the property of the whole world." "Socialism desires the final measure of bourgeois life as the kingdom of this world. The ascetic victory over the bourgeois life of this world, in the name of another world, is foreign to it." It affirms as a principle "the slavery of man to natural necessity, and not the rule of man over nature." Nevertheless, as between socialism and capitalism, preference is to be given to the former. "The bourgeois world will be forced to give way to the socialist world by necessity and by justice. Socialism is the necessary and just development of the *bourgeoisie*, of the bourgeois world order." [8] Accordingly, there is a relative truth, but also a relative untruth, in socialism: "Sacrificial spirit is just as foreign to socialism as it is to bourgeois capitalism. And the path to all creativity is through sacrificial spirit."

How shall the New City be built, then? Not from the old society. No conservative, or revolutionary, or evolutionary paths lead to the New City. No social evolution can produce the future kingdom of the God-manhood. Government, law, economics, science, cannot be transformed into Christianity, God-manhood, the City of God. It is not possible to advocate Christian government and Christian economics, because they have never existed; nor is it possible to establish them by way of evolution or revolution because they never will exist. All governments and all economic systems, by their nature, are non-Christian and contrary to the Kingdom of God. In order that the City of God may conquer the world, the entire old society, as well as all government, all law, all economics, must pass away. Even Lenin understood that before the "classless society" can be established, the state which was necessary until then must "wither away." *The new society shall be created not from the elements of "the world"; it shall be created, in the worldly sense, from nothing, from sources lying outside the terrestrial societal evolution, from the Spirit, and not from the world.* The new society is not a horizontal but a vertical movement. No hopes can be put in any social group or class, nor in any historical force, but solely in persons born of the Spirit. The radical error of all who seek to create a theocratic society lies particularly in the hope of deriving the new society from the old. "The Kingdom of God comes unperceived by 'the world,' and man enters it only to the degree of his growth in the Spirit. As long as a man is still outside the higher attainments of the Spirit, so long does he belong to the physical flesh of the world, and must participate in the evolution of the earthly society, must pay tribute to Caesar." [9]

In August, 1914, the first of the world wars broke out, which were destined, within a generation, to transform out of all recognition the whole world. Who could have foreseen the truly historic changes that were to follow in the wake of that titanic struggle? Empires that had lasted long centuries, such as the Russian and the Austrian, crashed to the ground.

For Berdyaev, who had long known that the ideas of "progress" which had been generally in vogue among the liberals were unrealistic, uncritical, mechanical, and emotional, the catastrophe was not unforeseen. Spiritually, he was prepared for it. But it brought a threat to his personal life that was surprising: he, one of the most fervent exponents of the "return to religion" movement among the Russian intelligentsia—even though these views were not traditional—was put on trial before a civil court by the Holy Governing Synod. The occasion for the action was the publication of an article, "Extinguishers of the Spirit," in which he had severely criticized that august body. The issue of the periodical in which the article had appeared was confiscated, and Berdyaev was charged with blasphemy. Not having been able to consult the article, I can pass no judgment on the merits of the case. But Berdyaev's lawyer had no doubt of the seriousness of the matter; in fact, he regarded the case as lost. Had Berdyaev been convicted, he ran the risk of being imprisoned, or even being sent into perpetual exile to Siberia. Fortunately, the trial dragged on through the war years because the court was unable to secure a sufficient number of witnesses. Those serving in the Army could not be recalled from military duty, and the outbreak of the Revolution terminated the whole procedure.[10]

During the period of the struggle which ended so disastrously for the czarist regime, Berdyaev "enthusiastically supported the war to the victorious end. No sacrifices frightened me," he wrote in 1918, when the Bolsheviks were already in power. "But now, I cannot but wish that the World War might terminate soon. One must wish that, not only from the point of view of the fate of Russia, but from the point of view of the fate of all Europe as well." For the whole Western civilization was in danger. "The life of the European nations is turned toward the elementary; it is threatened with barbarization."[11] During the war Berdyaev thought that Russia might bring East and West together; but the leaders of the Russian Revolution chose another task for their country. Berdyaev feared that Europe, in her weakness and exhaustion, might be conquered by Asia and America. "Now the result of the war is such that only the Far East — Japan and China, a race that has not exhausted itself — and the Far West, America, can win, really conquer. After the weakening and disintegration of Europe and Russia, Sinism and Americanism will rule — the two powers may find a common meeting point between them."[12] Berdyaev certainly missed the mark as far as the immediate aftermath of the First World War was concerned; whether the future trends will prove him correct remains to be seen.

Berdyaev had been unable to share the confidence of the liberal elements of the Russian society who supported the Provisional Government in the attempt to establish a democratic regime in the country. His sister-in-law writes in her *Memoirs:*

> "Nicolas Alexandrovich felt very pessimistic. I remember his ironic smile when our numerous friends spoke with ecstasy of 'the bloodless Russian Revolution,' sang praises of Kerensky'[illegible], and awaited the inauguration of a regime of freedo[illegible]. He knew that the bloodless revolution would end in a bloody one. He was very taciturn and sad."[13]

When the fearful judgment of the October Revolution — which Berdyaev had prophesied many years previously — befell Russia, he remained outwardly calm, although he had no faith in it, either. During the actual fighting he continued his writing, even when bombs were falling near his home. Nevertheless, he took some part in the events that were transpiring, for he allowed himself to be chosen one of the members of the Soviet of the Republic, i.e., the pre-Parliament. But he soon gave up his membership in this body, for the whole action seemed "stupid" to him. He likewise felt a similar sense of futility in regard to any co-operation with the Church: he attended some of the meetings of the First All-Russian Sobor, which had for its task the reorganization of the ecclesiastical structure, and which elected Patriarch Tikhon as the head of the new organization. He sensed that the external changes did not go deep enough, did not constitute the needed basic reformation. When the various reformist parties sprang up within the Church some years later — the Living Church, for instance — he kept aloof from all of them because the leaders courted the favor of the Government by denouncing the patriarch and his party. Berdyaev wrote of these groups, "Reformation, which I myself desire, is not accomplished in that manner."[14]

Consequently, although he retired from all public activity, he could not refrain from writing. For considering the almost apocalyptic scenes which accompanied the tremendous political, social, and economic overthrow of almost everything that had any connection with the old order, how could a responsible thinker of Berdyaev's caliber by-pass these momentous events without expressing himself? As a matter of fact, we need be in no doubt as to what he thought. For as usual, he took refuge in writing. Thus alone could he relieve his sense of deep loathing of the new masters of Russia. Of Lenin he wrote, "Philosophically and culturally Lenin was a reactionary, a man terribly behind the times; he did not reach the heights of Marx's dialectic."[15]

But his indignation against the "treason of the Russian intellectuals," whose weakness and irresponsibility had prepared the way for the Bolshevik seizure of power, was even greater. By that weakness the intellectual class committed suicide; but in their doom was involved the fate of the Russian culture, and the future of the Russian people. He expressed these seething sentiments in the unique book of his career, although in his spiritual autobiography he speaks deprecatingly of it. He writes in the latter work that he dislikes the book and that it does not express his real mind. It was not published in Russia — how could one expect the Soviet censorship to approve its publication? It appeared five years later in Berlin. The very title was provocative, if not misleading: Berdyaev called the book *The Philosophy of Inequality.*[16] Even the form was unusual for Berdyaev, for it was written as letters to his "noncomrades," to the men who did not agree with him. Berdyaev composed the book (with the exception of the Postscript) early in 1918. It is a passionate, vehement, often vitriolic, excoriation of those who had destroyed Russia in the Revolution — and he did not mean merely the Bolsheviks! There is nothing like it among his other writings; for that matter, it would be difficult to match it among any other writings. He lashes out with passionate eloquence that is more than half invective:

"To you who have poisoned the soul of the Russian people with a terrible poison, to you who are destroying Russia, I dedicate these letters. . . . At first your oppression was spiritual, for you ruled the weak souls of the Russian intellectuals; but now you have become persecutors of all higher, spiritual life, and have boycotted all who believe in higher spiritual realities and values, who acknowledge a religious goal of life. . . . You have established an unheard-of tyranny, threatening at last to destroy the human image. You have always hated freedom, have always been extinguishers of the human spirit, destroyers of the divine in man. You have ever bartered the human birthright for a mess of pottage of ephemeral well-being and of passing interests. You are destroyers of the eternal: you would pluck out of the human heart the sense of the eternal and the longing for the eternal. . . . I have long fought you to the extent of my strength. Now, even those who were formerly seduced by your spirit, all those enlighteners, progressives, and humanists who were content with the superficialities of life, who recognized no evil, who possessed the souls of aesthetes, innocently dreaming of the good of the people and happiness on earth — even they are beginning to know you. We long ago forewarned them, and pointed out whither the paths taken by the educated Russian society would lead, into which they have also enticed the Russian people. We have exhorted them about the awful responsibility that is incumbent upon the 'haves' of the ruling class; for they were doing almost nothing of a creative nature to prevent Russia and the Russian people from falling into the fateful abyss. Let them now remember *Milestones* and judge it more impartially!" [17]

He then proceeds to dissect minutely the revolutionary character of the Russian intellectuals, and to pass judgment on the Revolution itself. To begin with, Berdyaev sees in the Revolution an upsurge of titanic, elemental forces, explosively released by the outburst of a passionate resentment toward accumulated, historic wrongs. In its own character, no revolution is ever religious.

> "Revolution, every revolution, is by its nature antireligious, and all religious justifications of it are ignoble. But a revolution of grand proportions may have a religious meaning. One may look for signs of divine providence in it, 'the accents of God's judgment.' I see that meaning and those signs even in the most antireligious of all revolutions, the Russian Revolution." [18]

What, then, is the religious significance of the October Revolution? Like the French, the Russian Revolution is the divine judgment upon historic injustice, oppression, and sin, perpetrated by the Russian state and society. Moreover, just as all revolutions have ended in reaction, so shall the Russian Revolution likewise terminate.

Berdyaev incontinently attacks the Revolutionists; he pounds them with a verbal sledge hammer; his characterization of them is about as subtle as a plague. Their revolution is not radical enough. It is merely destructive. It has no transforming power because it has no spiritual force. For no external, merely mechanical change can produce really radical results; only a spiritual transformation can do that.

> "The revolution of the spirit has nothing in common with your external, material, political, and social revolutions. Marx never was a revolutionary of the spirit. Nietzsche was. But what has he in common with your external revolutions? He despised them as uprisings of plebeians. Dostoevsky was a revolutionary of the spirit. But you have ever regarded him a conservative and a reactionary. And what have you to do with the prophetic Vladimir Solovev, or what has he to do with you? All that was spiritually significant in the history of Russian thought and of the Russian creativeness in the nineteenth century is not on your side but is against you. The greatest representative of Russian culture, Pushkin, is not yours. You have abused and denounced him, opposed to him a stove pot and boots. Neither has Leo Tolstoy loved you; on the contrary, he has condemned your doings. Only second- or third-rate men are with you; not a single genius has been born, or has risen among you." [19]

Above all, Berdyaev accuses the Communists of instituting a collectivist system which destroys the highest value in the world, the human personality:

"You reject and destroy personality, all you heralds of the materialistic revolution, you socialists and anarchists, radicals and democrats of various shades, all you levelers and subverters, heralds of the religion of equality. You would like to convert men into atoms, and the human society into an atomic mechanism, into a collective of impersonal atoms. But in truth, man is not an atom, but an individuum, an individual, a differentiated being. Every man possesses a unique, individual lot in this life and the life beyond, in eternity." [20]

"Your human collective, that anthill of the future, the terrible leviathan, shall finally destroy personality as well as all other reality. . . . Your collective is a pseudo reality which will supersede all true realities after destroying them — the realities of personality, nation, government, Church, humanity, cosmos, as well as God. For every reality is a personality and possesses a living soul — man, nation, humanity, cosmos, Church, and God." [21]

"I know that you will decry as reactionary all I say, and will see in my ideas a justification of the social evils. But I have long ago ceased to regard your judgments as significant. . . . Inequality is the basis of the cosmic order and harmony, and is the justification of the existence of human personality itself, the source of all creative movement in the world. . . . Out of inequality the world and the cosmos were born. Out of inequality, man himself was born. An absolute equality would leave being in a state of equilibrium, in a nondifferentiated state — that is, in nonbeing." [22]

"You . . . love to make use even of Christianity in defense of your objectives, and do not scruple to refer even to the gospel in which you do not believe, and which you do not accept. But you cannot find anything in Christianity in your support except external sounds and a collection of words which are unintelligible to you. The inner Christian secrets elude you. Christianity acknowledges the absolute worth of every human soul and their equal worth before God. But one cannot derive any conclusion therefrom that would be favorable to external, mechanical equalization and undifferentiation. Christianity did not rise up or revolt against slavery at a certain stage of its development; it only acknowledged that the soul of the man in the social condition of slave has an absolute worth and is equal before God to that of the master. Slave and master could be brothers in Christ, and a slave could hold a higher position in the Church of Christ than a master." [23]

These views of basic " inequality " could easily be misunderstood or twisted to mean something different from what Berdyaev really intended. They were obviously written in a defiant mood, and were purposely provocative. It is obvious that their author had " long ago ceased to regard as significant " the judgment of his opponents. But to prevent a misconception of his meaning by friends and foes alike, it is necessary, in the first place, to point out what it was that Berdyaev rejected. He had in mind the indiscriminate leveling of the Russian society which prevailed during the first years of the Soviet regime when the proletarian class was seizing places of power and influence in order to dispossess the *bourgeoisie*. During this time there occurred extreme cases of " leveling," as, for instance, when the simplest factory worker was accorded equality in the management of the concern along with the engineer or the technical expert, or the university janitor was granted equality in the academic councils along with the rector and the professors. Berdyaev, with his characteristic verbal vigor, opposed such methods of securing " dictatorship of the proletariat," by insisting upon the hierarchical principle of social organization. Men differ in their physical and mental, not to say spiritual, endowments, he argued; consequently, they differ in the kind of social service they are able to render. This service, then, must likewise be hierarchically organized: in industry, specially gifted and trained men must provide the engineering knowledge and skill, or managerial direction, while others must render the necessary but subordinate service in the processes of manual production. One may obviously apply the same principle to the military, academic, professional, and political life, and so on through the entire organization of society.

As a matter of fact, life in the Soviet Union of today is so rigidly organized on this same hierarchical principle that, if anything, it is overregimented and excludes freedom of individual initiative. One of its chief characteristics is a rigid bureaucracy. In this the Soviet regime has gone to the opposite extreme from the equalitarian sort of society with which it began. There have arisen in the Soviet Union new social classes, as sharply differentiated and separated as those of the czarist Russia. The differences among the classes are economic, cultural, and social. In other words, the contention of Berdyaev that there are differences in human endowments and that human society must be organized hierarchically has not only been tacitly acted upon by the Soviet regime, but has even been carried to the point of extreme regimentation, which he detests as fully as all lack of differentiation.

On the other hand, Berdyaev's even more insistent contention that, despite natural differences, the worth and dignity of human personality must remain unaffected by external circumstances, has not been heeded, because according to the Marxist view it is not true. The Marxist regards man primarily as an economic unit, for economic forces are basic; man's entire mental life is regarded as a mere " epiphenomenon," dependent upon the economic substratum. It is in such a sense that the strictures of Berdyaev must be understood, for he wrote about the situation prevailing in 1918, not today.

This work, written during the catastrophic upheavals that accompanied the seizure of power by the Bolsheviks and their " transvaluation of all values," which they purposed to effect on the vast scale of the whole life of the Russian peoples, may be characterized as an outburst of irrepressible emotional revulsion, as a passionate protest against the revolutionary principles and ideas that were basically at variance with Berdyaev's convictions. For spiritually he belonged neither to the czarist nor to the Soviet regime. He stood apart, and high above both. He fought Communism with spiritual, not political, weapons. He had to write; but he could not publish, with the exception of his *Destiny of Russia*,[24] which appeared during that year. But even if *The Philosophy of Inequality* could have been published, its author would have deliberately courted death by such an act. Perhaps in czarist Russia he could have published such a diatribe and could have escaped with nothing worse than a trial or banishment to some remote province (as he had been banished in 1898) or to Siberia. In Soviet Russia, however, such plain speaking as Berdyaev had indulged in would almost certainly have been visited with condign punishment. At any rate, Berdyaev did not publish the work until five years later, after he had been exiled from Russia and had found refuge in Berlin.

But during those five years the passionate, emotional resentment that had consumed Berdyaev during the first year of the Soviet regime gave place to a deeper insight, a more Christian estimate of the significance of the fateful event. One can hardly imagine a more moving conclusion to a book than the Postscript of Berdyaev's *The Philosophy of Inequality*. In simple, straightforward, manly fashion, he acknowledges and confesses that mere resentment, a magnificently eloquent "I told you so!" is not on a sufficiently elevated spiritual plane to be worthy of a Christian. No matter how natural such a resentment may be, a Christian cannot be merely "natural." He must occupy a higher ground; he must try to judge *sub specie aeternitatis*. In moving words, with utter sincerity, because the words came from a man who humbly acknowledged his fault, he confessed that the previous pages of the book had been written before he had passed through his "spiritual catharsis." It is the "post-Revolutionary" Berdyaev who is speaking in the Postscript. That Berdyaev is characterized henceforth by the words of Bloy which he himself loved to repeat often: "*Souffrir passe, avoir souffert ne passe jamais.*" So important for an understanding of Berdyaev is the Postscript that we must needs scrutinize it closely. The book, he informs us, was written during the summer of 1918,

"in an atmosphere of painful spiritual revolt against the victorious Communist Revolution. In it are reflected, perhaps too strongly, negative emotions which at present no longer dominate me. At that time I as yet had not experienced spiritual catharsis; I had not yet felt the spiritual experience of the Revolution in its very depths; I had not thought it out to the end in the light of religion. Even now, in 1923, I accept the distinctions among the basic hierarchical social-philosophical ideas that I made in 1918; but my attitude is much more cleansed and liberated from the dominance of negative feelings, from all hate, even though those feelings were aroused on behalf of true ideas and the right faith. Revolution — atheistic and demonic by its nature — must be experienced with deepened spirituality and luminous religion. He who has brought away only the feeling of wrath and hatred, only a desire for restoration, has not experienced the Revolution spiritually and religiously. . . . Nor has he experienced the Revolution spiritually who has experienced it greedily. The landed proprietor or factory owner who desires above all else the return of his confiscated lands or factories, and vengeance upon those who took the property away from him, has not experienced the Revolution spiritually. The politician who is wroth above all else because his political party and his political ideology have not won, and bides his time to seize the rule and repay those who have been victorious in the Revolution, has not experienced the Revolution spiritually. The ideologist and thinker who is full of wrath because his ideas are persecuted, and is ready to join any power capable of revenging him for his nonrecognition and the crushing of his ideas, has not experienced the Revolution spiritually. The citizen who sees in the Revolution only the harm done to his interests and to his accustomed style of life, and daily expects the restoration of his interests and his lost style of life, has not experienced the Revolution spiritually. He alone has experienced it spiritually who has seen in it his own and his nation's unhappy share, who has discerned in it punishment for past sins, who has repented of not only the Revolutionary but the pre-Revolutionary falsehoods, who has acknowledged the necessity for enlightenment and transformation of life. Such a person becomes not only a Revolutionary or a pre-Revolutionary, but a post-Revolutionary individual, a man of the new era. Our counterrevolution should become post-Revolutionary, not pre-Revolutionary; and it should profess principles unlike those dominant during the Revolution, or those of the pre-Revolutionary period which brought about the Revolution. A spiritual experience of the Revolution cannot lead to a desire for restoration, i.e., the re-establishment of the old regime which has brought about the falsehood of the Revolution; a return to it would be senseless, and would condemn the people to an endless circuit. It is imperative that we abandon the endless circuit of revolution and reaction for a new kind of life — the life of creativity. We cannot oppose the "bourgeois" truth to the anti-Christian Communist falsehood, for there is no more Christ in the bourgeois type of life than in Communism, and one atheism gives birth to another. Communism is but the atheistic falsehood of the bourgeois world consistently carried out to its end.

"To me, revolution is not an external event; it is a reflex of something happening within me and with me, of my guilt, of my spiritual malady. If I, and every other I, had been spiritually sufficiently strong and had had genuine power of faith, the Revolution would not have occurred, but instead of it, enlightenment and transformation of life would have taken place. It matters not if I be called a "reactionary," for I am in reaction — a profound, spiritual reaction against falsehood and lie, against the inhuman and godless character of revolution. But one must understand the meaning of such "reaction." My "reaction" is not pre-Revolutionary, but post-Revolutionary. . . . It does not lead to a restoration of the pre-Revolutionary style of life, a pre-Revolutionary spiritual state. The Revolution has taken place, and it was as ugly as every other revolution. But one must go on to what is possible after it, and not back to what has come before it. For the antecedent conditions brought it about. We shall aim at creating conditions that shall not lead to a revolution again. Revolution must run its course and terminate itself, for it cannot be terminated externally.

"All these ideas have followed each other during the three years, and I thought it necessary to formulate them in this Postscript so that the ideas expressed in the book could be understood in their true light. No one should utilize them for a nefarious goal. . . . A spiritual understanding of the events that have transpired in the world during the few last years confirms the truth of historical pessimism which has a firm basis in Christian prophecies, and which I have long professed. That strict historical pessimism liberates us from all earthly utopias and mirages of a perfect social organization. But it does not liberate us from the duty of realizing Christ's truth as far as our strength allows. It is not easy to vanquish the radical evil of human nature and of the nature of the world; the final victory over evil consists of the transformation of the world, a 'new heaven' and a 'new earth.' But it does not, therefore, follow that we should consent to the rule of evil and to evil rule; that our wills should not be directed toward the maximum of truth in life." [25]

The problem of the Russian Revolution tormented Berdyaev. When some years afterward he once more returned to a discussion of the topic, his treatment was already set in a larger frame of reference: it is part of a much larger theme, the decline of the Renaissance era and the dark, dimly shadowed future. He discerned the necessity for a new period of spiritual, ascetic training of humankind — the "New Middle Ages," [26] as the title he gave his new book indicates. The second chapter of this work is devoted to " Considerations About the Russian Revolution." This portion of the book repeats many, perhaps most, of the ideas of *The Philosophy of Inequality,* published in the previous year. Even whole sentences are repeated, either verbatim or essentially unchanged. But the new book is permeated by a new spirit, the spirit of the Postscript of the previous work. It is as if Berdyaev published the book by way of expiation for the previous one; here, certainly, speaks the authentic, " post-Revolutionary " Berdyaev at his best both in depth of thought and in beauty of expression.

He has not modified his opinion as to the essential nature of the October Revolution: " The Russian Revolution is a great misfortune. Every revolution is a misfortune. . . . The Russian Revolution is repulsive. There have never been and never can be pretty, propitious, and beautiful revolutions." [27] But he is no longer eloquently saying, " I told you so! " in several hundred pages of diatribe. He is no longer disposed merely to put the blame on others. Although the external facts as to the Revolution remain the same, the interpretation of these facts is different. He sees things now from a Christian perspective:

> " Too great an indignation against the Bolshevik Revolution, too exclusive an ascription of every sort of thievery to the Bolsheviks, is not seldom the result of idealization of the Revolution, an unvanquished illusion that revolutions can be pretty and propitious. . . . Almost all prevailing judgments regarding the Revolution are based on the presupposition that it need never have happened, that it could have been prevented from transpiring, or, that it could have been managed reasonably and well, had not the rascally Bolsheviks gone insane." [28]

When Shakespeare wrote that " men at some time are masters of their fates: The fault, dear Brutus, is not in our stars, but in ourselves, that we are underlings," he expressed a sentiment which Berdyaev echoed in bewailing his own or his nation's misfortunes:

"It is spiritually false to suppose that the source of evil is outside myself, that I alone am the vessel of good. From such soil springs cruel and hateful fanaticism. To accuse the Jews, Freemasons, and intellectuals as alone guilty is no better than to accuse the *bourgeoisie,* the nobility, the old regime of it all. No; the source of evil is within myself and I should share in the guilt and the responsibility. That was true in relation to the old absolutism, and has remained true in relation to Bolshevism." [29]

"Bolshevism is my sin, my guilt. It is an affliction sent me from above. The sufferings which Bolshevism has caused me are in expiation for my guilt, my sin — our common guilt and our common sin. All are responsible for all. Only such experiencing of the Revolution may be called religious, spiritually enlightened. The Russian Revolution is a judgment upon the Russian people and upon me — a penalty and expiation both on the part of the people and on my part." [30]

"The Russian Revolution has fulfilled Dostoevsky's anticipations. He had prophetically laid bare its ideological dialectic and had depicted its image. Dostoevsky understood that Russian socialism is a religious question, a question of atheism; that Russian revolutionary intellectuals are not concerned with politics, but with the salvation of humankind without God. . . . *The Russian question is at present above all a spiritual question.* Russia cannot be saved unless it is spiritually regenerated." [31]

But what is true of Russia is equally true of the whole world.

"There is no basis for rosy historical optimism. Christianity does not teach it. The world is headed toward a tragic duality and a struggle of opposing spiritual principles. But on these paths a dispelling of illusions and a discernment of authentic realities have a great significance." [32]

Accordingly, Berdyaev's appeal to the whole Christian world rings with an earnestness and solemnity which possess a moving quality:

"Again there stands before the Christian nations the question whether they seriously accept their Christianity and wish to direct their wills toward its realization. If the Christian nations do not supremely exert their wills toward the realization of the Christian way;

if they do not put forth their utmost activity; then atheistic Communism shall conquer the world. A free spirit must act independently of whatever forces are dominant and victorious. Christianity is returning to the pre-Constantinian status, and must once more win the world." [33]

May God grant that the spiritual regeneration come, and that it be not a case of "too little and too late!" Certainly everything that has happened since these terribly somber words of Berdyaev were written, more than twenty years ago, has heightened their solemnity.

Despite Berdyaev's defection from Marxism, and his arduous and fervent profession and defense of the Christian religious world view, the new masters of Russia treated him at first with surprising consideration. He was included in the writers' guild. In fact, he was chosen one of the twelve writers who were considered so outstanding that the Government granted them special rations (they were jestingly known as "the immortals"). But the new regime's policy was inconsistent and subject to sudden changes. When the law regarding compulsory labor was passed, he was compelled to join the work battalion to which he was assigned and do his share of clearing the streets or work outside the town. His sister-in-law, who was assigned to the same labor detail, writes that Berdyaev's sufferings under these unaccustomed conditions of hard physical labor were great, even though he himself makes no mention of the episode. He was ill and had a high temperature. Nevertheless, he had to arise at 5 A.M. and go out into severe cold. Surrounded by soldiers, the labor detail was assigned the task of cleaning the ice off the rails on a railroad track outside Moscow. All day long they ate nothing. At the close of the day Berdyaev could hardly stand on his feet.[34]

Nevertheless, this experience was exceptional. He was not deprived of his apartment and was allowed to continue his accustomed writing. When many other writers, fearful lest they lose their professional classification, demeaned themselves by currying favors from the new commissar of education, Lunacharsky, Berdyaev refused to call upon this former fellow Marxist, whom he knew well in his youth. He even severed relations with a number of his friends — such outstanding literary figures as Vyacheslav Ivanov and M. Gershenzon — because of their too great " accommodation " to the new regime.

Under these circumstances it is no wonder that Berdyaev could hardly escape being arrested. One night in 1920 a Chekist (a member of the security police) appeared at his home and ransacked his study. Berdyaev quietly remarked to him: " You are searching in vain. I am an opponent of Bolshevism, and have never concealed my views. You will find nothing in my writings that I have not openly declared in my lectures and meetings." The Chekist, however, continued his search until morning, when he drew up his report: " Berdyaev confessed that he is an opponent of Bolshevism, because he is a Christian." [35] Thereupon Berdyaev was arrested and incarcerated in an inner cell of the Cheka prison. One night, at midnight, he was summoned for an examination before the dreaded master of the Cheka, the insanely cruel and fanatical Dzerzhinsky; the meeting was also attended by Kamenev and the deputy chairman of the Cheka, Menzhinsky. When permitted to state his views, Berdyaev spoke for forty-five minutes, summing up his religious, philosophical, and moral reasons for his rejection of Communism, but adding that he was not a political opponent of the regime. What a scene this must have been! In the end, Dzerzhinsky dismissed Berdyaev and allowed him to go home, but forbade him to leave Moscow. Indeed, the master Chekist ordered a state automobile to convey Berdyaev to his home — but since an auto was unavailable, a soldier carried out the order on a motorcycle.

Berdyaev thereupon extended his activity to a surprising degree. He greatly expanded his lecture and study courses in the Free Academy of Spiritual Culture, an institution Berdyaev had founded in 1918, which received the authorization of Kamenev himself. It was registered in the Soviet of Workers' Deputies. The academy afforded the only platform in all Soviet Russia where freedom of thought and expression prevailed. Berdyaev conducted there study courses and seminars, held public lectures, and even arranged disputations on controversial subjects. For instance, during the winter of 1920–1921 he delivered a series of lectures on Dostoevsky which were later reworked for publication.[36] Anyone acquainted with this work, the best exposition of the essentials of Dostoevsky's basic faith and thought, cannot but admire the daring of its author in defying the official "party line" of the Soviet regime in such a flagrant fashion. The same may be said about *The Meaning of History,* which was originally delivered as a course of lectures during the winter of 1919–1920. The public disputations in which Berdyaev participated were also of a challenging character: thus at one time when the Anarchist Club arranged a disputation about Christ, Berdyaev delivered his defense of Christ and Christianity in such an inspired manner that he himself regarded this speech as "his most successful."[37] It was later published under the title *The Worthiness of Christianity and the Unworthiness of Christians.* But it may be noticed in passing that the pamphlet was published in Warsaw; apparently it could not appear in the Soviet Union itself. On other occasions he spoke before larger audiences than ever before or afterward. For example, he delivered a lecture on religion in the Polytechnical Museum before an audience that comprised from 1,500 to 2,000 hearers.

The most surprising event of this period of comparative freedom of expression which Berdyaev enjoyed was his appointment, in 1920, to the chair of philosophy at the University of Moscow. He was elected to this position by the faculty of that institution, and held his post for a year. Nevertheless, he earned his living, not as a university professor, but as a member of the writers' union.

The situation changed suddenly in the late summer of 1922, when religious persecutions were begun by the newly organized antireligious front. Berdyaev was again arrested by the secret police. This time he was held in prison for about a week. The original Revolutionary leaders, many of whom knew Berdyaev personally, either were no longer in power or did not exercise their former influence. At any rate, Berdyaev no longer received the comparatively mild treatment that had been meted out to him formerly. He was banished from the Soviet Union, and informed that if he should attempt to return, he would be shot. He even had to sign a declaration to that effect.[38]

However, it was not until two months later that, in September, he and some twenty-five other members of the intelligentsia who proved too independent or intransigent in their ideologies and political views were deported from Soviet Russia. Before his departure, a cultured Bolshevik, the president of the Academy of Arts, told him, " The Kremlin hopes that when you find yourself in western Europe you will learn on whose side the truth is." Berdyaev remarks in his autobiography that he disappointed the Kremlin's hopes: " I have remained a spiritual opponent of totalitarian Communism both in Russia and in the West." [39]

4

The Exile

THE EXILED GROUP left Leningrad for Stettin by boat, and thence proceeded on to Berlin. They were kindly and hospitably received by the Germans, although the representatives of the Russian *émigrés* did not trouble themselves to welcome them. Berdyaev lived in Berlin for two years. He did not co-operate with the " white " Russians who were headed by his former friend Peter Struve, with whose political program he disagreed. With the financial help of the International Y.M.C.A. he organized the Religious Philosophical Academy, of which he became president. In this way he sought to perpetuate the work and influence of similar societies which he had sponsored in Russia. Moreover, there was organized in Berlin, under the auspices of the German Government, the Russian Institute of Sciences, in which Berdyaev taught and in which he served as a departmental dean.

Although he eagerly engaged in cultural activity which directly or indirectly served the interests of the Russian people, he refused to engage in political activity, particularly in behalf of the restoration of the old order in Russia. In the spirit of an Old Testament prophet he accused the *émigrés,* particularly the monarchists, of their sins of omission and commission which had brought about the Revolution. He did not believe in their sword. " The truly realistic struggle with the Bolsheviks is a spiritual struggle," he wrote in reply to a monarchist who had taunted him with holding to " a passive suffering of evil." [1]

As has already been mentioned, during the Berlin period Berdyaev published, in 1923, a book entitled *The New Middle Ages.*

It met with an enthusiastic reception, and was translated into fourteen languages. The work is significant because it bears witness to a new interest which henceforth engaged his attention with an ever increasing, even anguished, concern. For that matter, *The Meaning of History* also belongs to this category. Count Keyserling, with whom Berdyaev became personally acquainted in Berlin, helped him in publishing a German translation of the work. Berdyaev likewise met Max Scheler who, however, disappointed his expectations because of his overweening egocentricity, and Oswald Spengler, whom he regarded as " very bourgeois." Henceforth Berdyaev's interests, which hitherto had been predominantly Russian, even though they had ranged through the fields of philosophy over a whole gamut of related subjects, now soared to the consideration of the cosmic destiny of man. This does not imply that Berdyaev had never before given a thought to such a subject; it only means that henceforth there is an increasing emphasis on this theme in his thought and writings.

Berdyaev did not claim to be a historian in the ordinary, professional sense of that word; he prefered to call himself a " historiographer " and " metahistorian." For the historian's task is limited to the available written and archaeological source materials. Consequently, the span of time with which he deals — even such a historian as Arnold J. Toynbee, who undertakes to abstract the norms governing all the civilizations that have appeared during the " historic " time — is comparatively limited. If civilization is only some six thousand years old, the subject matter of the historian is pitifully meager in comparison with the precivilization period. It may be a mere one hundredth of man's earthly existence. Moreover, the historian qua historian does not raise the ultimate questions regarding the *meaning* of history — the whence, whither, and why of human life. These " damned questions," as Dostoevsky used to refer to them, cannot be answered merely from the point of view of recorded history, although the historical span must be considered as integral. Essentially, such questions are cosmic and metahistorical: they deal with beginnings and ends of history, of which historical science knows nothing and can know nothing. And yet they are absolutely essential. For without an answer to them history is meaningless, as " nonmetaphysical " science and philosophy rightly concede or affirm. Is one to conclude, then, that human life is meaningless? It is of prime importance to every thinking man how he answers these questions for himself.

Berdyaev applied to himself the terms " historiographer " and " metahistorian " just because his primary interest was in the whence, whither, and why. His answers must necessarily rest upon the " realistic mystical " insight of religious faith. Whether or not they be mere fancy each reader must decide for himself.

Although a discussion of his positive views on this subject belongs properly to the second part of this work, his repudiation of the dominant views contrary to his way of thinking must be treated here. It is expedient to include in our discussion several works that Berdyaev devoted to this theme. For thus we shall gain an integrated synopsis of his views which otherwise would have to be treated separately. Accordingly, I propose to deal with Berdyaev's spiritual development spanning fifteen years — from *The Meaning of History* (published in 1923, but written earlier) to *The New Middle Ages* (1919–1923), *The Bourgeois Mind,* and *The Fate of Man in the Modern World* (1934).

Berdyaev definitely ranges himself with the personalist or existentialist philosophy, and along with Dostoevsky and Kierkegaard he rejects Hegel's view of history. He charges Hegel with depriving man of personality. For Hegel, only the Absolute was real — the World Spirit which found its infinitesimally momentary embodiment and realization in man. " In human knowledge and volition as its material element, Reason attains positive existence." [2] Man's spirit is not his own; it is but the fleeting phase of the Absolute. Man is but a ripple on the vast limitless ocean of the Eternal and the Unconditioned. Without the ocean, there would be no ripple; by itself, the ripple has no separate, independent existence. As for world history, the history of nations, they too are but an evolving, developing Eternal Idea. Nations do not determine themselves; they are determined.

Hegel speaks of the " cunning of reason " in history, which overrides man in order to gain its ends, although man subjectively feels as if he were freely carrying out his own designs. In fact, it is illusory to speak of the " overriding " of man, for man does not, cannot, have a " will " or " purpose " apart from the Absolute. " It may be said," according to Hegel, as interpreted by Berdyaev, " that the subject of history is not man, not even mankind, but a nonhuman reason or spirit which, in the teaching of Marx, is transformed into nonhuman economics." [3]

It is against this dehumanizing philosophy of history, or this " historical " or " economic " determinism, that Berdyaev ranges himself. As we shall see later, this protest against " objectification " plays a large part in his philosophy. Man is a real being; he exists. History, then, is

> " the tragedy of the lack of agreement between what exists as human and personal on the one hand, and all objectification, which is always extrapersonal, nonhuman, antipersonal, and antihuman, on the other. Every objectification of history is nonhuman and impersonal. Man is fated to live in two different orders: that of existence, which is always personal, although full of superpersonal values, and that of the objectified world, always nonpersonal and quite indifferent to personal values. . . . He is compelled to realize that the processes of history are fatal, inhuman forces, quite indifferent to his fate, forces as merciless as they are nonhuman." [4]

In other words, man is the meeting point of the spiritual and the material orders. His spirit is not the product of natural forces. As far as he fails to live spiritually, as a person, he lives in a world alien to himself. When, in Berdyaev's language, he yields to objectification, his inner freedom is lost.

Berdyaev is in total revolt against the dominant secularist character of modern history. He denounces it in unmeasured, exaggerated terms. He is not a " detached," " objective " philosopher in this respect, but an earnest, flaming reformer and prophet. Secularist culture is corrupt in root and branch — not only corrupt, but dead. An ax is already laid at its roots, and it shall be cut down and burned. Berdyaev vehemently declares that

" the very substance of my philosophy is to have nothing at all to do with the thought of times which, so far as I am concerned, are over and done with. I look to the thought of a world which is to begin, the world of the New Middle Ages." [5]

The beginning of the modern period of Western history, which Berdyaev quite properly identifies with the Renaissance, is characterized by him as an outburst of creative energy unequaled since the amazing sixth century of the Greek era. The long incubating period of the Middle Ages, during which man's spirit had been disciplined by the ascetic training he had received in the Church, finally gave birth to the marvelous creative forces of the Renaissance. For the period of the Middle Ages was by no means culturally sterile; in fact, it was a time of great potential as well as actual vitality. Nor was it altogether spiritually unified and thoroughly Christian, as Roman Catholic apologists for the medieval " synthesis " would have us believe. In fact, Berdyaev makes an interesting suggestion in one of his [illegible] books that, in a sense, the medieval philosophy was more naturalistic, cosmological, ontological — in a word, Aristotelian — than is the modern, which is at least to a degree existentialist.[6] As in all ages, so in the medieval, the religious spirit struggled with the secular:

> " It was not only the most ascetic, but also the most sensuous epoch . . . which gave birth equally to the ideal of the monk and the knight, of the feudal anarchy and of the Holy Roman Empire; to the world denial on the part of the Church and the world domination by that same Church; to the ascetic exploits of monasticism and the knightly cult of the beautiful woman. This epoch emphasized dualism in all spheres of being and placed before future mankind unresolved problems: above all, the problem of comprising all activity within the confines of the Church, and of the subjection of all human life to theocracy." [7]

This lusty, virile period gave birth to the Renaissance. " Man came to this flowering with medieval experience, medieval preparation, and all that was authentically great in the Renaissance had a bond with the Christian Middle Ages." [8] Nor was it a mere rebirth of classical antiquity, as is commonly supposed; it had an abundant life and character of its own. The Renaissance man did not merely return to the world view of the Greek and Latin cultures — he could not do so even if he had wanted to. For, after all, he had lived through more than a millennium of Christian nurture which had become the flesh and blood of his being. He only expressed himself, his newly born spirit of self-assertion, in the beautiful forms of antiquity. The new wine of humanism was, for the time being, poured into the skins of antiquity, found conveniently at hand. But the humanism of the Renaissance man was his own. Above all, man believed in himself. Instead of *Te Deum,* he was now singing *Me Deum.* Even his Christian self was often expressed in ancient thought forms; if the terms were pagan, the content was not.[9]

At first, the humanistic self-assertion took the aesthetic form in the outburst of an astonishingly powerful artistic creativity such as the Western world had not witnessed since the days of Phidias and Praxiteles. Boccaccio, Dante, and Giotto were the chief representatives of the earlier, Christian phase of the Renaissance, the *trecento* — "the greatest age of European history and its culminating point." [10]

However, the artistic phase of the Renaissance carried the germs of death within itself. It distilled poisons from its own body that in the end caused the writhing agonies of the approaching end, which, according to Berdyaev, we are now witnessing. Hegel displayed an authentic insight when he formulated the same idea in the philosophical formula of a thesis generating its own antithesis. The Renaissance man cut himself off from his Christian sources of inspiration. His art became technically superbly finished, but inwardly cold, rigid. At first he strove to conquer nature by painting "naturally"; but in the end nature conquered him. He became merely a natural being: "but the natural man cannot draw upon inexhaustible springs for his creativeness; he drains himself dry, and only the arid surface of life is left." [11]

The same creative, self-affirming spirit manifested itself in the religious realm during the Reformation period. Man affirmed himself by repudiating the corrupt papal autocracy which had usurped the place between man and God. He insisted upon asserting the rights of his own conscience, upon his own immediate approach to God. Whether or not the words were actually spoken by Luther as tradition reports them — "Here I stand; I can do no otherwise. God help me!" — is of little importance for our purpose. It expresses symbolically the spirit of the Reformation as well as of Luther. Being a revolt, the Reformation was necessarily one-sided, overemphatic. Berdyaev's own characterization is noteworthy:

"Protestantism was not only a rupture with the Church, but also a healthy reaction against the deviations of Catholicism, against the degeneracy within the Church. Protestantism attempted to renew the freedom of Christ which had been completely lost. Protestantism affirmed the principle of personality which lay at the basis of Christ's religion: the false teaching of medieval Catholicism regarding man, and the false debasement of man's personality, brought about the protest, the relative correctness of which is beyond doubt. Protestantism was bound to make its appearance, because there existed in the history of Christianity no positive religious anthropology, and the vacancy was filled by a false anthropology. In the Protestant affirmation of personality and of freedom, the new man was initiated, the man of modern history." [12]

In its unfolding, in the later stages of modern history, the humanistic spirit of the Renaissance has developed, with almost fatalistic irresistibility, its inner contradiction, its inevitable antithesis — the denial of man. This is the lesson grandly taught by Dostoevsky. Perhaps Berdyaev learned it from his spiritual master. Dostoevsky, in almost everything he wrote, taught the truth that human self-assertion, the titanism of the man-god, leads to self-destruction. Such is the case with Raskolnikov, who thought he could commit crime without suffering punishment; with Ivan Karamazov, who realized with startling clarity that if there be no God, all things are permitted; with Verkhovensky, who caused suffering to himself and all about him; and above all, with Kirilov, who represents titanism pushed to the extreme limits of man-godhood. This latest stage of the Renaissance "*is an unfolding of ideas and events wherein we see humanism destroying itself by its own dialectic, for the putting up of man without God and against God, the denial of the divine image and likeness in himself, lead to his own negation and destruction.*" [13]

The disintegration of the humanist movement from inner sterility is the burden of the sad story of modern philosophy. The Renaissance self-affirmation found a philosophical mode of expression in the rationalist and empirical movements fathered respectively by Descartes and Locke. But Berdyaev, as we shall see later, having been nurtured in the German philosophical tradition, begins his real discussion of modern philosophy with Kant and the German idealists whom he knows thoroughly, and in whose thought he has steeped himself from his early youth. Kant, the cold rationalist and moralist, is the "continuator of Luther, the creator of philosophical Protestantism." "One must fight Kant," Berdyaev declared in one of his earliest books.[14]

"Kant is very dangerous, for in him are sown the seeds of the most hopeless and at the same time the mightiest philosophy of the ephemeral. The sons of the Kantian spirit attempt to organize humanity on a rationalistic basis, affirm rationalistic morals, rationalistic experience in which all transcendence, all passage to the eternal, are forever lost. . . . Kant was the creator of epistemological and moral values by which a large number of people of our cultural epoch live; but he dried up their souls, rendered them positivistic, taught them not to hold pure, living, and life-affirming hopes. Often it is said that Kant fought against rationalism, delimited it properly; but in reality he was the most subtle of rationalists, the mightiest of them all. It is characteristic of Kantianism that it appears as a surrogate, or substitute, religion. That arid, abstractly moralistic religion, substituting for the living saviour a dead categorical imperative, is extremely characteristic of the whole epoch in which religious hopes were abandoned." [15]

"It was Kant's genius that expressed the serious illness of humankind, for he formulated philosophically humanity's fatal cutting itself off from the roots and sources of being. The philosophy of Kant places man on the brink of a bottomless void and demands that man subjectively re-create the objectively lost being. Only lost, forsaken, and isolated man could and should have conceived Kant's philosophy.

That is why one cannot regard it as merely an epistemological doctrine, a system of theoretical philosophy which need not call forth too painful sufferings. Kantianism is a phenomenon immeasurably deeper and more terrible — a matter of life and being itself. . . . One cannot be a Kantian and profess faith in the reality of Christ's resurrection or expect a real end of history." [16]

However, in one of his recently published books, *An Essay on Eschatological Metaphysics,* Berdyaev returns once more to his first love, Kant, and speaks of the latter's system of thought with warm appreciation.[17] Not that he repudiates his former judgment that Kantianism is antipersonalist; but he now asserts that Kant has provided the necessary presupposition for the existential philosophy (which will be dealt with later) in establishing the reality of the autonomous noumenal, that is to say, the spiritual, realm upon which existential philosophy is grounded. Because of this discovery, Berdyaev ranks Kant and Plato as the two greatest philosophers in the entire history of human thought.[18] To be sure, these two giants among philosophers drew diametrically opposed conclusions from their premises: Plato held that only the world of ideas, i.e., the noumenal world, may be known; while Kant asserted, on the contrary, that only the phenomenal world is knowable, since knowledge derives its raw material from sensory impressions which the mind works up into concepts by the use of categories. And although Kant was too rationalistic and empirical to penetrate very far into the noumenal domain, yet he established its reality beyond all doubt. He thus prepared the way for a philosophy which recognizes the noumenal world as primary. Berdyaev's philosophy of existentialism derives from Kant.

Nevertheless, the immediate successors of Kant proceeded to play fast and loose with Kant's discovery in exactly the same way in which the epigoni of Plato have done: instead of guarding the precious distinction between the *two* realms — the phenomenal and the noumenal — they immediately proceeded to obliterate it by uniting them in one or another form of monism. There appears some fatality in the working of the philosophical mind: it seems to be irresistibly drawn to monism, as the moth is impelled toward the fatal candle flame. Accordingly, the systems of Fichte, Schelling, and Hegel are all monistic and, therefore, *ipso facto* antipersonalistic. For as long as a World Soul or an Absolute alone possess being, human personality must be in some sense unreal. Fichte held the antipersonalist view by making the Ego a bridge across the chasm dug by Kant, between the phenomenal and the noumenal. The Ego is not the human self, personality, but a universal, divine Ego. In Fichte's philosophy, accordingly, man is not a real person.

Likewise, the Hegelian Absolute which comes to self-consciousness in man is not, after all, a human personality but an impersonal Idea. Berdyaev writes of it:

> "True, the divine self-consciousness and self-knowledge are realized in and through man. But what comfort is that to me? The teaching that the Deity comes to self-consciousness in man, and that the World Spirit attains its height through philosophy which is man's work, might appear very gratifying to man's pride and elevating to his dignity. But that is to affirm that human independence exists not at all and man is but a function of the World Spirit, of the World Reason, of the Deity: he is but an instrument, a means, a way toward the realization of goals that are not human at all." [19]

This process of philosophical denial of man's noumenal existence culminated finally in the radically antihumanistic systems of Friedrich Nietzsche and Karl Marx. Of the two, Nietzsche was philosophically incomparably greater. Nietzsche was the great antihumanist. He hated man — the herd man — the common, ordinary, natural human being. Men were mean and low. He would be a benefactor who would rid the earth of the hateful human herds. But his hatred of the herd man was only the obverse side of his romantic admiration for the transformed, transfigured, heroic race of supermen. "The superman I have at heart; *he* is the first and only concern of mine, and not man: not the neighbor, not the poorest, not the sorriest, not the best," said Zarathustra.[20] The superman, the physical paragon, "the blond beast," possessed the Dionysian qualities which Nietzsche admired and deified in the Greeks and Romans: virility, courage, lust for life, victorious spirit, will to power, ruthlessness toward everything weak and degenerate. His opposition to Christianity (that is, to his conception of the debased, bourgeois Christianity of his day) emanated from his interpretation of it as a religion of slaves and weaklings, deliberately inculcating ethics of humility, submission, and love of enemies. He assumed, as a self-evident fact, that Christianity was no longer a living force. " The Great Pan is dead! " cried Zarathustra; but he said it with regret and sorrow. Since God was dead, Christian ethics had no relevance — at least he saw what many modern pagans do not seem to have perceived, that Christian ethics could not survive without the Christian faith. Consequently, Nietzsche undertook the task of creating new ethics, based on strength and beauty.

His basic error was his naïve supposition that the herd man by some miracle would give birth to the superman. In other words, he still retained from his Christian antecedents an essentially religious faith in the possibility of transforming human nature — Berdyaev would speak of it in terms of God-manhood — but he denied the Christian means and power for such a transformation. Since he provided none in its place, his basic assumption in regard to the transforming process is groundless, and his whole system sterile. One cannot make virile and romantically beautiful " blond beasts " out of the ordinary variety of herd men. Accordingly, one is left with Nietzsche's violent antihumanism. The result is pessimism, denial of the worth of man, impossibility of changing the situation, defeatism, futilitarianism.

As for Karl Marx, he was likewise antihumanist, even though he began his career as a humanist. In the end, he subordinated the individual to the class, and the class to an impersonal force in nature and history — the economic force — which blindly and relentlessly pushes its way through all opposition. This is the primary reality: everything else is determined in relation to the economic factor. For man's economic status makes him what he is. Despite this economic determinism, which obviously deprives man of any freedom of choice — the bourgeois capitalist is just as much its product as the proletarian — Marxism, with contemptuous disregard of the inescapable implications of its own premises, asserts that man has a choice, that he is free, and therefore responsible. The core of Marxism is the faith in the free, creative role of the proletariat. Thus materialism, *dialectical materialism,* turns into a kind of surreptitious idealism. Self-contradictory as all this is, devoid of elementary logic, it still manages to function as the greatest modern social revolutionary inspiration. But even then the spiritual content is ascribed to the social collective, not to an individual.

Summing up the effect of these two mighty antipersonalist faiths of the modern man, Berdyaev asserts that these two thinkers

"have, with the precision of genius, defined the two forms of self-negation and self-destruction of humanism. Nietzsche shows us humanism destroying and denying itself individually; Marx, collectively. . . . Nietzsche conceives man as degraded and ignominious; he aspires to his conquest; his will aims at the superman. The ethical teaching of Nietzsche does not admit the value of human personality. . . . In Nietzsche's teaching the superman replaces the lost God. . . . In the same way it [humanism] perishes in the superhuman collectivism of Marx. . . . But in him too humanism transforms itself into its opposite: into antihumanism." [21]

There have, of course, arisen philosophical protests against the dominant nihilism of the thinkers we have described. In western Europe, the most powerful of them was Søren Kierkegaard. "The melancholy and tragic Kierkegaard is now exerting on modern philosophy an influence toward an ontology of nihilism which is not found in Kierkegaard himself." [22] He rose with might and main against Hegel, and challenged his Absolute in behalf of a real existence of the human being.

Among the more recent of the "existentialists" the best known are Heidegger, Jaspers, and particularly Sartre. But although Berdyaev regards himself as an existentialist, there is a wide gulf between him and these last three. In fact, Berdyaev denies them the designation of "existentialists." [23] But with equal right and considerable justification they could turn upon him and deny him the propriety of calling himself an existentialist. Be that as it may, Berdyaev points out that in their system "the integral image of man disappears." In Heidegger's view, for instance, the chief character of human existence is care, anxiety, for it ends in physical death. Human life is but a preparation for death which terminates man's existence. In Heidegger's system, man's personality, his innermost being, is lost sight of. "Worry turns out to be more significant than the man who worries. Man is constructed out of worries, just as human existence is built up from death." [24] This is again a variation of the philosophy of nihilism — a philosophy of despair and absolute pessimism. The Freudian analysis of man, also, makes him out to be a being so obsessed by sexuality and the fear of death that the most lurid interpretation of Luther's doctrine of "total depravity," by comparison, pales considerably.

It is not surprising, therefore, that in view of such dominant philosophical nihilism and pessimism, modern theology should reflect the same tendencies. Karl Barth's crisis theology reflects the same antihumanist orientation which one finds in so much of the postwar culture. The world and man are bereft of all divine elements and are regarded as incapable of turning toward God. The Fall had utterly defaced the divine image in man. God had thus become "wholly other." There is only "one-way" passage between God and man — from God to man. On his part, man cannot initiate the process, cannot turn to God. He is literally "dead in trespasses and sins." The sole connecting link between man and God is provided by the Word of God: "*Deus dixit,*" but only when and how he pleases. And man only hears, he need not understand. Man has no part in the process of salvation; even his act of hearkening unto the Word of God is a miraculous work of grace. Moreover, the work of the Holy Spirit is limited; he must work only through the prescribed channel. He no longer blows where he lists. Thus God is everything and man is nothing. Worse than that, since God is wholly transcendent, not at all immanent, the world is literally left Godless. Here the extremes meet: atheistic secularism and the most impassioned modern theism agree. Berdyaev concludes, " This is a passionate reaction against humanism in Christianity which has resulted in a degradation, or even a denial, of man." [25]

The last of the affirmations of man, which has turned into a dismal subjugation and denial of the essential man, is to be seen in capitalism. The laissez-faire theory of economics has asserted an illusory economic freedom of man; utilitarianism has flaunted the silly theory that what is most beneficial for an individual likewise makes for the greatest happiness of society. As if the sum total of individual human selfishness has ever resulted in the greatest common benefit! The capitalistic form of economy created by the Industrial Revolution has brought about not only the new era of mechanization of life — which in the long run may be the most significant aspect of the era — but has given birth to the proletariat as well. The prevailing type of society, and this comprises both the capitalistic and the proletarian classes, for they are essentially at one in their avid desire for the " good life," is bourgeois. In his essay on this predominant type of the modern man,[26] Berdyaev mercilessly subjects the bourgeois to exquisite satire, delicious irony, biting sarcasm. He disdains the vulgarity of the bourgeois, his insatiate desire for the things of this world: for wealth, position, power, and respectability. The bourgeois is practical — above all practical; there is no " mystical " nonsense about him at all. He smacks of honest soil and toil, for he does not always belong to the " leisure " class. He " believes only in this world, in the expedient and the useful; he is incapable of living by faith in another world and refuses to base his life on the mystery of Golgotha." [27] When he is religious and righteous, and he may be that in his own way, his righteousness certainly does not exceed that of the scribes and the Pharisees — far from it! He is the first to cast a stone at the sinner,[28] for he has no love for publicans and sinners: " his predilections lie with the righteous Pharisees."

No wonder that the rich bourgeois finds it difficult to enter the Kingdom of Heaven; for he wants no other kingdom than that which he has on earth. Were he to manifest a desire for the Kingdom of God, he would cease to be bourgeois. Nevertheless, mere poverty as such possesses no saving qualities. " The poor man, envying the rich and spiritually enslaved by the desire of usurping the latter's place and wealth, is himself a bourgeois and his entry into the Kingdom is in no wise easier." [29]

This " bourgeoisization " and " proletarianization " of man has greatly contributed to the destruction of human personality. Capitalistic economy is particularly antipersonalistic. It has produced a moral jungle in which the large beasts devour the smaller. Both capitalistic and collectivist economics have speeded up mechanization which dehumanizes life. " We are witnessing the process of dehumanization in all phases of culture and of social life. . . . Man has ceased to be the supreme value; he has ceased to have any value at all." [30]

The primary means whereby the mechanization of modern culture is effected is technological progress. " The chief cosmic force which is now at work to change the whole face of the earth and dehumanize and depersonalize man is not capitalism as an economic system, but technics, the wonder of the age." [31] Modern man has become so fascinated by the mechanization of life and techniques in general that he has forgotten the purpose of life. This is happening on a vast scale. Exclusive concern with technical means supersedes and destroys life's ends. Organization supersedes organism. " *The supremacy of technique and the machine is primarily a transition from organic to organized life, from growth to construction.*" [32]

Moreover, in this mechanical-minded age, scientific ingenuity finds it easier to invent frightful means of destruction than beneficent means of construction. And these sentiments were held by Berdyaev before the invention of the atomic bomb! What would he say now?

To sum up, the Renaissance period is ended. The humanistic spirit it engendered has exhausted its vitality. It has disintegrated from inner sterility. It has transformed itself into its opposite: antihumanism. Modern man stands on the threshold of a new era.

Having removed to Paris in 1924, Berdyaev at last found a congenial refuge after the previous harassing experiences in his native land. For Paris became the center of Russian emigration, when life in Germany became too difficult and necessitated removal. He continued there his accustomed activities. He transferred to Paris the Religious Philosophical Academy. Moreover, two years later he founded a religious-philosophical review, *Put'* (*The Way*), which he continued to edit for fourteen years, until the outbreak of the Second World War put a stop to its publication. It contained a wealth of highly important material, including many articles of his own. Most of the religious-minded Russian *émigré* scholars contributed to its pages; accordingly, many articles that Berdyaev accepted for publication did not necessarily represent his own views. His own writings were often the most aggressive, as for instance when he attacked the promonarchist politics of the Russian hierarchs living in Yugoslavia (the so-called Karlovtsi group), or denounced the condemnation of Bulgakov's doctrine of sophiology by Metropolitan Sergius. Berdyaev also inspired the founding of a literary magazine, *The New City,* which represented the general cultural interests of the Russian *émigrés.* In these ways Berdyaev became the leader of the Russian " leftist " cultural movements, always opposing all " rightist " tendencies. Besides, he became the best-known Russian philosopher as far as the Western educated classes were concerned.

The International Y.M.C.A., under the leadership of Dr. John R. Mott and with the active aid of such of its able representatives as Dr. Donald A. Lowry, Paul B. Anderson, and H. H. Kuhlmann, has earned itself great credit for having provided publication facilities for these Russian intellectuals. The Y.M.C.A. Press has published not only practically all the major works of Berdyaev (who almost invariably wrote in Russian), but those of a large number of other Russian religious and cultural leaders as well. Among them the most remarkable are the theological treatises of Protopriest Sergius Bulgakov, then the dean of the Russian Theological Academy in Paris; the work of the ablest of the present-day Russian theologians, Professor George Florovsky; besides, the works of V. V. Zenkovsky, George P. Fedotov, Constantine Mochulsky, Nicholas Lossky, N. S. Arseniev, V. N. Ilyin, L. A. Zander, and many others.

The Paris period proved to be the longest and the most fruitful. For during nearly a quarter of a century which Berdyaev spent in the French capital he produced his most important works. Moreover, international recognition was generously extended to him, for his works were acclaimed throughout the educated world and were translated into many leading European languages — particularly into French and English. His fame is particularly well established in the English-speaking world, where he is often regarded as the most creative and stimulating of the religious thinkers today. In fact, in his autobiography he expresses his amazement at finding himself "respectable." There is no doubt that such is his status, since Oxford University recently conferred upon him the degree of doctor of theology, *honoris causa!*

Among the most important works that he published during this period may be named *Philosophy of Free Spirit,* published in 1927 and translated into English under the title *Freedom and the Spirit.* This work, which is devoted to the exposition of Berdyaev's religious views, received the French Academy prize in moral and religious sciences. It was followed in 1931 by a substantial book dealing with "paradoxical ethics," entitled in its English translation *The Destiny of Man.* This is one of the most mature and valuable of his writings. *The Fate of Man in the Modern World* (1934) harks back to *The Meaning of History,* for the main thesis of the later work is already sketched in the earlier volume.

Spirit and Reality made its appearance in 1937 and was devoted to the important subject of God-manhood. Perhaps along with it was published (although it is not dated) the very choice small work—one of Berdyaev's happiest creations—*I and the World of Objects* (*Solitude and Society* in the English edition), which deals with the basic concept of objectification. This was followed in 1947 (although it was written in 1941, in the midst of the war) by his *Eschatological Metaphysics,* which expounds more fully than any other of his writings his central ideas of existential metaphysics conditioned by his concept of the end of the present and the inauguration of the new aeon. These books comprise an excellent exposition of the basic concepts of Berdyaev's philosophy wherein he sets forth the antithesis between personal existence as freedom and true reality, and all objectification as alienation, slavery, and depersonalization. He ranges himself with the philosophers of the type of Pascal, Kierkegaard, and Saint Augustine. The book *Slavery and Freedom* (1939) summarizes in concentrated form all his ideas, ranging over the whole gamut of his thought, as they are singly presented in his previously published books. Of a similar character is *The Divine and the Human* (1947).

His last book of essays is entitled *Toward a New Epoch* (the English translation was published in England in 1949), although Berdyaev made references to other works upon which he was engaged shortly before his death, and which may still appear in print. Altogether different from his other works is his spiritual autobiography, significantly entitled *Self-knowledge,* which was published in its original Russian edition in 1949. It was written, for the greatest part, in 1940; Berdyaev brought the story up to 1947 by appending two additional chapters. It is not an autobiography in the usual sense of the word, but rather a "history of his spirit and of self-knowledge." Nevertheless, it is an invaluable work, absolutely essential for a fairly adequate understanding of his thought, not to mention its value as a source of knowledge of the main events of his life which was hitherto unavailable. In conclusion it may be remarked that Berdyaev's writings abound in repetitions, so that the same idea is treated in many books and with wearisome verbal similarity. Berdyaev himself confesses that he is not a discursive thinker and that his literary style is aphoristic; consequently he has been much misunderstood on that account. The repetitiousness is particularly annoying in his autobiography.

Besides the literary activity which was always primary, Berdyaev took an active part in a number of organizations in which he desired to make his influence felt. He was particularly interested in student work. Thus, for instance, he co-operated, even since the Berlin period, in the work of the Christian Student Movement. He was looked upon by the Orthodox youth not as a true Orthodox but as " a modernist, a freethinker, a heretic," for most of the official religious leaders were under the influence of the " rightist " Karlovtsi hierarchy, against which Berdyaev was in constant opposition. " He left . . . [the Student Movement] when the rightist currents revealed themselves in it," as he himself reported. It may be remarked that many times Berdyaev saw " rightist " tendencies in movements that others considered quite moderate. They were " rightist " from his own, often extreme, point of view.

Furthermore, he organized the Paris meetings of the Russian Orthodox with the French Roman Catholics and Protestants. These meetings were initiated in 1926 by the Religious Philosophical Academy, of which he was president. Roman Catholics were represented by such outstanding intellectual leaders as Jacques Maritain; R. P. Gillet, of the Institut Catholique, and later the general of the Dominican Order; Abbé Labertonnière, who represented radical Catholic modernism; and others. French Protestants sent as their spokesmen Marc Boegner, and Wilfred Monod who represented the radical social group in Protestantism; the Orthodox were represented by Bulgakov, Berdyaev, and several other outstanding leaders. Of course, even in these meetings, Berdyaev did not pretend to speak in behalf of official Orthodoxy, but for his own free religious views. Berdyaev found himself " to the left " of the position of most of the participants, whatever their religious affiliation. All were, in his eyes, more or less traditional and conservative. " Western Christians," he wrote, " Catholics as well as Protestants, were likewise in the grip of religious reaction, although in distinction from the Russian Orthodox, a reaction of a highly cultured form: they felt the need of a return to the past and sought firm authority and tradition. I perceived with sorrow that the Russian religious movements are foreign or little known to Western Christians, although the same must be said of the present generation of Russians." [33]

The equivocal position of Berdyaev *vis-à-vis* his own Orthodox communion caused him considerable uneasiness and embarrassment: for the Westerns were at first inclined to look upon him as the very embodiment of Orthodoxy and "almost the voice of the Church." Such a role could be played perhaps by Bulgakov, but not by Berdyaev. It was with considerable astonishment that the non-Orthodox learned of the true relation of Berdyaev to the traditional Orthodox circles. This inherent difficulty in the end led to his rupture with most of the members of the latter group, including the professors of the Orthodox Theological Academy, of which Bulgakov was the head. Although there was no actual break with Bulgakov, Berdyaev henceforth greatly limited his contacts with him. Berdyaev likewise continued to regard Professor G. P. Fedotov in a friendly fashion and came to his defense — in his usual spirited manner, to say the least — when he thought that the Academy treated Professor Fedotov unfairly. There were, as usual, two sides to this question in which Berdyaev displayed his customary impetuosity. To be sure, Berdyaev's religious views differed often greatly from the accepted Orthodox position, and a conflict between him and the exponents of the more traditional Orthodoxy was inevitable. Berdyaev repeatedly admitted that he felt himself to be a "leftist" or "modernist" (a term he greatly disliked) even in comparison with liberal Catholics and Protestants. "I felt it keenly at international meetings at which Protestants predominated; but these Protestants were much more conservative, traditional, and authoritarian than I who represented Orthodoxy. In the end I felt isolated and suffered by reason of either not being understood or by being misunderstood." [34]

Furthermore, Berdyaev attended many international congresses: thus in 1927 he took part in a conference held in the Austrian Alps, in which representatives of the Roman Catholics, the Orthodox, and the Protestants participated. He also took part in many of the annual "Decades of Pontigny," held each August, at which the elite in philosophy and literature met. His lecture tours took him to England, Germany, Austria, Switzerland, Holland, Belgium, Czechoslovakia, Hungary, Poland, Latvia, and Esthonia. Since his whole outlook was essentially ecumenical, he likewise interested himself actively in movements looking toward the federation or union of Christian communions into one ecumenical body.

Berdyaev's circumstances were greatly improved when one of his English friends, Florence West, who had married a very rich Frenchman, left him a villa in a small village southwest of Paris, at Clamart sur Seine. Not far from this village, in Meudon, Jacques Maritain had his home. Berdyaev's home became renowned for cordial hospitality and served as a meeting place for religious and cultural private gatherings.

There Berdyaev and his gifted wife — she was a poet — held regular Sunday evening "open house" attended by his Russian friends, such as Professors George P. Fedotov and Constantine Mochulsky; by American Y.M.C.A. leaders engaged in work among the Russian *émigrés,* Dr. Donald H. Lowry and Paul B. Anderson; as well as by clergymen, both Catholic and Protestant, and other intellectuals. Among them was the Russian convert to Catholicism, the daughter of the former czarist ambassador to France, Hélène Iswolsky, who has written a charming description of these meetings in one of her recent books.[35]

Sitting at the large, round dining room table, Berdyaev carried on a fascinating philosophical or religious discussion which sparkled with brilliant flashes of spiritual insight. Always in earnest, he was quickly moved to indignation by all injustice, compromise with evil, or insincerity. On such occasions he indulged in vehement outbursts of anger; thereupon his wife would calmly remark that he talked like his grandfather.[36] This would prove sufficient to bring him back to his usual urbane and kindly self.

Berdyaev was passionately fond of animals. He had a favorite cat, Murya. Somctimes, in the midst of a lively discussion of some profound theme, the philosopher would suddenly manifest signs of anxiety, get up, and go into the garden to look for her. When she died, Berdyaev was heartbroken. He devoted several pages to her in his autobiography. In another book he actually remarks, " I cannot think of the Kingdom of God without a place in it for my Murya." [37]

When the Second World War broke out and the Germans invaded France and Paris was about to fall, Berdyaev's friends urged him to leave his home. At first he refused; but in June, 1940, he did leave. He chose to seek refuge in Pilat, near Arcachon in the Bay of Biscay. But a few days after his arrival the German Army occupied this strategic spot. Nevertheless, the Berdyaevs (with Mrs. Berdyaev's sister, who had lived with them for many years) were in no way molested.

Although Berdyaev himself makes no mention of the incident, Miss Iswolsky tells the story of Berdyaev's first encounter with a Nazi officer, which occurred on the Pilat beach. He was accosted by the German warrior and interrogated as to his identity and profession. Berdyaev gave his name and answered the latter part of the question by saying that he was a philosopher. But when the Nazi seemed to have been considerably puzzled by Berdyaev's professional occupation, the latter attempted to explain. He found it difficult, however. In the end, he asked the German where he came from. The latter replied that his home town was Königsberg. Berdyaev thereupon remarked that the greatest German philosopher, Immanuel Kant, was born and lived all his life in Königsberg. To that the Nazi warrior replied with a shrug of his shoulders that he had never heard of him.[38]

Early in September of the same year Berdyaev returned to his home in Clamart; although his friends urged him to emigrate to the United States, he refused to go either there or anywhere else.

When Germany attacked the Soviet Union, its faithful ally

hitherto, the Germans in France began a mass arrest of the Russians living there. Many friends and acquaintances of Berdyaev were imprisoned. Although Berdyaev openly proclaimed his sympathy with the Red Army and refused to co-operate with the German occupational forces even in the remotest way, he was not molested. Several times he was visited by the Gestapo and subjected to a searching investigation, but no direct charge was ever brought against him. This deference on the part of the Gestapo puzzled him considerably, for he knew that they were not particularly squeamish in their methods, until he learned that he had found a protector among the members of the ranking Nazi hierarchy. It was this unknown disciple who prevented his arrest.

These war years were a time of the most acute suffering for Berdyaev, both physical and spiritual. In 1942 he fell ill and had to undergo an operation. But much more painful were the tortures caused him by a spiritual conflict in which he engaged; under the stress of the cataclysmic events of the war he sometimes doubted whether God could be good and loving, although he never doubted that God existed. He found himself particularly in revolt against many traditional doctrines of Christianity. He felt as if he professed an entirely different religion. " Nevertheless, this revolt against God took place within me in behalf of God, in the name of a higher understanding of God. Just the same, I experienced a sense of God-forsakenness, of the loss of grace. To experience a sense of being forsaken of God does not signify the rejection of the existence of God: in fact, it presupposes God's existence." [39] Above all, Berdyaev concerned himself with thoughts of death and immortality, and these meditations entered partly into his book of unusually beautiful essays, entitled *The Divine and the Human.*[40]

With the liberation of Paris, a new life began for Berdyaev as well as for all France. Nevertheless, fresh sufferings were in store for him: in September, 1945, his beloved wife, Lydia, died. " This was one of the most torturing as well as the most significant experiences of my life." Berdyaev pays her a tender and exceedingly moving tribute in his autobiography; " she was of an immense spiritual help to me in all my life."

Berdyaev's autobiography ends with the year 1947. In the addendum comprising that year he returns once more to the theme of his relation to Soviet Russia. During the war, he experienced something of a revival of his pride in Russia, for the whole world was filled with admiration for the bravery and sacrifices of the Red Army as well as of the Russian people. He even considered returning from his exile, but in the end he decided against the idea. Speaking of the Soviet authorities, he wrote: " They would, perhaps, permit me to return to Russia. But what could I do there? The question of my return home is very painful to me. But a return to Russia, particularly for a philosopher, has no sense." [41] The mood of elation and pride quickly passed, and Berdyaev suffered a disappointment with the conduct of the Soviet masters of Russia subsequent to the war. " Freedom has not increased; rather the contrary." The Church had once more become the subservient tool of the Government. " In the official Church life, in the supreme Church hierarchy, conservative tendencies prevail, a desire to return to the sixteenth and the seventeenth centuries." [42] " A critical attitude on my part to much of what is transpiring in Soviet Russia (I know very well what is wrong) is particularly difficult because I feel the need to defend my native land before the world which is inimical to her." [43]

Despite the mounting sufferings, however, Berdyaev continued to plan new books which he hoped to be able to complete. He makes mention of several titles of books on which he was currently engaged. Among them he mentions " The New Spirituality and Mysticism " and " Truth and Revelation." Whether these works were completed before his death, or whether they will be published, I have no means of knowing.

Berdyaev died suddenly, and without a previous serious illness, on March 24, 1948. On the morning of that day his sister-in-law, who continued to keep house for him after his wife's death, found him sitting at his desk — dead.

PART TWO

THE FAITH BERDYAEV LIVED BY

5

Berdyaev's Existentialism

WE HAVE HITHERTO considered Berdyaev as a man in revolt. But he was not merely negative. He lived by a positive faith and knowledge, which he expressed in his philosophy. One of his books begins, half-seriously, half-facetiously, with the remark: "The philosopher's position is truly tragic: almost nobody loves him."[1] And yet, he devoted a lifetime to philosophy.

But before proceeding to amplify Berdyaev's philosophical development, and as a preliminary step toward understanding his views, it is essential that we take note of the very important differences which exist between the presuppositions of the German-Russian and the Anglo-American cultures. The former derives from Kant and the post-Kantian idealism and romanticism, while the latter goes back primarily to John Locke and the English empirical school.

It was John Locke who exercised an overwhelming influence upon the Founding Fathers of the American Republic, particularly upon Thomas Jefferson. The Declaration of Independence echoes Lockean principles from beginning to end. Locke's views of the nature of man proved to be the norm of the American concepts of government, of ecclesiastical and religious policies, and of the laissez-faire economic theory as defined later by Adam Smith, who derived his concept of man from Locke. The latter, basing his thought upon the new physics of his friend Sir Isaac Newton, defined nature as consisting of "material substances." These were wholly subject to mechanical laws. His own contribution to the empirical philosophy consisted mainly in the new theory of the nature of man, whom he compounded of "mental substance" and a material body. The two substances were wholly different. Accordingly, Locke was a relative dualist. Bishop Berkeley, by applying the Lockean empirical principles more rigorously, denied the existence of the " material " substances, although not of the " mental." David Hume, the most logical and consistent of the English empiricists, negated the existence of both the material and the mental " substances." According to him, man was a transitory association of sense impressions and recollections — a stream of sensations and nothing more. Since knowledge is derived solely from sensory data, mental life consists, in his view, exclusively of apperceptions of colors, odors, tastes, and other sense impressions. On such a basis there is no possibility of experiencing " substances." F. S. C. Northrop summarizes the English empiricist epistemology by declaring that for it " minds and material objects are mere shorthand names for . . . associations of sensed data." [2]

The resultant Anglo-American concept of man based on such flimsy presuppositions must necessarily be atomistic, individualistic, lacking in any fundamental principle of social cohesion. No wonder that the Aristotelian-Thomistic principle that man is naturally a political, social animal, and therefore that society derives from the intrinsic social nature of man, and not from some superimposed divine or human fiat, has lost all cogency. Lockean and particularly Humean men could have no essential, necessary relation with one another. Society became an aggregate of intrinsically isolated, atomistic human monads on the order of a heap of sand. The only concept of government that would fit this norm was that of the social contract, which was given its best-known formulation by Rousseau but originally had derived from Hobbes and Locke. According to this theory, the " founding fathers " of the primitive human society voluntarily banded themselves together in order to gain centralized defense of their common interests. Locke himself designated the defense of private property — not of human or social rights or values — as the chief function of government. No wonder, therefore, that the culture derived from the Lockean presuppositions has placed property rights above all other human rights! It likewise follows logically that in such an acquisitive society the dominant economic view should be Adam Smith's laissez-faire theory, which extols the free and unimpeded play of economic forces and individuals. This theory has survived with considerable vigor as the favorite economic norm in the United States, while in Britain it has been modified somewhat by the hedonism of Jeremy Bentham and the utilitarian theory of John Stuart Mill. The American political and economic ideas of both major political parties still derive from the fountainhead of Lockean philosophy. And what is more, the dominant empirical temper of the American people explains the vogue that the instrumentalist pragmatism of John Dewey enjoys.

The two world wars made the Anglo-American peoples keenly aware that Germany, and more recently Soviet Russia, was dominated by cultural presuppositions very different from their own. The difference has manifested itself chiefly in the repudiation of the Anglo-American concept of democracy. The reason for this basic cultural antithesis is that the Lockean philosophy was never generally accepted by the Germans or the Russians. Instead, the tremendous philosophical insights of Kant, which admittedly inaugurated a new era in the history of Western philosophy, to a large degree superseded all previous German philosophical tradition. But even so the most influential forms of the German idealistic philosophy were those of Fichte, Schelling, and Hegel. The latter defined the State as

> "that form of reality in which the individual has and enjoys his freedom; but on the condition of his recognizing, believing in, and willing that which is common to the Whole. And this must not be understood as if the subjective will of the social unit attained its gratification and enjoyment through that common Will; as if this were a means provided for its benefit; as if the individual, in his relation to other individuals, thus limited his freedom, in order that this universal limitation — the mutual constraint of all — might secure a small space of liberty for each. Rather, we affirm, are Law, Morality, Government, and they alone, the positive reality and completion of Freedom. . . . The State is the divine Idea as it exists on earth." [3]

The Germans, who for almost a century and a half have been nurtured on the Hegelian notion that the categorical " ought " of the rational spirit of universal history is identical with the " is " of the State, naturally looked upon their culture as far superior to the Anglo-American, or to any other. Because they thought of the Lockean notion of democracy as philosophically outmoded and discredited, they regarded any social system based upon it as necessarily obsolete or at least inadequate. That is still their view of the matter. Only a change in the philosophical creeds of either one or the other, or preferably both, of the cultures is likely to produce a change in their political or social systems.

Russian culture of the nineteenth century was almost wholly dependent on German philosophy for its basic assumptions, as Berdyaev's own analysis in his book *The Origin of Russian Communism* amply demonstrates. Kant, Schelling, and Hegel have exercised the most powerful influence upon Russian thought, whether Westernist or Slavophile. Feuerbach and Marx have produced — as is evident from the Communist conquest of Russia — a more decisive revolution in that country than in their own native Germany. The dominant cultural tradition is in both cases Hegelian — in the leftist, Marxist direction and the more conservative, rightist orientation. No wonder Russian Communists have the same contempt for the Anglo-American concept of democracy that the Germans have hitherto exhibited! They are keenly aware that the American democracy resembles a heap of sand, although they fail to see that theirs, on the other hand, is like an anthill, as Dostoevsky used to say about Europe in general. Consequently, he would indeed be utterly blind who would still regard the widely differing philosophical concepts as mere innocuous, inconsequential abstractions.

These elementary but basic considerations of the differing cultural patterns are essential for an understanding of the philosophical assumptions of Nicolas Berdyaev. As a cultured Russian, he was brought up, as has already been mentioned, in the traditions of Kantian and post-Kantian German idealism. To the end of his life he remained thoroughly imbued with them. Accordingly, there is much truth in the criticism of some of his Russian fellow exiles — if criticism it be — that he was more a German than an Eastern Orthodox thinker. But in that case the criticism must be applied to the entire movement of the Russian religious renascence of the last hundred years. For although he was steeped in German thought, Berdyaev was thoroughly Russian; he judged the German ideas from the Russian point of view. As he himself has reminded us, Russia has a culture essentially *sui generis,* for it has not passed through the Renaissance period. The Russian forms of thought — as, for instance, the Russian attitude toward private property — are vastly different from those generally accepted in western Europe. For the Russian thinks "eschatologically," in terms of the final end and of perfection. He is an "out-and-outer," either for Christ or Antichrist. Moreover, there are anarchistic elements in the Russian soul which in Berdyaev take the form of excessive emphasis upon freedom of human personality. In all this and much besides, Berdyaev, despite the elements in him of undoubted German provenance, shows himself a true Russian: he himself defines his philosophy as "above all expressing the original Russian religious philosophy tinged with eschatology."

We are now ready to consider Berdyaev's philosophical development in somewhat greater detail. He began as a convinced Kantian. But as has already been pointed out, he discerned in Kant and his idealistic successors an antipersonalism which led him to repudiate this aspect of the whole German idealistic philosophy. One must fight Kant, he declared: "Suspect that philosophy for which reality is illusory, personality is illusory. Do not believe that philosophy; seek another!" [4]

Another aspect of Kantian philosophy which apparently became a source of torturing concern to Berdyaev was its epistemology. Since for Kant the *Ding an sich,* the existential subject, when considered by "pure reason," i.e., from the empirical, mathematico-scientific point of view, is not knowable, it follows that only the phenomenal object is knowable. Moreover, when the sensory data are perceived by the mind, which is an active, not merely a passive, receptive organ, the impression is ordered and fashioned by the forms and categories inherent in the mind. It was in this way that Kant resolved the devastating Humean skepticism and began a new era in Western thought. Nevertheless, since the empirical principle that there can be nothing in understanding that is not first in the senses was retained by Kant, he held that scientific knowledge must necessarily deal with appearances only, i.e., with phenomena; it is unable to attain knowledge of the noumenal, i.e., spiritual reality. Only the " practical reason," the ethical, intuitive mode of understanding, is capable of dealing with the noumenal reality — freedom, immortality, God. This was the radical dichotomy bequeathed by Kant to his idealistic epigoni. They, in turn, overcame it by transforming his dualism into monism, by sacrificing human personality altogether and by positing as the sole existent and knowing subject the Ego, the World Soul, the Absolute Idea, or some other abstraction which made the existence of human personality unreal. Berdyaev regarded this antihumanistic epistemology as one of the greatest errors of the nineteenth century German idealism.

Nevertheless, in his latest books, Berdyaev returns to his first love, Kant, and points out that since the monism of Kant's successors was a perversion of Kant's fundamental dualism, the consequent epistemology was not his. Plato and Kant, he asserts, " must be acknowledged the greatest and most original philosophers throughout the history of human thought." [5] Kant's grand discovery was the fact that the true noumenal reality was within, and is attainable only by means of the moral sense, not by " scientific " knowledge. His own solution of the mode of nonsensory understanding, by means of " practical reason," i.e., the ethical consciousness of the categorical " ought," was by no means conclusive or definitive, because it did not go far enough. Nevertheless, by his insistence upon the dual nature of reality and the dual mode of apprehending it (*Vernunft* and *Verstand,* the knowledge of phenomena and the understanding of noumena) he prepared the way for the existential philosophy.

From this point of view Berdyaev characterizes the various extant philosophical systems by contrasting the existential with the nonexistential; they differ in:

> "(1) the primacy of freedom over being or the primacy of being over freedom, that is the first and the most important; (2) the primacy of the existential subject over the objectified world or the primacy of the objectified world over the existential subject; (3) dualism or monism; (4) voluntarism or intellectualism; (5) dynamism or statism; (6) creative activism or passive observation; (7) personalism or impersonalism; (8) anthropologism or cosmism; (9) philosophy of the spirit or naturalism. These principles may be combined differently in different systems. I decidedly choose the philosophy that affirms the primacy of freedom over being, of the existential subject over the objectified world, dualism, voluntarism, dynamism, creative activism, personalism, anthropologism, and the philosophy of the spirit."[6]

One cannot but be grateful to Berdyaev for stating the case so succinctly and adequately. At least, there can be no question as to how to understand him or how to interpret his meaning. Nor can one charge him with inconsistency as far as his previous philosophical development is concerned: for he had been feeling his way toward this particular philosophical conclusion from the very beginning, although he did not possess full clarity from the very first. But then who does? The existential point of view was at least implied and employed as early as 1911 in his *Philosophy of Freedom*[7] and a few years later in *The Meaning of Creativity,* although at that time he had not used the term "existentialism." In this sense, he ceased to be an idealist, for he did not identify being with thought. But, as has already been shown, Berdyaev qualifiedly differentiates himself from the fellowship of such existentialists as Heidegger and Sartre, for his is not a nihilistic philosophy of despair. He traces his spiritual ancestry through Dostoevsky to Kierkegaard, Pascal, and Boehme, and even in a sense to Augustine.[8] He defines existentialism as that philosophy which, "in the first place, is determined by the existentiality of the knowing subject himself. A philosopher of the existentialist type does not proceed in the experience of knowing by means of objectification, does not place the object against the subject. His philosophy is the expression of the subject itself as it is engrossed in the secret of being. Existential knowledge of the object is impossible."[9] Accordingly, besides the difference that religion or denial of religion causes between the two groups of existentialists, there are other equally basic differences. The two groups start from dissimilar presuppositions and draw therefrom widely divergent, even contradictory, conclusions. Taking that into consideration, it is unfortunate that the term "existentialism" is applied to both groups, for this practice will undoubtedly lead to a great deal of confusion. If the term "personalism" were not itself subject to similarly diverse interpretation, it would perhaps be better to use that term to designate Berdyaev's philosophy. Nevertheless, he himself seemed to give preference to the term "existentialism."

Berdyaev places subject, the only real center of existence, against the world of objects and the objectified world. It is in this sense that he denies the primacy of ontology as against that of existentialism. His book *Solitude and Society* (the original title of which, *I and the World of Objects,* seems to be far more expressive of the theme than the title of the English translation), and the more recently published *Essay on Eschatological Metaphysics* — not to speak of passages in many of his other books devoted to this subject — are explications of this idea, which is immensely important for the understanding of his entire world view. Stated in the boldest relief, his basic principle is that personality, the existent subject, is primary; while being, the ontological object, is secondary. In other words, being is a product of thought, a rationalized concept; existence creates essence. This constitutes the substance of Berdyaev's dualism — the polarity of spiritual freedom and objectified necessity, not that of spirit and matter. He does not recognize "the autonomous reality of matter."[10] Consequently, Berdyaev inverts the Cartesian dictum, "I think, therefore I am," and asserts instead, "I am, therefore I think." Thought is not the product of matter, nor does it exist by itself, in isolation, any more than the grin of the Cheshire cat can persist "on the vacant air" after the cat has disappeared. Thought necessarily presupposes a thinker. Ontological reality does not exist antecedently to the perceiving subject; he creates it. Only the subject is free; the object is contingent and determined. Consequently, the identification of the " objective " with the " real," as made in naïve realism and as uncritically assumed in most positivist world views, is an error. Scientific knowledge deals solely with objects; as such it is eminently justified within its proper limits and immensely beneficial and useful when devoted to good ends. At no time does Berdyaev disparage science or lack an appreciation of its immense value. Science is and must remain an integral part of any worthy culture of the future. But there are no inherent meanings in objects; meaning is imparted to the object by the existential subject. Science, therefore, since it deals only with objects, cannot find or yield any meanings, whether positive or negative. Its sphere is that of the " how," not of the " why." Whenever science attempts to assign meanings to objects, it oversteps its province. Meanings are created solely by personalities, and their recognition belongs to philosophy or religion.

The basic assumptions of existential philosophy led Berdyaev to the formulation of a new epistemology; for he had always been deeply disturbed by the dominant theories of knowledge. He held that man, as a spiritual being, is not outside the noumenal reality which he has no means of comprehending. On the contrary, man is on the inside, and hence participates in the reality. He is a microcosm and a microtheos, the meeting point of the material-mental and the spiritual; therefore, he knows reality through himself, and this knowledge is itself reality. " I, the knower, abide in the reality from the beginning and am an inalienable part of it. I know reality in myself as man and through myself as man. Only a being can know being." [11] " I can know nothing when I immerse myself in the object; I know all only when I immerse myself in the subject." [12] " Truth is not that which has being, but is the meaning, the logos of that which has being." [13]

Nor is the process of knowing to be pictured under the analogy of the projection of a picture on a screen — a *tabula rasa* — as

John Locke conceived of it and as naïve realists still hold. The perceiving subject is not passive, but creatively active; he contributes to the act of knowledge, as even Kant has taught. " Knowledge is always a creative possession, and a transcendence, of the object." [14] For intuition implies no mere perception of the object, but also a penetration into its meaning. This is a creative act. Accordingly, intuitional knowledge deals with meanings rather than with the nature of being as such. Thus reality is illuminated through the knowing process: " Being cognizes itself and through this cognition is illuminated and expanded." [15] " Knowledge of truth is communion with truth and life in it." [16] Accordingly, all spiritual existents and values — God, freedom, truth, meaning, righteousness, and whatever else there is — pertain to the existential, noumenal, not to the objectified or phenomenal realm.

Furthermore, understanding is not exclusively intellectual or conceptual: the emotive and voluntaristic elements are also involved in it and contribute to the sum total of the intuitive, conative process. Accordingly, Berdyaev taught that understanding is integral — not merely intellectual, conceptual, rationalistic. In this he followed the tradition firmly grounded in the Russian renascence by his predecessors, Khomyakov, Solovev, and others, as well as the traditional German distinction, derived from Boehme and followed by many German philosophers, between knowledge and understanding. Had this distinction been more generally adhered to, a great deal of confused and naïve discussion of God's existence would have been made unnecessary. For the discussion rests upon the uncritical assumption that he is a substance, an object. Since he cannot be perceived as an object, he is said not to exist. But God cannot be an object of knowledge as so many " philosophies of religion " try to make him. When God is treated in an " objective " way, one only learns what certain men have thought or taught about him, but one does not learn to know God. Only when the human spirit meets the divine Spirit in an existential encounter is there an immediate, real understanding of God. Countless learned tomes dealing, supposedly, with God have missed this elementary although absolutely basic fact. Were the distinction between the knowledge of objects and the understanding of existents more generally adhered to, Berdyaev insists, such naïve misunderstanding as that mentioned above would be avoided.

The existential knowledge of God is also the true basis of mysticism. Whenever mysticism is considered from another point of view, it is misapprehended and consequently denied — as happens in the theology of Barth and Brunner. For true mysticism is the core of religion, " the depths and the heights of the spiritual life." As Rudolf Otto defines it, mysticism " enters into the religious experience in the measure that religious feeling surpasses its rational content . . . to the extent to which its hidden, nonrational, nouminous elements predominate and determine the emotional life." [17] Religion conceived otherwise may even hide God; but truly understood, it translates with conscious awareness, and often in conceptual forms, that which in mysticism, in the existential encounter, is given immediately, intuitively. Thus, for instance, the historic dogmas are but attempts to translate into symbolic, even though conceptual, terms what was immediately perceived in mystical apprehension. Whenever they are objectified, i.e., treated as if they were rationalistic, logical, scientific definitions, they often become fossilized into absurdities, which then wrongfully serve as an external authority. Religion of the spirit knows no external constraint in the sense of a force compelling submission. Any attempt to " impose " religious truth is irreligious in itself. Truth must be existentially experienced in order to be spiritually apprehended and freely received. Its conceptual formulation is of secondary importance; in no event can it ever be more than a symbolic adumbration of the living, throbbing, authentic, spiritual experience. Were it possible to define religion " scientifically " it would be dead. A God whom man could comprehend would not be God. For no spiritual existent can be known " scientifically "; it is a subject, not an object. That insight the modern man owes to Kant. For the human spirit may commune with the divine Spirit, but such a communion cannot be verified by a scientific analysis. It is impossible to measure piety by taking a man's pulse — as has actually been attempted by a " scientific " religious research scholar. Christianity, then, may be said " to be the most mystical religion in the world and at the same time not mystical at all but historical, ethnic, and amazingly adapted to the average level of people, to the mediocrity of their lives." [18]

But there exist different types of mysticism, and not every kind is compatible with Christianity. All monistic, antipersonalist types are *ipso facto* anti-Christian. The Hindu personality-denying mysticism can never be harmonized with the Christian. The same repudiation of human personality is found in Neoplatonism. " Plotinus is the clearest and the most gifted exponent of the mysticism of ' the One.' Plurality and individuality do not possess for him metaphysical reality. Man is lost in God." [19]

This Neoplatonic mysticism has passed over into Christianity. It is found in the pseudo-Dionysian *corpus* and, Berdyaev thought, in the mysticism of Meister Eckhart. But Berdyaev did not share the fairly common view that Eckhart was a pantheist or panentheist.[20] For such a charge is possible only when Eckhart's mystical intuitions are forced into the strait jacket of rationalistic theological formulation. Since he taught that the *Gottheit* was above all being, i.e., was supraontological, and therefore outside the antithesis of subject and object, the accusation of pantheism, which can be understood only as identifying the *Gottheit* with being, is obviously self-contradictory. Eckhart, therefore, rightly repudiated it in his " Defense," although he was, nevertheless, condemned on that charge by the papal Curia. But Berdyaev does charge Eckhart with antipersonalism, by asserting that for the latter creation " lacked essential reality and value. All that was created was an empty nothing. Even the existence of man was a sort of sin." [21] It was in this sense that Eckhart, according to Berdyaev, made God everything and man nothing. But Berdyaev misunderstood the great Dominican mystic in this respect, that he chose to place an exclusive stress solely on one pole of the latter's thought — the creatureliness of man —

and ignored the other pole of Eckhart's thought. In this, which Rudolf Otto calls the " Gothic element," man is all but identified with God. To affirm either one of the two extremes exclusively is to distort Eckhart's thought. Only a combination of the two poles does him justice.

Berdyaev rejected all mysticism of the monistic type: " Monistic movements of that sort are foreign to me because the problems of personality and of personal destiny have always been central to me." [22] Monistic mysticism is necessarily antipersonalistic. But Christian mysticism is personalistic: it involves an experience of the revelation of God in the soul of man. The transcendental gulf between God and man is bridged and the transcendent becomes immanent. But in no case is the eternal distinction between the creature and the Creator, the human and the divine, obliterated. Mystical union is not the merging of a raindrop with the illimitable ocean, the loss of identity on the part of the human spirit in the limitless vastness of the divine Spirit. Christian mysticism is distinguished from all others by three characteristics which must invariably be present: personality, freedom, love. Wherever any of these three aspects is missing, we are no longer dealing with Christian mysticism.[23] Or otherwise expressed, Christian mysticism is the *theoria,* the intuitive vision of the Eternal; like faith, it is " the assurance of things hoped for, the conviction of things not seen." [24]

As for himself, Berdyaev declared that he was primarily a " *homo mysticus* " rather than a " *homo religiosus*." That is, for him the intuitive, spiritual awareness of God and his eternal verities took precedence over the historical revelation of God as found in the Scriptures or in the experiences of other men. " What differentiated me from men who regarded themselves as wholly Orthodox was the fact that the historical revelation was for me secondary in comparison with the spiritual revelation. The inner revelation of the spirit is real. Historical revelation is symbolical, is the symbolism of the spirit." [25]

And yet, despite the undoubted importance of the mystical, intuitive element in religion, Berdyaev's stress upon it betrays something of a lack of balance, or an inadequate recognition of other legitimate forms and aspects of religious experience. Baron von Hügel, in his sober, catholic diagnosis of the elements that make up Christianity, recognizes in it three basic aspects: the institutional, the intellectual, and the mystical. He too regards the intuitive, immediate, mystical aspect of Christianity as the highest. And yet he insists on the absolute necessity of the other two and deprecates any tendency toward an overemphasis upon any one of the three. Berdyaev too acknowledges the legitimacy, even the necessity, of the intellectual formulation of the intuitive insights of religion. In fact, he stresses this aspect of Christianity quite adequately, although he is acutely aware of the difficulties and dangers of reducing the ineffable vision of God to bald, rigid, rational concepts. More than many, perhaps than most, religious thinkers he insists upon the distinction between the ineffable, inexpressible, nonconceptual, intuitive apprehension of religious truth (which he calls apophatic) and the logical, rationalized definitions of theology (which he calls cataphatic). But as for the institutional aspect of religion, he is preoccupied mostly with its "objectified," all too human, debased, and corrupted, features which so often sadly disfigure the historic forms of Christianity. Perhaps he fails to do justice to the necessities and conditions under which the Church has to live.

Of no less importance in the philosophy of Berdyaev is his concern with the "objectified," i.e., imagination-constructed world. In fact, this concept holds an equal rank in his system with that of the priority of the spiritual over the material and is its correlative. Its sphere of operation is mainly human society, but nature is included as well, although in a secondary fashion. In fact, everything, including God, may be and generally is liable to objectification. In its simplest form, the term means just what it says — namely, converting something which in its proper nature is a subject, a spiritual entity, into an object, a thing. In the case of nature it is making an improper use of, or putting a wrong valuation upon, an object. The most reprehensible, as well as the commonest, of such objectifications is that of treating a human being as a thing, a commodity. When industry or economy exists for the purpose of making profit rather than for the satisfaction of human needs, and consequently labor is considered as a commodity to be bought in the labor market, an objectification, i.e., dehumanization, takes place. But so it does in all other social relations: when political systems are used for the advantage of a privileged group, whether it be by democratic or by totalitarian regimes; or when governments squander human lives in aggressive, imperialistic schemes of aggrandizement; when members of a family regard each other as means of convenience or pleasure, or in any other way than as persons. In short, wherever man is used as a means rather than an end, objectification takes place.

But dealing with a man as if he were a thing is not the only method of objectification: any other wrong social attitude belongs to this category as well. Treating others with hatred, prejudice, injustice, disdain; dealing with them as if they were on a lower plane racially, socially, intellectually; treating them wholly in external (professional or official) terms of relations; in short, dealing with others in anything less than the terms of communion proper to spiritual beings constitutes a mode of objectification.

The result of objectification is degradation, depersonalization, dehumanization. For whether or not one is conscious of the implications of one's act, by treating another human being as if he were a thing, or assuming a wrong attitude toward him, one thereby denies to that person the recognition of his spiritual status. Any real personal communion on such a basis is, of course, impossible, since communion presupposes a spiritual intercourse. Consequently, most social relations are conducted upon a lower, external, impersonal level rather than upon one that is inwardly personal. Society comprises a vast interrelationship of such impersonal contacts, and consequently possesses no cohesive, integrating, unifying principle; hence it is at the worst a heap of sand, and at the best an anthill. Democratic societies are likely to be the former; totalitarian, the latter. This is what Berdyaev means when he speaks of the " fallen world." For the real human community is spiritually knit together in a communion that is possible only in the intimate "I-Thou" relationship.

The practice of objectification is so habitual, so constant, that most men regard it as wholly normal. When that happens, it profoundly affects their own personal life: they become "self-alienated." The process of objectification, or the propulsion of self into the external relations, empties the person of his inner, spiritual potentialities. He accommodates himself to the level prevailing outside himself, becomes just like the other members of his social group, degenerates into a normal, average citizen. Mass education levels society to a dead uniformity. Instead of living his own free, or even creative, life as a real person, a center of spiritual reality, such a man transfers his whole conscious life into those external, wholly secondary relations of the objectified world. He becomes merely a butcher, a baker, a candlestick maker, a technician, a businessman, a scientist, or a politician. The real person in him atrophies. Or at least, he becomes a stranger to his real self, suffers the fate of "self-alienation." His motivation henceforth is from the outside. He acts as he is expected to act by the requirements of social custom, by expediency, or by conscious imitation of those he admires. For we are what we love. He becomes a slave, for anyone who is not motivated by the inner promptings of his real self loses his freedom.

Furthermore, objectification takes place not only in regard to human beings and society, but in nature and in the use of things. Berdyaev calls this process "idol-making." Money and the financial structure of modern society have become gigantic idols which are worshiped by vast masses of men. But power, the sheer lust for domination over others in all aspects of life, is likewise a case of objectification, of idol-making. Exploitation of natural resources for the sole or predominant sake of enrichment may be included in this category as well. All such exclusive lavishment of one's life on something less than the highest aims of personality entails loss of freedom, enslavement, and hence depersonalization. "Man's life consisteth not in an abundance of the things which he possesseth." By living exclusively for the sake of wealth or power, one becomes "an outcast" from the real world of spiritual, personal values. He becomes " rich in things and poor in soul." He becomes a bourgeois.

It follows, therefore, that all objects are the creation of subjects, who in turn are the creation of God. The " fallen " world is man-made. Men have created it by means of objectification, of wrong imagination. A man in the grip of passion creates his own world of sin and suffering which is real to him. Hence "the objectified world is one of slavery and fall. But into the real and free world enters the whole cosmos which does not exist in the phenomenal, objective world. This relation may be expressed as follows: the phenomenon is the objectified world, the natural and social world of necessity and slavery, of hatred, of governmental rule; the noumenal world is spirit, freedom, and creativity; it is the world of love and sympathy; it is the entire cosmos. The so-called 'other' world is for me no other, but is by preference my world." [26]

This is another way of saying what the German idealists, and particularly Schopenhauer, have said — that the world is my idea. But for the German idealists, it was ultimately the suprapersonal Spirit or Absolute Idea which realized itself in nature and man, while for Berdyaev it is the human spirit which is the agent of objectification. Nevertheless, German philosophers were familiar with the concept of objectification. For instance, Karl Marx, during his early, idealistic period, formulated his basic concept of social injustice in terms of " *Verdinglichung,*" i.e., as the treatment of the proletarians as things, as a commodity. For this concept German idealism is indebted to Boehme. The " sage of Goerlitz " spoke of it as " imagination." According to him, both Adam and Lucifer fell because of wrong imagination, i.e., because they thought in terms of material rather than spiritual categories. For thought, imagination, whether good or bad, are creative. Faith creates its own reality. Love is holy imagination. But evil imagination is creative as well. The question is not whether or not a man exercise imagination, but what controls his imagination; for thereon hang the issues of life. Sin is subordination of oneself, by means of wrong imagination, to natural objects, to passions, to self-assertion; it separates the sinner from the spiritual realm of freedom and thereby enslaves him. "Whatever property is lord of thee, its servant thou art." [27]

Schopenhauer also adopted Boehme's basic concept that the ultimate reality and inmost nature of all that exists is *will.* "Phenomenal existence is idea and nothing more. All idea, of whatever kind it may be, all *object,* is *phenomenal* existence; but the *will* alone is a *thing-in-itself.* As such, it is throughout not idea, but *toto genere* different from it; it is that of which all idea, all object, is the phenomenal appearance, the visibility, the objectivization. It is the inmost nature, the kernel, of every particular thing, and also of the whole. It appears in every blind force of nature and also in the preconsidered action of man; and the great difference between these two is merely in the degree of the manifestation, not in the nature of what manifests itself." [28]

These examples of the concept of objectification as drawn from Boehme and Schopenhauer throw considerable light on Berdyaev's use of it. Without identifying himself with everything Schopenhauer asserted about the nature of will — for instance, that the blind forces of nature may properly be called will — he does nevertheless affirm that personality constructs and projects concepts objectified in the social, political, and cultural order of society and of history. These objectifications of human will — whether " fallen " or redeemed — then dominate a given era of society or history. It is in this sense that the objectified world order is the product of human will. Since fallen humanity cannot but will sinfully, selfishly, the social order is necessarily sinful.

Nevertheless, objectification serves a useful purpose. For the sinful, fallen society could not exist and perpetuate itself without some kind of myths: men believe in " the divine rights of kings," in the sanctity or infallibility of papal pronouncements, in the " sovereignty of the will of the people," or in " the messianic mission of the proletariat." These fictions of imagination strengthen the collective bond without which society would fall apart. Lacking the true spiritual unity, society must resort to false but useful myths in order to prevent disintegration. Even

Plato could not construct his ideal Republic without the generous use of " noble lies." But likewise, these myths are the source of evil, injustice, exploitation, and oppression.

Nor does the assertion that the objectified world is the creation of man's imagination and will imply that it is therefore unreal. What it does imply is that the world created by wrong imagination, selfish will, lies in evil, that men stand in wrong relations to each other when they hate rather than love. They subject themselves to outward necessity because they surrender their freedom; they have become strangers to their own real selves. " Objectification is the process of ' self-outcasting,' of exteriorization, of submission to the conditions of space, time, causality, and rationalization." [29] Man's enslavement to these conditions is indeed real, but not necessary, not existential. He could free himself from them, if only he would.

As an illustration of the process of objectification we may cite Berdyaev's two concepts of the Church: it exists, on the one hand, in its spiritual, noumenal entity and, on the other hand, as an objectified social institution. " The Church is, in its depths, the life of the spirit, a spiritual life; it is supernatural life independent of social laws; it is communion, a brotherhood of men in Christ, the sacramental life of Christ in human communion, a supernatural communion with Christ." [30] Its real character has been succinctly characterized by Russian religious thinkers by that untranslatable word " *sobornost.*" But what a tragic contrast there exists between this concept of the spiritual nature of the Church and its historical manifestation as a social institution! As in all objectification, the embodiment of the idea is painfully inadequate at best, and in some extreme instances is even contradictory to the spiritual character of the Church. As a concrete institution it may be but an instrument of lust for power, greed, obscurantism; it may even alienate men from God and stifle spiritual life. It may be what the Grand Inquisitors of historic Christendom have made it. There may be more honest faith in God outside it than inside it. Such is the tragedy of the duality of the Church in its spiritual and objectified aspects.

Since social realities as a rule represent an objectification of the will of the fallen man, the only way to change the world is to change man. The source of evil is the alienation of man from the spiritual realm. But Berdyaev's solution differs from that of Schopenhauer, whose cure consisted in the complete denial of will in so far as he propounded the harmonization of the human and divine wills in the voluntary surrender of man to God. Human will is not to be eliminated, but rather transformed by the action of God's grace, into divine-human will. The complete transformation of the temporal world — the end of the world, as Berdyaev terms it — will take place when men cease objectifying their evil wills, desires, and imaginations, and live in the "communion of saints." This will be the coming of the Kingdom of God. But that event will not occur in time; it is of eternity.

6

" *As It Was in the Beginning* "

WE ARE NOW READY for the application of Berdyaev's basic philosophical principles to his world view. As for the faith whereby he lived, Berdyaev arrived at it the hard way. His conscious acceptance of the basic Christian view of life was a matter of gradual enlightenment rather than a violent change. He disliked to apply the term " conversion " to his experience, if that term be understood as a return to a previously lost " faith of our fathers," or an acceptance of some traditional, authoritative, dogmatic system. Berdyaev experienced no such conversion.[1] He had not been brought up in his youth in the traditional teachings of the Orthodox Church. His father shared, in a loose way, the views of Tolstoy, and his mother held to her own French Catholic mother's religious ideas and practices. Berdyaev grew up without any definite religious commitment, but, on the other hand, without any violent repudiation of religion. He asserted that he was never " a skeptic, nor a materialist, nor an atheist." Very early he experienced a torturing concern in regard to evil in the world, and therefore felt himself a stranger to this world, while at the same time he experienced an overpowering sense of the existence of another world wherein freedom reigns. Thus he was a born Platonist. To this was later added the conviction of the supreme worth of human personality which he derived from Kant. He wrote that when he consciously acknowledged himself a Christian, he did not feel so much a sense of personal sin or the sinfulness of men in general as the fact of evil and the consequent loss of freedom. " I experience sin not as disobedience but as the loss of freedom." [2] Accordingly, Berdyaev never wholly accepted any traditional, dogmatic system of Christianity but regarded himself as " a representative of free religious philosophy." [3] Early in his life of faith he wrote:

" For us, religion does not rest upon any external authority, nor on the constraint of factual reality. Religion is the product of mystical experience, given meaning by reason — mysticism illuminated by the Logos. They say: The Gospels are historical books; Christ is a historical fact. But I should have never mystically sensed and rationally comprehended who Christ is and what he is for me unless there had been revealed within me the truth of God-manhood, of the Trinitarian character of God and salvation. These truths of reason must combine with my mystical experiences. I have never been able to understand the blind submission to the authority of the Scriptures, or of tradition, the authority of the external, irresponsible factuality. I can penetrate the words of Christ and bow before them only when reason discloses their meaning and my free, mystical experience succeeds in feeling their whole depth. Otherwise, both Christ and the Gospels remain for me only historical facts similar to any others. Submission to external authority of whatever historical Church, the traditional dogmatism which repudiates free inquiry and new prophecy, is a treason against the supreme worth of the Eternal Reason. There is not, and cannot be, any other authority in the world save the authority of free Reason within. But the truths of reason remain abstract and dead unless they unite with the living, concrete incarnation of the world meaning of history." [4]

Such was the " *confessio fidei* " of young Berdyaev, written in 1906. One feels that the words smack of rationalism, even though he already partly understood the religious significance of mysticism. Contrast them with the lyrical outburst in which he expressed his mature experience of God's reality, not based upon any sort of discursive reasoning or logical argument, but wholly derived from spiritual intuition:

" It is impossible to ask whether there be a reality which corresponds to the experience of great saints, or great mystics, of men living on a higher spiritual plane; for that is not a spiritual question, but one arising only within psychology, naturalism, and naïve realism. . . . Spirit is, and spiritual life does in fact appear and manifest itself. . . . God and the divine, Spirit and the spiritual, are given in experience, in life; they reveal themselves, they are apprehended; they are not given in reflection." [5]

"The fact that within me the spiritual life is born, that I seek God, that I desire the divine in life and that I love the divine in life, is the highest in the world and is the very justification of existence of the world. No power on earth can persuade me that it is an illusion, a self-deception, and not life itself. For it is the only life without which all is but dust, fantasy, and nonbeing." [6]

Nevertheless, Berdyaev found himself closer to Eastern Orthodoxy than to Roman Catholicism or Protestantism, because Orthodox doctrinal teachings are less rigidly defined than those of the other confessions, and therefore allow greater freedom of interpretation. Moreover, he did not wish to exist in spiritual isolation. "I profess a spiritual religion; I am a free Christian, but not separated from the Church, i.e., I do not wish to be a sectarian." [7] "I have never pretended that my religious views bear a churchly character. I sought truth and experienced as truth what was revealed to me. Historical Orthodoxy appeared to me inadequately ecumenical, parochial, almost sectarian. I am not a heretic, and least of all am I a sectarian; I am a believing freethinker. My views are free, completely free, but are related to the primitive faith." [8]

Berdyaev had spent half a century in hammering out his system of thought on the anvil of experience. Because his exceedingly versatile mind led him to investigate several directions at the same time, and because it had been his lot to live through a chaotic, decadent period, he had to think his way through many devious mazes. He did not always follow the right path, but whenever he found himself astray, he had the courage to change his course. Nevertheless, from the beginning he had been led, as if by a lodestar, by the dazzling ideas that human personality is the most precious thing in the universe and that its most precious possession is freedom. In a special sense, Berdyaev is the philosopher of freedom par excellence, "a captive of freedom." His entire life and thought are a commentary on the text, "What shall a man give in exchange for his soul?"

Berdyaev's concept of spiritual freedom — at once the most

tragic and the most exalting fact about man — is derived from Dostoevsky's Grand Inquisitor. Berdyaev accepted it as basic. All his lifework is but an elaboration, a detailed application of the idea to the various phases of his philosophical world view. Others have attempted the same task: for instance, Vasily Rozanov wrote a volume on the theme.[9] But Berdyaev made it the criterion whereby he judged all, but principally the nature and destiny of man. Man, both "fallen" and "transformed," was his chief concern. He was a Christian anthropologist. In this respect he differed from his lifelong friend and fellow exile, the recently deceased Sergius Bulgakov, whose theological interests were centered about the concept of sophiology — the problem of the divine immanence in, and the transformation of, the entire cosmos. Although the latter interest was by no means ignored by Berdyaev, he did not make it central: he preferred to search the very depths of the human heart. All other questions he viewed only in relation to the concept of man's spiritual freedom.

Whence came freedom? The answer to this basic question could have been comparatively simple: Man was created by God in God's own image and likeness, was endowed with a freedom which was inalienably part of his nature since it was an integral concomitant of the divine image. Furthermore, that divine image, including freedom, was not lost, blotted out, or totally vitiated in the Fall, but, although marred, was nevertheless essentially preserved. Such a view could have come fairly close to that generally held by the Eastern Orthodox Church, and therefore could have been regarded as one of the historic Christian doctrines.

Unfortunately, the matter was not so simple as that for Berdyaev. In fact, he regarded such an interpretation as altogether unacceptable. Occasionally in his writings he even asserts that it is a source of atheism; for it amounts to the assertion that God is the source of evil, or is responsible for the evil consequent upon man's misuse of freedom. For if man, endowed with God-given freedom, succumbs by means of that freedom to temptation, and hence entails upon himself the ruinous consequences of sin, God must have foreseen the results. It is he who, with full foreknowledge of the consequences, endowed man with the fateful gift of freedom which brings many of his creatures misery and perdition. No wonder that some sensitive souls, like Dostoevsky's Ivan Karamazov, could not accept God's world order, involving as it does evil and suffering, and were driven into atheism! One must not forget that Dostoevsky's own gnawing doubts were expressed in Ivan's words just as much as his alternate mood of faith was expressed in the triumphant speeches of Father Zosima and Alyosha Karamazov. For theodicy is a characteristically Russian problem and dominates even Russian anarchism and Communism; it certainly was a lifelong concern of Berdyaev's.

The matter was made even worse — in Berdyaev's view — when great Christian theologians, such as Augustine, Luther, and Calvin, acerbated the problem by attempting to solve it by the doctrines of predestination and foreordination "cataphatically," i.e., in terms of rigid rationalism, by the use of intellectual concepts; rather than "apophatically," i.e., by intuitive insight into its spiritual character, an insight not capable of conceptual formulation. For by the use of the former method they not only denied man's freedom in any real sense of the word, but further explicitly made God responsible for man's eternal destiny. According to these theologians, some men, by God's immutable decree, before all ages and without any consideration of their merit or demerit, were predestined to eternal glory and bliss; while others were foreordained to everlasting damnation. This "terrible" view, as formulated by Calvin, at least "had the tremendous advantage of being a *reductio ad absurdum*." [10] Had Calvin and the other predestinarians left the matter in the realm of religious experience, as a quite proper feeling on the part of every soul that has experienced God's justifying grace of something freely granted rather than of something that man had earned, Berdyaev would perhaps have accepted it. Had they said with Pascal, "I would not have sought Thee hadst Thou not first found me," I dare say that Berdyaev would have assented to such a statement of predestination. But he objected to the inadmissible translation of an ineffable experience into terms of conceptual theology which makes God appear unjust. Berdyaev's dislike of Barth rests on this and similar aspects of his teaching.

Unable to accept the traditional Biblical view of the origin of freedom, Berdyaev developed a highly complex view of his own. Although at first he had adopted a concept not greatly dissimilar to the prevailing view,[11] subsequently, abandoning the earlier concept for reasons already stated, he developed his own on the basis of Jacob Boehme's theosophic teachings. Henceforth, this doctrine became fundamental to all his later thinking, and he expounded it repeatedly and almost *ad nauseam* in his later writings.[12] Berdyaev looked upon Boehme as the "greatest mystic-gnostic of all ages,"[13] and above all "the greatest Christian gnostic." Boehme did not belong to the Neoplatonic tradition of mysticism, but developed an original form of mysticism which postulated the ultimate origin of all that exists — including the divine Trinity — in the dark abyss of the *Ungrund*. The reader must be warned, however, not to regard Boehme's symbols and myths as concepts of discursive reason, but rather as attempts to describe direct intuitive visions. As such, Boehme's descriptions belong to the realm of mystical, rather than systematic, theology. The basic difference between him and the previous Christian mystics of the Neoplatonic tradition is that he does not regard the Godhead primarily as being but as will.[14] German idealism of the nineteenth century drew heavily upon him. Schopenhauer is particularly indebted to him; but so is Hegel. Boehme held that at the beginning there existed pure, naked, indetermined, aimless, contentless will. This is the chief characteristic of the primal *Ungrund*, which is beyond all positive comprehension or description. This concept imparts voluntaristic, rather than ontological, character to all Boehme's thinking, which links him more closely to the Rig-Veda and the Upanishad than to the pseudo-Dionysian *corpus*. This is not to suggest, of course, that Boehme knew or drew upon either of these sources. Independently of the Rig-Veda, Boehme held the same basic insight which is expressed in one of the Rig-Veda in the words:

"Therefore rose Desire in the beginning—
Desire, the primal seed and germ of Spirit."

The primal will, according to Boehme, manifested itself in a dynamic dialectic which resulted in a threefold movement: in the first place, the indeterminate will (Father) realized itself in the Eternal Mind (the Son), and then the process turned upon itself in the Spirit, who went out of both. This was the eternal theogonic dynamism which assumed the aspect of the Trinitarian dialectic.

The world of nature is likewise the result of the dynamic will or desire which brought out from the indeterminate "nothing" a determinate, created "something." Boehme spoke of this cosmogonic process as "imagination," and applied the same term to every other process of exteriorization or objectification. "All things are either wills or the imagination which is the objectification of wills," Brinton writes in his illuminating exposition of Boehmian mysticism.[15]

The *Ungrund,* then, comprises evil as well as good. Mysticism of the Neoplatonic tradition commonly minimizes, or practically denies, the existence of evil. For an Augustine, evil is only an absence of good. Boehme holds that evil is real, not illusory. Good has its substratum in evil which is a necessary stage on the way to maturity, to good. Evil may be regarded as a case of arrested growth or development: like a green apple, it would normally ripen into good, wholesome fruit, had it been allowed to mature. It is unwholesome only when unripe.

Berdyaev's own exposition of this difficult concept not only repeats the basic Boehmian tenet—with some important differences—but expands it in some particulars. Boehme's *Ungrund,* which Berdyaev interprets to mean the primal freedom, is to be found in the Godhead. Not so Berdyaev's. For him, the *Ungrund* —the primal freedom—is outside the Godhead, in the primal meonic stuff. It is the "primal, irrational, dark, and indetermined freedom. It is not itself evil, but makes evil possible; it comprises potentiality of evil as well as good. . . . It lies outside God, outside of being, is pre-existent to all being which is already determined."[16] God himself, i.e., the divine Trinity, is derived by a theogonic process from the *Ungrund* or the Godhead: "From the *Ungrund,* the abyss, are born light and God; in it occurs the theogonic process. Thence also flow darkness and evil as shadows of the divine light. Evil has its source, not in the born God (i.e., in God the Creator), but in the ground or pool, in the abyss, from which flow both light and darkness."[17] On another occasion Berdyaev speaks of this same "ground of God" as "the dark nature of God."[18] The *Ungrund* from which God is born by a theogonic process obviously cannot be the creator of anything; only God is the Creator. The doctrine may be summarized as follows: the divine Trinity is realized in eternity by a theogonic process; thereupon, God creates the world.

But it must be reiterated that the *Ungrund* cannot be grasped conceptually, for it transcends all human concepts — it is a myth, a symbol. Accordingly, it may be spoken of only in terms of negative, mystical theology. The divine Trinity, on the other hand, may be expressed positively, although the categories of "Father," "Son," and "Spirit" are symbolic. Hence, God the Creator differs from the Godhead, the "ground of God." Since freedom derives from the *Ungrund,* God did not create freedom and is therefore in no sense responsible for its consequences. He is not to be held accountable for the misuse of freedom on the part of man — for wars, suffering, injustice, and evil of the world order. Man, accordingly, was not created by God alone, for along with God's creative act, freedom, derived from the *Ungrund,* has also entered the resultant amalgam.

Since freedom is uncreated, is the world created? Berdyaev departed in this respect from Boehme, who held that both the theogonic and the cosmogonic processes were the result of the same primal Will-to-Be. For himself, Berdyaev answered the question of creation in the traditional way, that God created the world out of "nothing." But this "nothing" is further defined by the Platonic term *τὸ μὴ ὄν* as distinguished from *τὂ οὐκ ὄν*; the former, "meonic" nothing possesses a potentiality of being, a desire to be; the latter does not.[19] In the act of creation, the "meonic" nonbeing has consented to become being. Or, as Berdyaev has expressed it elsewhere in a more picturesque phrase, God created the world out of a potentiality which was driven by "a hunger to be something."[20] Thus he stressed the voluntaristic character of nonbeing. One is forcibly reminded of Gautama Buddha's characterization of the ultimate and basic nature of man as the blind clutching after existence, the instinct of self-preservation, the will to live, the inborn, insatiable, driving desire to be. Accordingly, Berdyaev held that the formerly undifferentiated, indeterminate nonbeing which had been "beyond good and evil" became differentiated and determined, and hence morally cognizable. Thus God's creative act brought about a moral differentiation between good and evil.

The doctrine of "uncreated freedom" drew upon Berdyaev more criticism than any other of his views. He was aware of it, and even came to the conclusion that he was alone in holding the doctrine.[21] And no wonder. For this highly speculative theory raises more serious problems than it allays or solves. Evgeny Lampert, in his recent treatise dealing with Berdyaev, declares that this is "probably the most disastrous conclusion of his [Berdyaev's] whole philosophy; and one that seems in fact in no way warranted by his fundamental presuppositions."[22] I am reluctantly constrained to agree, in the main, with this judgment. Granting the authentic character of Boehme's genius, and the vivifying influence he has exerted on many religious thinkers and philosophers, his insights nevertheless have sometimes been contrary to basic Christian conceptions.

Perhaps it may be deemed proper to offer a few considerations as to the grounds of my dissent from Berdyaev in the instance under discussion. In the first place, I do not feel convinced that God's endowment of man with freedom makes him responsible for man's abuse of that freedom. I honor Berdyaev for his unusual sensitiveness toward the fact of evil, but I dissent from his assertion that the traditional Christian doctrine of creation makes God responsible for the consequences of man's freedom. Secondly, Berdyaev's "uncreated freedom" theory really does not free God from responsibility for at least consenting to use the "meonic" stuff in creation, although he knew it contained freedom. Did not God know what the consequences of freedom would be? How much difference is there between God's creating freedom, and his using matter which contained it? Furthermore, Berdyaev's theory posits two sources or agents of creation: God and the "meonic" stuff comprising uncreated freedom. This theory denies creation in the Christian sense of that word. The Creator-God becomes a Demiurge who fashions the cosmos out of the pre-existent potential matter; it does not help much to call this material "meonic nothing." In vain did Berdyaev attempt to deny such an implication. The world, he wrote, is not "an emanation from God, it is not born, nor did it evolve, but was created, i.e., it was absolutely new, something that had never been before."[23] How could the world be said to be "new" when it was created out of pre-existing matter containing "uncreated freedom"? And the final objection — although it may be only to the phrasing of the concept — has to do with the whole idea of the "birth" of the divine Trinity. If the divine Trinity is in some real sense "born," even though it be out of "Godhead" or the "*Ungrund*," the whole absolutely basic concept of the eternal existence of the divine may be in grave jeopardy. It does not help much to have Berdyaev's assurance that "the theogony does not at all signify that God has a beginning, that he originates in time, that he develops in the world process, as Fichte and Hegel have held; it signifies that the inner, eternal life of God reveals itself as a dynamic process, as an eternal tragedy, as a struggle with the darkness of nonbeing."[24] For, my dear Nikolai Alexandrovich, the language you employ does mean that the divine Trinity is not eternal in the present form, and therefore need not remain eternally in that form, for the divine Trinity was derived, "born," from the Godhead of which nothing positive can be affirmed. Of course, the theogonic process did not take place "in time," since time itself is a creation. Perhaps the wisest thing to do would be to take refuge in the negative mystical theology and to say that the concept is altogether beyond positive, conceptual formulation.

An ineffable event cannot be expressed in terms of discursive reason. But this excellent advice, which Berdyaev so often gave to others, in this instance he himself failed to follow. I repeat regretfully that this cure of Berdyaev's for the fancied slight upon God's character by reason of his "responsibility for man's freedom" appears to be worse than the disease. Had Berdyaev initiated his discussion of human freedom with an assumption of it on empirical grounds, his argument henceforth would have remained wholly valid and cogent. Nevertheless, since he arrived at the concept of man's freedom, no matter by what devious route, one may regard the resulting view as to that extent consonant with the Christian world view.

But, as has been said many times, not only is freedom, good, derived from the *Ungrund,* but evil as well. This problem, which has been the despair of theologians of all ages, is a specifically and characteristically Russian problem. Russian thinkers have agonized over it, have been tortured by it, more cruelly than any others. Dostoevsky in particular was almost morbidly fascinated by it. Whence evil? And since evil exists, how can the God of love be kept free from blame for it? Berdyaev replies to the first question: Evil derives "from the same dark, indeterminate *Ungrund* whence good and freedom came. Its source is the unfathomable irrationality, the indeterminate possibility and relentless will-to-being of the primal Will. For evil is the necessary presupposition of good and freedom. Accordingly, it is real — not merely "an absence of good." Were there no evil, there could be no good, as there could be no light without darkness. Thus freedom presupposes both good and evil, for there could be no freedom without the two alternatives. Evil, therefore, is by nature spiritual. Greeks and Persians were inclined to identify evil with matter. In Orphism, and from this source, in Platonism and Neoplatonism, spirit was thought to be imprisoned, enmeshed, in the flesh. Salvation was conceived as the liberation, escape, from the bondage of flesh, or matter. Such, however, is not the Christian view. Matter may be put to evil or good uses; but the decision is made by the spiritual agent who alone is capable of making an evil or a good choice. Nor is God the Creator the source of evil. He is not evil and he sends no evil. He is the supreme good, and there is no evil in him.

Furthermore, let no one jump at the conclusion that there exist two co-ordinate, independent, ontologically real principles — on the order of the Persian Ormazd and Ahriman, or the Manichaean Good God and the Demiurge, or the Christian medieval notion of God and the devil. In this particular, Berdyaev departs from Boehme, who held that evil, as we have seen, is but immature good. Berdyaev comes closer to Schelling's conception, for evil is not noumenal, not real in the same sense as good. It is irrational, for were it to partake of reason it would be in some sense the work of the Logos — Reason — and, therefore, equally real with good. Since it is irrational, it cannot be grasped by reason, cannot be understood. Therefore, it is in its very essence an antinomy. To demand a rational, logical explanation of evil is to misunderstand its very nature. "Evil is nonbeing and has its roots in nonbeing, in the primal nothing. But nonbeing cannot possess meaning, which is always ontological. If evil possessed meaning, it would thereby be transformed into good." [25] Berdyaev then pens a passage of such lyric beauty, of such unparalleled spiritual insight, that I cannot resist quoting it in full:

> "Above all, evil is a lie. It always pretends to be what it is not. It always seduces by deception. The devil is a liar; he has no source of life of his own, no being of his own. He steals all from God and perverts and caricatures it. The devil's strength is fictitious, illusory, deceptive strength. There is no kingdom of evil as of positive being, existing alongside the Kingdom of God and the divine Being. Evil always bears a destructive, negative character, for it destroys life and being, and annihilates itself. It comprises nothing positive. Many teachers of the Church have taught that evil is nonbeing. The completely destructive, nonontological character of evil reveals itself in our social experiences of the evil of life.
>
> "All that we indisputably regard as evil bears a destructive character, and contains within itself no positive being. Animosity, hatred, envy, vengeance, corruption, egoism, love of gain, jealousy, suspicion, avarice, megalomania, greediness, destroy life; they undermine the strength of the man who is dominated by such passions. Every evil

passion devours itself, bears within itself the seeds of death, both for man and for life. In all evil passion there is something devouring; in it is revealed evil infinity. Evil plunges man into an illusory, unreal, and fictitious life. There is nothing ontological in such a life." [26]

By asserting that evil has its origin in nonbeing, and is nonexistential, Berdyaev does not, of course, affirm that it is unreal in the sense in which Mrs. Mary Baker Eddy employed that and other similar phrases. Evil in the phenomenal sense is real enough and its effects are all too obvious all about us. Suffering too is real. But it is not noumenally real in the sense in which good is real, for it does not ultimately endure. It is essentially an exteriorization of "wrong imagination," as Boehme would say. Nevertheless, a certain contradiction still inheres in the concept: for by making it a component part of the *Ungrund,* Berdyaev in some real sense affirms its existence.

We come at last to the baffling, soul-tormenting question as to why suffering is permitted, why even the innocent and the good should sometimes be afflicted with almost unbearable suffering. The agelong cry, "Why do the righteous suffer?" has often been raised to mock faith in the God of love. Ivan Karamazov—and one must remember that Ivan is just as much an alter ego of Dostoevsky as Alyosha—does not accept God and his world, "respectfully returns the ticket" to God, because of the tears of even one small child suffering innocently, because the world is full of unredeemed evil, agony, pain, and hopeless sorrow. And that was written long before the two world wars! The answer of Berdyaev, who was ever sensitive to the fact of evil, and consequently was deeply interested in the problem of theodicy, is drawn chiefly from his existentialist point of view and is that God does not cause evil and does not punish men for it; concrete evil is created by the objectification of evil desires and imaginations of men.

"God created concrete beings, persons, creative existential centers, and not the world order which signifies the fall of those creatures and of their ejection into the external, objectified sphere. . . . God is to be found in the child who has shed a tear and not in the world order by which that tear is justified. . . . God is not the world Providence, that is, not the Ruler and Sovereign of the universe, the Pantocrator. God is freedom and meaning, love and sacrifice; he is the struggle against the objectified world order. . . . He suffers along with man and strives together with man against the falsity of the world, against the intolerable sufferings of the world. There is no need to justify, we have no right to justify all the unhappiness, the suffering and evil of the world with the help of the idea of God-Providence and Sovereign of the universe. That is difficult. But we must turn to God for the struggle on behalf of freedom, righteousness, and of enlightenment of existence." [27]

Berdyaev detects in the concept of God as Sovereign, which was established in Latin theology by Tertullian, a concept foreign not only to his own Eastern tradition but also to the spirit of the Gospels. The concept of God as an autocratic monarch, as an Absolute Will, is not derived from the supreme revelation of God in Jesus Christ, but from a pre-Christian and non-Christian, e.g., Roman, Latin, idea of the divine. It is an objectification of the political concept. In Christ, God reveals himself, not as an Oriental despot, an all-devouring fire, but as suffering love. Even in Elijah's vision of God the prophet recognized him in the "still, small voice." God is love, justice, truth, not hate, injustice, lie. He is Spirit, not substance, force, power. "He has less power than a policeman." [28] He is in silence rather than in sound. He is freedom, not authority. He is not Sovereign, but Deliverer from the thralldom of the world. Sovereignty, authority, are human concepts, belonging to the realm of the fallen world. Love needs no authority, for it does not rule: it attracts, draws, does not drive. In short, God does not justify evil; in Christ he takes it upon himself. "One can believe in God only in the event that there exists God the Son, the Redeemer and Liberator, the God of sacrifice and love." [29]

But besides this "existential" view, Berdyaev shares with Dostoevsky a profound insight into the remedial, redemptive function of suffering. Not all suffering is borne by men in a redemptive way: it depends on what attitude they take toward it. Taken in Ivan Karamazov's way, suffering embitters, crushes, fills man with passionate resentment against God. Only Christianity imparts meaning to suffering which makes it an indispensable means of ennobling human life. Accepted in this Christian spirit, suffering purifies, purges; it provides the necessary spiritual catharsis as nothing else can do. There are some good people whose greatest deficiency is that they have not suffered enough. They have not been refined by the trial of fire; consequently, they lack sympathy with those who have suffered. They may make up the deficiency by holy imagination; but the best way is by actual experience of suffering. Its significance then lies in the enrichment of life brought about by a struggle with evil within and without. Even Arnold Toynbee in his *Study of History* reminds us of this same lesson in connection with the rise of civilization: the creators of the Egyptiac civilization faced the desperate conditions caused by the gradual desiccation of their territories, and conquered the adverse situation by removal into the Nile Valley; those of their original society who neither changed their habitat nor their way of life either paid the penalty of extinction or remained close to the savage level. As an athlete cannot develop muscles unless he undergoes strenuous, persistent exercise; as a butterfly cannot obtain the wing rigidity necessary for flight except by a violent struggle in freeing itself from the chrysalis, so a human being must wage a spiritual war against the powers of evil in order to gain the crown. The main concern of a Christian is not that the cup of suffering pass away, but that he be given sufficient strength to drain it to the bottom.

Recapitulating the whole argument, then, Berdyaev stoutly holds the essentially Biblical and Christian doctrine (despite the additional Boehmian speculations which may or may not be regarded as aberrations) that man is a being created by God in His own image and likeness. Against all other theories, ancient and modern, he maintains that the Biblical teachings alone deal with the whole man — with his origin, true nature, significance, and destination.[30] Nevertheless he asserts that the Old Testament doctrine is incomplete; accordingly, it must be supplemented by the supreme revelation of the divine intention in regard to man which was made in Jesus Christ, the God-man. Many Christian theologians, Berdyaev thinks, have not perceived the relevance of this truth. Hence, their anthropology is seriously faulty.

But what necessity, if one may use that word, was there that God should create the world or man at all? Was it a whim, an inscrutable pleasure, on his part? Was it for his own glory and praise, as certain traditional theologies assert? Was it for some other reason which would make God's action essential, justifiable? Berdyaev sees such motivation in the nature of love. Self-contained love is egoism, not love at all. Love presupposes an object and a going out toward that object. If God be love, and love cannot exist in a vacuum but must go out to a beloved object, then a free man and the world are necessary to God. "God so loved the world . . ." There exists in God, therefore, a longing, a yearning for a loving response on man's part, which is inseparable from love. This the mystics, particularly Eckhart, designated as being "born into God." [31] But love must be freely reciprocated if it is not to result in a poignant sense of frustration, the sharpest pain. No human love would feel satisfied with less than a free response, for there can be no constraint in love. That is why man whom God created must be a free being, capable of reciprocating, returning freely, the yearning love of God. It is only in this sense that one can understand the daring words of the seventeenth century disciple of Eckhart, Angelus Silesius, which Berdyaev used as a motto for his *Meaning of Creativity,* and which sound almost blasphemous to our sober Western ears: "I know that without me God cannot live a moment; did I not exist, he must of necessity give up the Spirit." [32]

Again one discerns how deeply rooted in Berdyaev's conviction are the words of the Grand Inquisitor, spoken to Christ: "Thou hast desired free love of man, that he should freely follow thee, charmed and taken captive by thee." No wonder that Berdyaev has no patience with the theological concept of the master-slave relationship as regards the position of God toward men. God does not desire a man over whom he can rule, but a man who can answer his call and with whom communion of love is possible.[33] Not even God may use the human personality as a means, for "all personality is an end in itself."[34]

But just because man is a free spiritual agent, he is not only capable of responding to God's love, but also of repudiating it, affirming himself, falling away from God. This is not only possible, alas! but the general, universal experience. Man has revolted against God. That is the basic fact of the Christian world view. The explanation of it—predestination or the story of the eating of the apple in the Garden of Eden—may be totally rejected or may be regarded as a mythical, poetic version of the religious intuition. But the fact of the sinfulness of man remains for all, Christians and non-Christians, religious and nonreligious, to account for and deal with. At present it is seen in its blackest colors, and in an exaggerated form, by such positivist students of human nature as Sigmund Freud, whose analysis "out-Herods Herod," or, more correctly, "out-Luthers Luther." The Fall is a spiritual fact of primary, absolutely basic importance. It is silly to deny or minimize it. A theology that does deny it argues itself out of significance and becomes futile. "They that be whole need not a physician, but they that are sick." If man be not a sinner, if the gospel of Jean Jacques Rousseau be true that natural man is indeed fundamentally good, corrupted only by his environment, e.g., the civilization, then religion as a redeeming, transforming power is not needed and a redeemer is superfluous.

Berdyaev certainly is not among those who deny the reality of the Fall. But he differs considerably from many who accept it in the traditional, literal way. He regards it as a spiritual event—the proud, rebellious self-affirmation of the human spirit—which took place in the pre-existent, spiritual realm. Reinhold Niebuhr likewise insists that a literal understanding of the Fall as a historical event occurring at a particular time is to be deprecated. To him it is "a symbol of an aspect of every historical moment in the life of man."[35] For Berdyaev, the human spirit is pre-existent; it was created by God in eternity before time began. In this he shares Origen's opinion;[36] but he is not alone in this respect among the Russian religious thinkers, for S. L. Frank holds it as well.[37] Human personality "is not a product of the process of generation and is not created at the moment of conception," but is created by God in the spiritual world, in eternity.[38] The terrestrial existence of each human being is preceded by a "prologue in heaven" like that of Goethe's *Faust*. Human spirit has a "celestial" as well as terrestrial history. Moreover, the celestial prologue conditions the spirit's terrestrial existence. By "celestial," of course, is not meant some remote geographical region in the sky but the pre-existent realm of spirits.

The revolt itself took the form of self-assertion on the part of the human spirit. This spiritual event finds a more fitting adumbration in the extra-Biblical myth of Satan's rebellion against God — such as is depicted in Milton's *Paradise Lost* — than in the myth of the Garden of Eden.[39] Berdyaev actually writes of the event in terms of the Satanic myth: "The spirit that belonged to the highest hierarchy of existence was the first voluntarily to fall away from God, committing the act of self-assertion in spiritual pride; with him began corruption and overthrow in the hierarchy of being."[40] But be the mythical imagery as it may, what is signified thereby is clearly a spiritual rebellion against God which was the cause of the Fall. God did not hurl anyone from his presence; the revolting spirits of their own free will separated themselves from him. It was their act that caused the break. In the same view, the unknown writer of the *Theologia Germanica,* using the imagery of the Garden of Eden, says that had not Adam asserted his own "I," he could have eaten seven apples and yet not have sinned thereby. That has ever been the view of mystics. Berdyaev's interpretation, therefore, is consonant with the *essential* features of the Christian doctrine: that man is God's creature, endowed with freedom, created in God's image and likeness, but that he fell away from God through self-assertion.

How has the Fall affected man's nature? There is, unfortunately, no unanimity in the Christian understanding of this basic issue. In Roman Catholic theology man, as originally created, is conceived as having possessed only the natural endowments, intellect, memory; but the "supernatural" virtues, the *donum superadditum,* of faith, hope, and love have been added by a special action of God's grace. Thus man has lost in the Fall only the superadded virtues which really never had formed part of his original nature. As for his natural endowments, they were but slightly affected. Accordingly, his original human nature was not corrupted.

In the classical Protestant formulation of this doctrine, the original nature of man comprised both the "natural" and the "supernatural" virtues. As the result of the Fall, the latter virtues of faith, hope, and love were totally lost, while the former were seriously damaged and vitiated. It is this view that goes under the unfortunate, and really inaccurate, term of "total depravity." In its most radical form in which alone the term could be properly used, and which was asserted by Martin Luther, it was claimed that after the Fall nothing was left of the image of God in man but the mere empty name. Luther characterizes the loss of the divine image as complete: the natural endowments are "utterly leprous and unclean." For "death crept in, like leprosy, over all the senses. So that now, we cannot reach the comprehension of this image of God by our intellect, nor even in thought. . . . Wherefore, when we now attempt to speak of that image, we speak of a thing unknown. . . . Of this image, therefore, all we now possess are the mere terms—'the image of God!' These naked words are all we now hear, and all we know."[41] Luther found his true disciple in this matter in Karl Barth, who restates it in his own extreme manner by asserting that the "*imago Dei*" has been completely lost. Barth assails Emil Brunner with what appears unnecessary vigor for the latter's mild admission that although the "material" image is lost, the "formal" is not; for in this manner Barth thinks that Brunner has provided a potentiality of contact with God, a "capacity for revelation." Barth does not think well of the notion.[42]

The Orthodox theologians in the main hold that although the image of God was marred in the Fall it was by no means lost: "man's divine likeness and spiritual life are not destroyed but merely damaged by the Fall, and the image of God in man is besmeared."[43] Berdyaev ranges himself on the side of the tradition of his own Church. Man "remains a spiritual being, although sick and broken, and has retained his religious consciousness. For the Word of God could not be addressed to a being deprived of free religious consciousness. There is liberty in man which precedes the action of revelation and grace."[44] "Grace acts upon liberty, for it can act solely upon it."[45] In defense of this view, which is basic for him — and should be for everyone else, for to cure a disease the physician must first diagnose it correctly — he argues with his accustomed vigor against the Roman Catholic and the Lutheran-Barthian theories of the status of the fallen man. Barth, for instance, denies that the natural man is capable of responding to God's grace or that there is anything left of the original image of God in man. But in that case, Berdyaev counters, the whole saving process would be initiated, performed, and consummated by God alone. Man would have no part in it. This is really another form of Monophysitism or pantheism. God is everything, man is nothing. God would save a man who really does not *want* to be saved, or who even refuses to be saved. This again smacks of the gospel of the Grand Inquisitor, who is set upon saving the world forcibly, against its will. There is no freedom, liberty, in this scheme; but these are of the very essence, if God wishes a free response to his love.

7

Redemption I: God-manhood — the Redemption of Man

SAD INDEED is the condition of the man who by pride and self-assertion cuts himself off from the only true source of being and chooses the path that leads to nonbeing. Berdyaev's favorite concept apropos of the Fall is that it results in the loss of freedom. Its consequences are self-centeredness, pride, lust, self-assertion, which result in pain, suffering, futilitarianism, a return to nonbeing whence man was evoked. For to assert oneself is to destroy oneself. Human history is replete with such results of human sin, both individual and corporate. It is a terrible tragedy, particularly because it is self-caused, self-inflicted — in fact, that is the most tragic thing about it. God does not will that man should suffer. He afflicts no man. Nor is man's suffering the result of impersonal fate. Omar Khayyám's view is unacceptable to the Christian:

> "The Moving Finger writes; and, having writ,
> Moves on: nor all your Piety nor Wit
> Shall lure it back to cancel half a Line
> Nor all your Tears wash out a Word of it."

No, human destiny is not externally determined by some mysterious demonic or divine force. It is within. Man is terrifyingly free: his destiny is bound up with the freedom of choice between good and evil, although this is not to be understood in the Pelagian sense. But alas! man has ever habitually chosen evil. This has imparted a tragic character to human history. "The freedom of evil is the real foundation of history. And the ancient tradition of man's fall, the fall of Adam and Eve, which relates in a short story what has happened in the history of being prior to the origin of the world process, is an account of the beginnings of history which lie beyond the boundaries dividing our time from eternity."[1]

The central event in the spiritual history of mankind — the "metahistorical" revelation of the eternal in the midst of time — is the appearance of Jesus Christ. For "God was in Christ reconciling the world unto himself." In his incarnation, in the assumption of flesh on the part of the Logos, God's love toward alienated, sin-enslaved mankind was revealed. In this basic doctrine of the incarnation, Christianity is unique; it alone teaches that God became man, the God-man. In Christ, God suffers in his longing for man; he woos man to return unto him who alone is the source of true life. God himself shares in man's suffering by taking on himself the sins of mankind. This is the predominant view of the atonement of the Eastern Fathers. On the basis of this interpretation, human love is engendered as a response to the divine love: "We love him, because he first loved us." Berdyaev thinks of Christianity as the religion of the second birth. "Except a man be born from above he cannot see the Kingdom of God."[2] This experience of spiritual birth is absolutely basic, fundamental: humanity which has been plunged into suffering and misery as the result of self-assertion must freely choose to retrace the steps by which it has descended. Man must repent of his sins in order to gain forgiveness and remission of sins. This is "*metanoia*." "The endless threads do not stretch from the past to the future" as in the Hindu notion of the karma, but 'are cut.' "[3] "He who does not know that inner work of obedience and renunciation cannot rise upward."[4]

Redemption, then, is the work of God, who grants the grace of the Holy Spirit; but man must voluntarily and freely receive it. For the Holy Spirit can work only upon human freedom, nothing else. Were grace to act without man's co-operation, predestination would be the accurate descriptive term for such an action. But, on the other hand, man cannot save himself apart from the divine grace. Christianity is not a religion of man's unaided attainment of salvation; or, in the words made forever memorable by Luther, man is not saved by works. "After the Fall, man cannot save himself, cannot return to the primal source of being freely by his own natural powers, because he is no longer free. His nature is damaged, enslaved by the element of evil, and has returned halfway to the sphere of nonbeing. Freedom must be returned to mankind and the world by an act of divine grace, by the participation of God himself in the judgments of world history. . . . Mankind itself cannot redeem sin, for its sacrifice and bloody torments are not equal to the transgression of abandonment of God and cannot forgive its own sins." [5]

But despite this Anselmic-sounding formulation of the part that divine grace plays in redemption (found in one of the early works of Berdyaev) he is even more insistent upon the part played by human freedom. He is conscious of the tension between these two statements and takes refuge in the paradoxicality of the whole concept and impossibility of treating it in logical concepts.[6] Consequently, as has been mentioned, he violently repudiates the view that man's nature has been so totally vitiated as to be completely unable even to respond to God's grace. He counters it with his own spiritual experience:

> "Freedom has brought me to Christ and I know no other path to Christ but the one of freedom. . . . Those who have repudiated authoritarian Christianity can return only to a Christianity of freedom. . . . Although it is grace that has brought me to faith, it is grace experienced by me as freedom. . . . Those whose religion is authoritarian and hereditary will never understand properly those who have come to religion through freedom and through the immanent partaking in the tragic experiences of life." [7]

He sums up his understanding of the work of Christ in redemption by saying:

> "Redemption and salvation of the world by Christ consists in the renewal of human nature, damaged by the Fall, by a restoration to man of the freedom which he had lost in the original defection from God. Christ became, by way of salvation, the freedom of mankind. To oppose him is slavery, a fettering of oneself to the devil. But the

Son of Man appeared to the world in the image of the Crucified; God appeared to the world incarnate, not as a czar, not as a ruler of the world, but as one oppressed and crushed by the might and evil of the world. Here is hidden the great secret of the freedom of humanity . . . man can and should be saved in freedom, by loving the Crucified in whom he had recognized his God. The appearance of Christ in the world has made man infinitely free, but that freedom brings with it a tragedy such as has not hitherto been seen — the tragedy of the final freedom of choice and the eternal danger of seducement and substitution." [8]

In accordance with these views, Berdyaev repeatedly repudiates and denounces the traditional Western juridical theory of redemption formulated by Saint Anselm of Canterbury in his *Cur Deus Homo?* To assert that God's honor had to be " satisfied " before his wrath could be appeased, and that only an infinite satisfaction through the voluntary death of a God-man would do it, is a confusion of spiritual and legal concepts. " To regard the universal tragedy as a judicial process between God and man, initiated by God on account of a formal transgression of his will by man, is quite unworthy." [9] Redemption is not a judgment, but a transforming process. Christianity is a religion of redemption, not a legal transaction. If God were a God of justice, and were to take account of human iniquities, who could stand? The process of redemption is initiated by the forgiveness of sins, all sins — even atheism and denial of Christ — offered in Christ and accepted freely and humbly by man, who otherwise would have no means of securing release from his guilt. " Man cannot forgive himself his sin and baseness; he is unable to forget the evil past. But Christ has borne on himself the sins of the whole world; he can take away sin and forgive it. Forgiveness and obliteration are possible only in and through Christ. Man cannot forgive himself sin and evil, and live down its consequences; he is freed through Christ." [10] Redemption is the work of love, not of justice; of sacrifice on God's part, not a propitiation of an angry deity. It is a dual process: both God and man share in it. Moreover, its goal is the transformation of the human into the divine-human, theanthropic personality. It is not, therefore, merely a restoration of the original state of man before the Fall, but an attainment of a higher stage of being. Thus Christ has ushered in a new era of spiritual history. It is in this sense that his coming was a unique event in history.

The incarnation, accordingly, is a revelation of both the character of God and the nature and destiny of man. God cannot be known from nature alone, or from human imaginings, no matter how exalted or noble. His supreme revelation is in Jesus Christ alone. Berdyaev derives his conception of God primarily from the implications of the incarnation of Christ, rather than from the idea of the Creator in the Old Testament or other sources. But he interprets it from the point of view of his existential philosophy which is nowhere more sharply differentiated from the rationalism or naturalism of some other thinkers than in his doctrines of God and man. For he repudiates all conceptions that rest upon external authoritarianism and upon the objectification of human political or other relations in regard to God when he is regarded as the Absolute, the principle of concretion, the all-inclusive Unity, or any other symbol or figure of speech in this category. The God of Berdyaev is not the Absolute, an abstract principle, an *actus purus* such as was conceived of by Aristotle, and by Saint Thomas Aquinas who in this matter followed Aristotle to a great degree. One cannot pray to, nor have communion with, the Absolute any more than with the law of gravitation, or the principle of concretion. No intellectual abstraction has a meaning or existence apart from the living thinker: the Absolute is not the living God, the God of Abraham and Isaac, of the Hebrew prophets, and least of all, of our Lord Jesus Christ. Pascal knew that the God of the Bible is a living fire, a spirit with whom man may enter into communion.[11] Nor is God a Sovereign, a Pantocrator, an all-embracing Power. Berdyaev's rejection of this concept has already been dealt with.[12]

The essentially pantheistic idea that God is all in all, that God is everything and man is nothing, is a dangerously lopsided, inadmissibly exaggerated half-truth. Some half-truths are worse than a whole lie—just because they contain an element of truth.

God is a Person, a Spirit, but men too are persons, spirits, even though in the former case we deal with an uncreated, eternal Being and in the latter with created, dependent beings.

Above all, Berdyaev rejects the assumption that God is being, an object among other objects in the world. God is never an object, always the subject.[13] Any other view is an attenuated, naïve materialism. There can exist only a personal relation, a spiritual communion, between God and men. Just because the intimate I-Thou relationship is relatively rare, both among men and between men and God, does not prove that it does not exist.

But the incarnate God-man has revealed not only the true character of God, but the nature and destiny of man as well. "Man partly is and wholly hopes to be," sang Browning. But to discern the potentialities inherent in man, one must regard him from the point of view of the revelation in Christ. Therefore, it is literally, realistically, true that only he who believes in God — particularly the Christian God — can also believe in man. In view of the failure of Renaissance humanism, considered earlier in this book, and of the subversion of secularist humanism into anti-humanism which we are witnessing today, there can be no doubt of the truth of this thesis. Accordingly, the Biblical anthropology is much more realistic than any of the dominant secularist brands: it does not regard the natural man as good, as did Rousseau and the Romantics; nor does it see in him a mere peripatetic chemico-biological laboratory driven by a number of natural impulses but devoid of all spiritual significance or potentiality; nor as a stream of associated sensations, as do the various modern secularist anthropologies. Christianity exalts man, recognizes in him a spiritual being whose destiny transcends the span of his natural life. In regard to the Christian view of man, Berdyaev wrote:

"I became a Christian not because I ceased to believe in man, in his worth and high destiny, in his creative freedom, but because I sought a deeper and surer basis for that faith. In this regard I have ever felt a difference between myself and the majority of men who were converted to Christianity, whether they were Orthodox, Catholics, or Protestants. My faith cannot be shaken by the unusually low status of man, for it is not based on what man thinks of man, but what God thinks of man." [14]

Berdyaev has learned both from Kant and from Christianity that from the point of view of its ultimate destiny, human personality is "the highest hierarchical value in the world." [15] Man is never a means, always an end in himself. This conviction runs like a red thread through all his works: "Above all," he asserts in his second book as a manifesto against Communism, "we acknowledge the absolute worth of man as an end in himself, and that idea cannot be arrived at by the empirical path." [16] All exploitation of man, therefore, whether by an economic order or by society or by government, is a denial of this fundamental, axiomatic truth of Christianity. For man is treated by them as a means, an object, a thing. But in reality he is "a greater value than society, nation, government, although he is often crushed by society, nation, and government which make themselves idols of the objectified, fallen world." [17] For since personality bears the image and likeness of God, and the state does not, personality belongs to eternity, while government belongs to this world.

Since Berdyaev's faith in the supreme value of man was perhaps the basic difference between him and the orthodox Marxists in the early days of his active life, he returned to this theme many times. In an article, "The Human Personality and Superpersonal Values," [18] he writes:

"The existence of personality is a rupture in the world, a break in the ongoing world process. It is a proof that the world is not self-sufficient. There enters into the world a being which bears within itself an image not of this world, but of a higher Being — the image of God. It is a being called to an active life in time, but predestined for eternity; a self-contradictory being, the meeting place of two worlds. Accordingly, there exists an incommensurability between personality and the world. The relation between personality and the world cannot be measured by a mathematical number, nor can it be described as the relation of a part to the whole. No nonpersonal goals may be acknowledged in relation to which a person is a means. . . . Man is a being which transcends itself toward that which is more than man and more than human. The transcendence belongs to the existential marks of personality. . . . The lie of humanism consists in the acknowledgment of the self-sufficiency of man, in asserting that man may realize the fullness of his humanity without the super-human, without God. But the integral humanism which envisages the realization and completion of humanity only in relation to a higher spiritual principle, opposes this false humanism. The final, integral, humanity, the final, integral realization of personality, are unthinkable within the limits of this world and presuppose a transcendence to another world. The supreme worth of human personality as not only an individual but as also a social principle, points the way to that world."

Nevertheless, this is not a confusion of individualism with personalism. Indeed, Berdyaev draws a sharp distinction between the two. Individuality belongs to the natural, biological category. Natural man — the psychic-physical, biological organism — may indeed be all that the physical psychologist, or psychiatrist, biochemist, anthropologist, or sociologist says that he is. But then animals and plants, as well as stones and manufactures, share individuality with him to a degree. "An individual is part of the species, he springs from the species, although he can isolate himself from the species, oppose and struggle against it. The individual is born by means of the biological, generic process; he is born and dies." [19] For all that originates in the world of time and space is conditioned thereby; it is only temporal. It does not and cannot possess immortality. The earth can produce only mortal individuals.

But not so personality. Personality is of the spiritual, not of the natural, order; as such, it belongs to the noumenal, not the phenomenal, world. It is not generated; "it is created by God," [20] although in the pre-existent realm. Thus it originates not in the temporal world, but in eternity. Accordingly, personality is a manifestation of the eternal in the temporal order. "Personality is not an object, not a thing, not a natural substance, not an objectification of the psychic life as is taught by the science of psychology. . . . Personality is spirit and therefore opposed to a thing and 'thinghood,' to the natural phenomena." [21] Mature personality is to be regarded as the realization of God's idea for the particular human being, the supremacy of the image of God in man over his physical nature. In this respect, personality surpasses the other component parts of human nature, as well as the world of matter. Nevertheless, this admittedly dualistic anthropology does not imply that the spirit is a foreign substance in the body-mind organism; nor does it suggest the Platonic image of a skillful charioteer driving a pair of wild horses. Personality is a whole, an organic and harmonious unity of body, soul, and spirit, but with spirit in command since it is, hierarchically, the highest principle. It is "unity in trinity." Personality is "the entire image of man in which the spiritual principle has the mastery over all his other powers, both mental and physical. The unification of personality is created by the spirit." [22]

Thus the harmonious integration of personality is a task to be achieved; "temperament is given naturally; character is a conquest and attainment, and presupposes freedom." [23] More than that, it is a duty, a moral obligation. Whether or not a man achieves personality during his lifetime is not a matter of indifference. He is a moral failure unless he achieves it. "Man ought to be free, he must not be a slave, for he ought to be a man. Such is the will of God." [24]

Since there is no personality without a struggle, what are the means whereby it is to be realized? Highest of all is love. It is only through love that personality may be achieved. For without love there is no goodness, no virtue whatever. "Love is the intuition of personality." [25] It cannot be developed in a vacuum. It presupposes a loving contact with other personalities — the "I-Thou" communion being of its very essence. Individuals know no communion with each other, for communion is a spiritual concept, while individualism is not. Moreover, the highest communion can exist only between the human and the divine Spirit.

Furthermore, the attainment of personality entails pain and suffering. The reason why men do not strive after the goal of free personality is that they are unwilling to pay the price of suffering. Dostoevsky knew this well; that is why he regarded suffering as essential to the Christian way of life. "The realization of personality is the attainment of inner freedom, when man is no longer determined from the outside. A being living in necessity and constraint does not as yet know personality."[26] This requires fearlessness and courage, as well as asceticism. Every hierarchically ordered life presupposes asceticism in the sense of putting first things first. The spiritual must rule the material-mental. Men seeking a comfortable life, abundance of things, or at least avoidance of pain, cannot attain personality. Eudaemonism, the bourgeois ideal of life, is the enemy of personality.

The result of the process of redemption is freedom. Man lost his freedom in the Fall and became a slave to his own passions, to the lust of the flesh, the lust of the eyes, and the pride of life. His redemption is effected by Christ, for he is free. He is bound by nought but love. Therefore, "if the Son . . . shall make you free, ye shall be free indeed." Accordingly, through Christ, the redeemed man regains his lost freedom; he becomes master of himself and slave to no one and no thing save God alone, whose service is perfect freedom. "A free man does not desire to lord it over anyone." Likewise, he ought not to be a slave. But alas! even the redeemed man must beware lest he become a slave to a vast variety of things, good, bad, and indifferent: for he may be enslaved even by seemingly good things, "in acquisition of knowledge, in morals, in religion, in art, in political and social life." Of course, the bad and the indifferent things always enslave. "The will to power, to domination and rule, is not a free will nor a will to freedom. . . . The caesar-dictator, the hero of imperialistic will, places himself under the sign of fate. He cannot stop, he cannot place a limit to his will, he goes farther and farther toward his ruin."[27]

The redeemed man, then, by being free and no longer a slave, is a transformed man. But despite the transforming process, man does not cease to be human, nor does he become divine; he is changed into divine-human. Accordingly, the Chalcedonian formula that Jesus Christ possessed two natures in one person is true of redeemed personalities as well — but with a difference.

For the redeemed man differs from the God-man Jesus Christ in that his is not an incarnation of the uncreated God but the union of a created spirit with the eternal Spirit. God-manhood, or theanthropy, deification, theosis, is Berdyaev's answer to all basic human problems. "The secret of Christianity is the secret of God-manhood, the secret of the meeting of two natures which are united but not commingled. Man does not cease to exist, but he is deified and retains his humanity in eternity. I regard this concept as fully orthodox, although in orthodoxy it is inadequately developed and often obscured by a Monophysite bias." [28] Humankind must be transformed, for one cannot make a good world without good men and women any more than one can make a silk dress out of calico. Men must be transformed from self-assertive, self-centered, lust-driven, power-mad, ambition-ridden, cruel, vengeful, domineering, proud individuals into persons who manifest "the fruit of the Spirit [which] is love, joy, peace, patience, kindness, goodness, faithfulness, gentleness, [and] self-control." The terms used to designate this transforming spiritual process—God-manhood, theanthropy, deification—are easily recognized as being derived from the Eastern Orthodox tradition. Irenaeus used them, and in this he was followed by Berdyaev's predecessors and contemporaries in the Russian renascence movement, particularly Vladimir Solovev. Berdyaev did not shrink from sharing the daring language:

> "The idea of God is the greatest human idea. The idea of man is the greatest divine idea. Man longs for the birth of God in himself. God longs for the birth of man in Himself. . . . In the depths of the divine life there exists pre-existent humanity—the drama of the relation between God and his 'other,' the divine and the human." [29]

Perhaps to the sober Western taste such usage appears intemperate, dangerously loose, even blasphemous, although one could find many examples of it in the West. The mystics commonly used it; even Luther did. Berdyaev follows Angelus Silesius in the instance quoted above. Nevertheless, the rationalistic contemporary West is apt to think that the terms tend to obliterate the everlasting distinction between the creature and the Creator. They smack even of the pantheistic concept that man loses himself in God as a drop of rain loses all identity by falling into the ocean. But is that what God-manhood means to Berdyaev? One must admit that his use of such ecstatic phrases is often vague, even inexact. When he speaks of the "theosis, deification, attained through man's freedom and creativeness, and enriching the very divine life itself," [30] the phrase sounds unbearably pretentious. But fortunately he has given us at least a few explicit statements which dispose of such misapprehensions.

In the first place, he steers clear of all notions of a mystical extinction of man in God which is sometimes charged against mysticism in general. In Berdyaev's concept of God-manhood the human element is not absorbed, annihilated, in the divine, but is transformed into divine-human.[31] God is not "the wholly other" from the human point of view, nor are God and man identical. Berdyaev writes:

"Human personality is human only when it is divine-human. . . . Human personality is a theandric being. But theologians will cry out in alarm that Jesus Christ alone was God-man, and that man is a created being and cannot be God-man. Such an argument remains within the confines of theological rationalism. Even though man be not God-man in the same sense in which Christ is the unique God-man, nevertheless there is a divine element in man. There are, so to speak, two natures in him. There is within him an intersection of two worlds. He bears within himself the image that is both of man and of God, and is the image of man only in so far as he realizes within himself the image of God." [32]

This is somewhat reassuring, provided one knows precisely what Berdyaev's terms mean. And that is still not quite clear. In the next quotation the matter is defined more distinctly:

"Theosis, which is at the basis of Eastern Christian mysticism, is neither a monistic identity with God nor a humiliation of man and the created world. Theosis makes man divine, inducts him into the divine life, while at the same time it preserves his human nature. Thus instead of the human personality being annihilated, it is changed into the likeness of God and the divine Trinity. . . . Man is not identical with the cosmos or with God; man is a microcosm and a microtheos. Human personality may be filled with a universal content." [33]

And finally, "the Christian world has raised up the ideal of the saint, i.e., of a man completely transformed and enlightened, of the appearance of a new creature that had conquered its old nature. This is the highest point that the new, spiritual man can reach." [34]

Furthermore, one may liken the "theandric" personality, as the Eastern Fathers used to do in connection with the two natures in Jesus Christ, to an iron incandescent with white heat. The iron is not the heat, and the heat is not the iron; nevertheless, the heat interpenetrates the iron. Moreover, it is only in that state that iron is malleable, capable of receiving a new shape. Cold iron cannot be changed. So it is with human nature: unless the love of God interpenetrates man's heart, he is incapable of the transforming, sanctifying process. If that is what Berdyaev means by "theosis," perhaps our Western fears of his exaggerated, intemperate language rest more on an appearance of evil than on its reality.

And, finally, the concept of the redeemed man necessarily comprises, in Berdyaev's estimation, a release of consecrated, creative energy. This is the burden of his early, significant work *The Meaning of Creativity*. It is an "anthropodicy"—a justification of man—as he tells us, for there are "theodicies" enough already. He suggests that perhaps the only way to write a convincing theodicy is by way of an anthropodicy. He severely criticizes the traditional Christian teaching about man, of the Church Fathers and of the current Catholic and Protestant theologies, as deficient because it does not stress the duty of the redeemed man to use all his powers toward the creation of a redeemed human social order. The gospel is presented by them as a message of salvation from sin alone. Christianity, as commonly understood, is too exclusively a religion of redemption. The emphasis centers upon the "fallen" man, rather than upon the redeemed and transformed man. The Church is regarded as a hospital for the curing of sick souls. There the work of redemption stops. But this is not enough; it makes the redemption negative rather than positive. The sinner becomes good; but what is he good for?

> "There can be but one solution for this tragic problem of Christianity: religious awareness of the truth that the religious significance of life and being is not exhausted by the redemption from sin, but that life and being have positive, creative tasks. . . . Salvation from sin, from perdition, is not the final goal of religious life; for salvation is always *from* something, while life should be *for* something. . . . The goal of man is not salvation alone, but a creative ascent; but for the creative ascent salvation from evil and sin is necessary. The event of redemption is religiously subordinated to the event of creativity." [35]

Since man was created in the image of God, he also shares the gift of divine creativity. "That the image and likeness of the Creator cannot but be creative is an anthropological truth which has not been perceived with adequate force and fullness by the preceding religious epochs. Religious consciousness was filled with the mystery of the redemption of human nature, but the mystery of the redeemed human nature was hid from it." [36] But redemption precedes the life of creativity, for only a free man — that is, a redeemed man, liberated from bondage to sin — is capable of creativity in the truly noumenal realm. For "only the free man creates. From necessity only evolution is born; creativity is born of freedom. When we speak, in our imperfect, human language, of creation from nothing, we speak of creation from freedom." [37] "The unfree, a slave, cannot enter the Kingdom of God; he is not a son of God, but is subjugated by the lower spheres." [38]

Nevertheless, that is not to deny the ability of the natural man to realize his selfish purposes in the objectified social order. Consequently, it must be understood that there are two freedoms: divine and demonic. The first is revealed and inaugurated by Christ, for he is the liberator. The demonic freedom, on the other hand, has made its appearance after Christ's earthly ministry, for its final form is opposition to Christ. "Demonic freedom appears only in the eighth day of creation as a false imitation of creative freedom. Demonic creativity effects only nonbeing; it steals from God in order to set up a caricature of being, a false imitation." [39] Nevertheless, the social order created by means of this demonic force confronts the redeemed and unredeemed with most of the tragic problems with which they have to deal.

Finally, it may be added that "the creature does not create being—that is effected by the Creator alone. It is not capable of effecting a personality—that is effected by God alone. Personality is created by God in eternity. Every attempt on the part of the created being to create a being, a personality, leads only to the making of an automaton, a lifeless mechanism. Such an attempt is always demonic—it is black magic. . . . The creativity of created beings may be directed only toward the increase of the creative energy of a being, toward the growth of beings and their harmony in the world, toward the making of new values, new approaches to truth, goodness, and beauty, i.e., toward the making of a cosmos and cosmic life, toward the pleroma, the supermundane fullness." [40]

To sum up, then, the task of creativity is the freeing of life from the dominance of the temporal. For creativity is no longer within time, but partakes of the eternal. Moreover, it is the task of freeing oneself from all slavery to all external conditions, of acting not from motives of gain, acclaim, praise, but from inner freedom. "A creator is neither a slave nor a master; he is one who gives and sacrifices. All dependence of one man upon another is morally abasing. . . . Where the Spirit of God is, there is liberty." [41] And finally, the task of creativity includes the transformation of the social order, which at present is dominated by selfish, evil purposes of men, into a free theonomic society, i.e., one in which men voluntarily accept the will of God in all their relations. Accordingly, the ethics of creativity is not merely personalistic, certainly not individualistic; it has a vital concern for society. Berdyaev speaks of it as the "eighth day of creation, continuing the creation." [42] In it, the Creator and the redeemed, transformed creature co-operate in molding the creation more closely to the divine ideal. For the ultimate divine plans are not completed as yet. "God had foreseen something better for us, that apart from us they should not be made perfect." [43]

8

Redemption II: Sobornost *— the Transformation of Society*

ONE of the fundamental differences between Berdyaev and other existentialist philosophers or theologians is that his philosophy does not issue in despair. He is "realistic" in his view of the "fallen" man and of the present plight of society; but he is neither hopeless nor indifferent as to the possibility of the redemption of society. He is not a devotee of the "necessity of desperation." Nor is he exclusively "apocalyptic," expecting the redemption of the world by a divine fiat at the end of history. In fact, there are few modern thinkers who lay such a stress on man's duty to transform human society as does Berdyaev. But the chief difference between him and a whole bevy of secularist would-be transformers of society is that he does not believe the feat can be effected by mere external changes: only transformed human beings can effect a fundamental, radical change in society. Accordingly, only theanthropic personalities united by the bonds of love into a nucleus of redeemed society, and engaged in a creative endeavor to produce new values, can transform society.

Christianity saves man, the concrete human personality, for it is concerned with worth, quality. But the purpose of the salvation of the individual believer is not exhausted by his own personal transformation and destiny; it finds a fuller realization in the realm of society. This idea played an essential role in the thinking of the Eastern Fathers: "For the classical Greek patristic Christianity was not a religion of individual salvation alone. It was directed toward a cosmic conception of Christianity; it held the idea of the enlightenment and transformation of the world, of the divinization of the creature. Only the later Christian consciousness began to value more the idea of Hades than the idea of the transformation and divinization of the world."[1] The exclusive preoccupation with one's own salvation Berdyaev condemns as a "satanic caricature of Christianity,"[2] and

"the minimalist ethic, an ethic of transcendental egoism. It invites human beings to settle down comfortably while other people and the world are uncomfortable; it denies responsibility of all for all, and rejects the oneness of the created world, the oneness of the cosmos. In the realm of the spirit, there is no self-contained and isolated personality. The ethics of personal salvation leads to the destruction and overthrow of the idea of paradise and of the Kingdom of God. Real heavenly bliss is impossible for me if I isolate myself from the cosmic whole and care about myself only. . . . Hence, individual salvation, or salvation of the elect only, is impossible."[3]

Thus in a true sense an exclusively individual salvation is contrary to Christian ethic, for the salvation of one human being is necessarily linked with that of others and with the transfiguration of the whole earth. It is only in this sense that the hoary saying of Cyprian, *"Extra Ecclesiam nulla salus,"* may be regarded as true. There is no salvation by oneself alone. One is saved among others, along with others, for others.

Moreover, the ultimate goal is universal, for Christianity is ecumenical in intent and scope. God's intention embraces in loving arms all his creatures, provided they choose to return to his embrace. There can be no thought of a "chosen race" in some exclusive sense, or a special group of "elect" who were predestined to eternal bliss before all ages. Salvation is intended for all men; more than that, it embraces "all things to the last bit of vegetation."[4] In this Berdyaev associates himself with another distinguished member of the Russian religious renascence, the late Father Sergius Bulgakov, who developed the idea of the redemption of the whole creation — animate and inanimate — in his concept of Sophia. This is a somewhat exotic formulation of the doctrine of the continuing divine creative process — the eighth day of creation — by means of which all things are brought closer to the realization of the divine idea for each individual thing. It recalls Saint Paul's words that "the creation itself will be set free from its bondage to decay and obtain the glorious liberty of the children of God."[5] The concept seems to have practically dropped out of Western theology, but has been preserved in the Eastern tradition.

History, then, is not only the record of the consequences of human freedom in the social realm, but also the scene of the redemptive process. It is, undoubtedly, a terrible tragedy, owing to the habitual choice of evil on the part of the fallen man.

> "Only for that reason is the world process a terrible tragedy, only for that reason is history bloody and at its center stands the crucifixion, the cross on which the Son of God himself was crucified; only for that reason there stands at its center God's suffering, for in truth God desired freedom; because the primal mystery and drama of the world are the mystery and drama of freedom in the relation between God and his other self which he loves and by which he desires to be loved; and the meaning of that love is only in freedom."[6]

But the historical process is also one of redemption from sin and a return of the creature to the Creator, a free union of man with God, and the final relegation of evil to the sphere of nonbeing.[7]

The transformation of society cannot be effected forcibly, either by God or by man. God does not desire it that way; and man should not. Again, Berdyaev is only echoing the lesson he has learned from Dostoevsky's Grand Inquisitor. The Church, which is the society of transformed persons, and which has for its aim the transformation of man and society, works not through external, forcible means, but through the inner regeneration of men. To charge Christianity with the failure to dominate society — to prevent wars, for instance — is to misunderstand its nature and function.[8] Berdyaev himself wrote a short treatise dealing with the everlastingly reiterated Marxist criticism that Christianity inculcates passivity in relation to the evils of the world; that it teaches men to do nothing "but to pray and be humble."[9] Although there is much truth in the criticism as applied to some quietistic interpretations of Christianity, such is not the case with Christianity properly understood. A Christian is one whose duty it is to seek the Kingdom of God; this is no mere passive wishful thinking, but an earnest activity. It must, however, be admitted that no historic form of Christianity has fully realized this social task. Russian Orthodoxy has failed, perhaps more than other Christian Churches, because it expected the Russian Orthodox Government to realize the Christian social ideal. Nevertheless, the failure was not one of Christianity, but of Christians. It is a human, not a divine, failure.

Moreover, Berdyaev never wearies of repeating that this task of transforming the world must never be conceived of in terms of legalism, or as regimentation imposed by some outward religious forms upon human life. He regards the period of such enforced Christianization by governmental means as a semipagan stage. "Christianity was greatly corrupted by being the ruling religion of the State; and the Church was seduced to the use of Caesar's sword which it employed to conquer those whose religion differed from the ruling faith."[10] One of the Church's great historic sins was the acknowledgment of a man — pope, emperor, czar — as the head of the Church. The only head of the Church is Christ. In all this Berdyaev's view is reminiscent of the fundamental theses of the Czech religious thinker of the fifteenth century, Peter Chelčický,[11] and after him, the Anabaptists and other representatives of the "Left Wing of the Reformation." No compulsion can bring anyone into the Kingdom of God; it cannot be attained without a free acceptance of God's grace, without a spiritual rebirth. Christianity is the religion of the cross. "Realization of the Kingdom of God on earth, of earthly happiness and earthly justice, without the cross and suffering, is a great lie for the Christian consciousness, is one of the temptations rejected by Christ in the wilderness when the kingdom of the world was shown him and he was asked to bow before the devil."[12] God compels no one to believe in him, to accept the proffered grace, and to enter into communion with him. But to reject God is only to choose one's own perdition.

This is, perhaps, as fitting a place as any in which to consider

Berdyaev's attitude toward his own communion — the Russian Orthodox Church. In this regard he worthily continues the tradition of his illustrious predecessors in the native religious movement — Khomyakov and Solovev. He regards the hierarchy not as authoritative in matters of faith or conscience, but in the realms of administration and ritual. For him, Orthodoxy knows no "infallibility" of the episcopacy, singly or collectively. He refers to the pronouncement of the Orthodox patriarchs, issued in 1848, which declares:

"Infallibility is to be found exclusively in the ecumenicity of the Church, united in mutual love; and the unchangeableness of the dogmas and purity of the rites is entrusted not to the hierarchy alone, but to all the members of the Church, which is the body of Christ."[13]

Accordingly, the truth of Christianity is not in the keeping of the hierarchy, or the clergy alone, but of all members of the Church, lay and clerical alike.

"The hierarchical organization of the Church, historically, inevitably, as the result of the canons, is a phenomenon of a secondary, and not primary importance. The spiritual life alone and what is seen in it, are primary. By it alone the Church retains its sanctity. The assertion of the primacy of the outward hierarchical authority is a self-deception and an illusion."[14]

Furthermore, it is often assumed that the ultimate authority of Eastern Orthodoxy is to be found in the doctrinal decisions of the seven ecumenical councils, as if the truth therein formulated received its validity from these councils. But this is putting the cart before the horse. The dogmas proclaimed by these councils are not true because they were asserted by ecumenical councils, but the councils are authoritative and ecumenical because they proclaimed true dogmas. The councils possessed no authoritative, ecumenical character until they were so acknowledged by the religious consciousness of the whole Church.

"Even the ecumenical council, the highest organ of Orthodoxy, does not possess formal authority. The ecumenical council does not possess formal, juridical characteristics, sensibly perceptible; it has no legal nature. One should not make an idol of a council, nor should one absolutize it. A council may turn out to be a robber council, even though it possess all appearances of legality. A truly ecumenical council is one in which the Holy Spirit really rules. And the true, spiritual character of an ecumenical council manifests itself and is confirmed in the free conscience of the members of the Church. The Holy Spirit works in the members of the Church, in the ecumenicity of the Church, and establishes the difference between truth and lie, between the authentic and the substitute." [15]

In view of this exceedingly strong emphasis of Berdyaev upon the "social application of Christianity," we must give some attention to his ethical teaching. To this subject he devotes particularly his book *The Destiny of Man,* which bears the subtitle "An Essay in Paradoxical Ethics," although other references to ethics are scattered throughout all his works.

In the first place, then, in his conception of Christian ethics Berdyaev opposes all legalisms. He particularly castigates Kant and Tolstoy for their failure to understand the spirituality of Christianity. "Kant and Tolstoy were strangers to the true secrets of Christian religion, but they were brilliant representatives of Christian morality as the morality of law, the morality of obedience, but not of creativity." [16] Kant sacrifices man to an abstract "categorical imperative," a sense of duty which is conceived as a system of external, ethical imperatives, a universal law, a principle of action binding uniformly and without any exception upon all. His system is mere legalistic pedantry. Tolstoy, the severe critic of every form of historic Christianity, mercilessly denouncing every falsity and lie in man and society, also conceives his "gospel" in terms of abstract moralism and legalism. His "five laws of Jesus"—be not angry; do not commit adultery; take no oaths; resist not evil; and do not make war—are still laws.[17] He reduces the Sermon on the Mount to a number of precepts, and vulgarizes it by naïvely assuming that it is not only "practical," but easily observable. This is a return to Pharisaic Judaism: salvation by observance of legalistic rules. Thus, for instance, Tolstoy seems to put smoking and murder in the same category.

"For L. Tolstoy, Jesus Christ was not the Redeemer and Saviour, but a great teacher of life, the herald of rules of life, of moral commandments. It seemed to L. Tolstoy that to realize Christianity in life is easy, that it is easier to live in accordance with the law of love than according to the law of hate as the world lives; that all this is easy, advantageous, and intelligent. . . . He demanded of men the maximum in the realization of divine commands . . . [but] he was not capable of realizing moral maximalism in his own life. Love was converted by him into a grace-lacking law and a source of condemnation. L. Tolstoy expressed many critical truths and many true judgments about the sins of the Christian world and of Christians. He justly denounced the unchristian character of society and culture. But he failed to discern Christianity itself behind the Christians. . . . Pride of reason prevented him from becoming spiritually a Christian; he did not accept Christ inwardly; Christ remained for him an external teacher of life." [18]

Berdyaev declares, on another occasion:

"I have never been a Tolstoyan and nonresister, and not only do not doubt the principle of legitimacy of the use of force and the sword . . . but have also written much in defense of that thesis." [19]

But the Christian gospel is not "practicable" in the usual utilitarian or eudaemonistic sense of that word. The absolute truths of the Sermon on the Mount, the gospel conception of spirituality, cannot be applied directly to the life of the unregenerate human society. "It is very clear that the gospel cannot be used as the basis for government, the economic life, the family and civilization; and that it is impossible to justify by the gospel the use of force on which history depends. . . . The gospel commands are utterly unrealizable and impossible as rules." [20] This is an exceedingly unpopular and hard saying; one expects that this conviction of Berdyaev is likely to be unqualifiedly and indignantly rejected by many. For there are many Christians, both lay and clerical, and of every conceivable denominational variety, who argue that the world indeed "lies in wickedness and evil," but all would be well if only "the Christian pattern of life" were substituted! They assume that governments, economics, science, may become Christianized. They criticize the

Church for having "failed" to make all relations of life Christian. But Berdyaev understands with illuminating clarity that the Christian life is far more complicated, far more difficult, than these advocates of "simple truths of Christianity" imagine. For a Christian must live on two planes — under law and under grace — for as long as we live we are citizens of both the secular and the spiritual orders. A Christian is always under a tension — and there is no escaping it completely.

Berdyaev subjects the life of the Christian to three types of ethics: of law, of redemption, and of creativity. The ethics of law [21] comprises the pre-Christian, pagan morality. It is exemplified not only in the Old Testament and the Pharisaic Judaism, but also in Aristotelianism and Stoicism. But this legalistic spirit, congenial to the Roman mind, has entered into historic Christianity as well. Saint Thomas Aquinas contributed not a little to the making of legalism a permanent part of the Roman Catholic system. It was against this feature of the medieval theology that both the mystics and Luther rebelled. But scholastic Lutheranism once more introduced legalism into religion. Kant, as has already been mentioned, was the philosophical formulator of the legalistic moralism implicit in the Lutheran denial of the freedom of will.

The ethic of law is necessary for the "fallen" man, for in his sinful state he does not acknowledge any other ethic. Human society, composed of unredeemed, "natural" men, must necessarily be held together by external compulsion or legalistic restraints, for otherwise it would fall apart. Since it is an aggregate of individual atoms, bound together by no inner sense of free cohesion, which only love can supply, it must be held together by force. That is what the apostle Paul meant by the famous injunction: "Let every person be subject to the governing authorities. For there is no authority except from God, and those that exist have been instituted by God. Therefore he who resists the authorities resists what God has appointed, and those who resist will incur judgment. For rulers are not a terror to good conduct, but to bad." [22] Accordingly, Christianity does not reject government as such, as some perfectionists have done; force, law, government are necessary, and the latter wields force and imposes it upon society.

The Christian, as a member of society, is subject to law equally with the non-Christian. Just because he is also subject to grace does not excuse him from obedience to the constituted authorities. Love does not exclude justice. The State is necessary, although it belongs to the "fallen" world. There can be no Christian, or ideal, State. For a State must be based on force; it has the duty of preserving order in a world which otherwise would destroy itself and the human society. No culture or civilization is possible without the function of the State.

Furthermore, the ethics of law must be looked upon as necessary for human society as long as it remains in its "fallen" condition. It is admittedly lower than the ethics of redemption. From this point of view, it can never be equated with the Christian ideals or standards. The kingdom of Caesar can never be identified with the Kingdom of Christ. Or, in other words, there is an abiding difference between the State and the Church: the State can never do the work of the Church, nor the Church of the State. It is a grievous blunder to confuse the functions of the two. The State, the highest principle of which is justice, can never be based on the Sermon on the Mount, for it would then cease to be a State. And the Church, on the other hand, the highest principle of which is love, should never resort to the forcible methods of the State. Its kingdom is not of this world. Therefore, it cannot do the work of the State. There is, and must remain, a difference of the nature and functions of these two entities: but both are necessary to human society at a certain stage of its development.

The Christian, therefore, "lives both by law and by grace." He cannot "resign from the world" in the sense of refusing his duties and obligations to society, as Thoreau is said to have "resigned from the United States." Moreover, the idea that humankind has moved to a higher moral level has been shown by two world wars to be wholly groundless. We live with "our own ancestors." Both the legal and the redemptive levels are present; we have not outgrown them. In fact, there has been an alarming moral retrogression! Accordingly, "man's life, his freedom and rights, cannot be made to depend exclusively upon the spiritual condition of other men, of society, and of government. His life, freedom, and rights must be safeguarded also in case the spiritual condition of other men, of society, and of government proves to be a low one, or is not sufficiently enlightened by grace. . . . It is impossible to wait for a regeneration of society by grace before human life is made tolerable."[23]

But obviously there may occur instances of conflict between law and conscience. In such cases the Christian must obey God rather than men. This has been the relation of law and grace ever since the beginning of Christianity. The great teachers of the Church — Roman Catholic, Protestant, and Eastern Orthodox — have held the same view. A Christian must obey law if it be not contrary to his grace-enlightened conscience. In case it is so opposed, the Government must be withstood no matter what the consequences. It is in this respect that the permanent tension of the Christian life is experienced: if the Christian pitches his standard too low, conforms to the world standards too much, accommodates himself from opportunistic motives to bourgeois morality, he all but surrenders his own proper ethical standard — the ethics of redemption; and if he "renounces the world" as the monastic orders did, or certain radical Protestant groups have tried to do, he ceases to be "the salt of the earth" and fails in his Christian duty of being in the world, but not of the world.

Nevertheless, the Christian's proper ethical standard is the gospel ethics of redemption. For him the love of God and man is the supreme motive of life and action. The redeemed man, no longer a slave to sin, is living in the liberty of the sons of God; for "where there is love, there is liberty." Saint Augustine put it in the memorable phrase, "Love God and do as you please!" Without love, there is no goodness of any sort. "Knowledge completely alienated from love turns itself into the will to rule, and becomes demonic. Without love everything turns into the demonic, even faith; likewise without freedom everything turns into the demonic."[24] Because love is basic to Christian ethics, it must hold supreme place in the personal life of the individual, in the Christian family, and in the ecumenical Church; but it can never become the basis of action on the part of government or secularized society, because love excludes force, without which the latter cannot exist.

Therefore, the truly Christian standard of life is ever at variance with the standards prevailing in "the world." The blessedness of the Christian involves humility; he is to be "poor in spirit"; but the worldling despises the humble, and is pretentious, proud, and wants to be regarded as "smart." Certainly, those who mourn are not counted by the world among the blessed. And as for the meek inheriting the earth, such notion is denounced as slavish morality by the Nietzsches, Marxes, and Hitlers of our days, as it has ever been by the "practical-minded" of all ages. And so it is with all the rest of the Beatitudes:

"Do not resist evil by force. But the world sees good in resisting evil by force. The sun rises equally over the good and the evil. The world sees good in the sun rising only over the good. Love your enemies, and bless those who persecute you. The world sees good only in loving one's friends, and not one's enemies. Accordingly, only Christianity breaks the magic circle of vengeance. The tax collectors and the wayward precede others into the Kingdom of God. The world thinks that the good, the just, the pure, who had fulfilled the law and the norm enter first. One must enter the narrow gate. The world enters the wide gate. That defiles which comes out of the mouth, i.e., the defiled condition of the human heart. The world thinks that what enters the mouth defiles — that the attitude of people and surroundings gives offense. The gospel calls us to the carefree life of the birds of heaven and the lilies of the field, and recommends that we take no thought for tomorrow. The world bases its life upon care and ceaseless thought for tomorrow. One should leave father, mother, and wife, and even hate them, if they hinder him from seeking the Kingdom of God. The world demands, first of all, love of the nearest, of father, mother, and wife. It is hard for the rich to enter the Kingdom of Heaven. The world esteems the rich, renders them honor, and accounts them the first. The blessed are by no means those whom the world accounts blessed — those who weep, the meek, the merciful, the pure in heart, those who hunger and thirst after righteousness, and so forth. The world accounts as blessed the rich, the distinguished, the strong, those who rule, the famous, the laughing ones, and so forth. Those who take up the sword shall perish by the sword. The world defends its existence by the sword." [25]

It follows then, that the ethic of redemption is wholly incompatible with the worldly standard of values. Moreover, it cannot become the basis of the "practical" life of the world, for it is the absolute revelation of the life of the Kingdom. "Be ye perfect, as your Father in heaven is perfect." But no human being can be perfect, not even as a human being, to say nothing of being perfect as God! To strive after perfection is to be doomed to failure; not to strive after perfection is to be doomed to mediocrity, that is, to become a complacent, self-satisfied worldling. Therein consists the inescapable, essential tension of the Christian life! And woe unto the Christian who does not feel it! For then he is almost certain to have accommodated himself to the easy virtues of the world. The function of pain is to give warning of a disease; it would be fatal not to feel pain when disease gnaws at the vitals. A Christian has no business feeling smug, or having a "good conscience," for, as John Stuart Mill has said (more forcibly than elegantly), it is better to be a dissatisfied Socrates than a satisfied swine.

The task of adjusting one's life to the two ethical levels, that of the ethics of law and the ethics of redemption, or to the prevailing secular standard of values and the gospel standard, is exceedingly difficult. Our Lord did not say it was easy, did not solve the problem for us. For any such solution would almost necessarily become a rigid regimentation of life, a new legalism. Much of it has developed in Christianity anyway. There are many who regard the Sermon on the Mount as if it were a rule of life instead of the absolute ideal, unattainable by mortal man in the present aeon. The redeemed man is left free to make the adjustment in the light of the developing standard of his own conscience. The Spirit makes that conscience ever more sensitive. For that reason, no external standard can be set up which would or should be normative for all, or even for the same person at all times. Every spiritually free being must decide for himself. Without such spiritual struggle there could be no growth.

Nevertheless, there is something characteristically Russian, almost anarchistic, in the steady emphasis upon the ultimate spiritual issues of life and the impatience with the "interim ethics" which necessarily have to be considered before the conditions of the Kingdom supervene. For the Russians are "apocalyptic people." They strive for the absolute norms — either the supreme good or the supreme evil. Berdyaev, along with Dostoevsky, shares this characteristic to a pre-eminent degree. He judges life from the point of view of absolute ethics; such judgments must necessarily produce an acute tension between what should be and what is.

In the third place, Berdyaev develops the theme of ethics by adding a third category — the ethics of creativity. For each human being is an idea of God and has for his supreme task the full realization of that idea. In this task of attainment of personality, man exercises his creative powers. Thus, each has a unique task to perform. "Creativeness, a creative attitude toward all life, is not a man's right, but his debt and duty. The creative attitude is a moral imperative in all spheres of life. . . . The way of creativity is also the way of moral and religious perfection, the way of realizing the fullness of life."[26] The transformation of the world is not solely God's task, but man's as well; it is a theandric enterprise. God works partly through men. Creation is not complete; it is still going on. We are living in "the eighth day of creation." The ethics of creativity differs from that of redemption inasmuch as it deals with the creation of values, which is the special, divinely given task of each particular, redeemed man. These values differ in accordance with the gift granted him by God. Man's part in the process is that he dedicate his gifts — whether they be in science, art, labor, government, economy, or in some humble skill — to the ends of the Kingdom, rather than to either his own or purely secular purposes. This is done by means of holy imagination. For a creator embodies his imagination in stone, poem, picture, government, economic order, or social custom. The way of redemption depends upon a purified, God-centered will working through a powerful, holy imagination toward the creation of true social good. Men of good will, but likewise of creative imagination, must "grasp this sorry Scheme of Things entire, . . . and then Re-mould it nearer to the Heart's Desire." For Christianity is not passive, static, quietistic; it is dynamic, creative, revolutionary. If, instead of devoting the best creative imagination to destructive ends, science were to utilize its tremendous potential for human good; if political imagination were devoted to peace instead of to war and expansion; if economic skills were utilized for the good of all rather than for the benefit and profit of the few, then many of the world's ills would be eliminated, or at least lessened.

On the other hand, not every kind of creativity is good; it may also be evil. "One may create not only in God's name but in the devil's name as well. But on that account, one should not surrender creativity to the devil, to the Antichrist." [27] Moreover, if Christianity should fail in the task of creativity, the Antichrist would surely assume control. In fact, he has already assumed control to an alarmingly large extent, and with great success. At present, he utilizes the creative arts and literature largely for his own purposes. Beauty is notoriously abused by the Antichrist as a seductive, alluring bait. It is the failure of Christians to use these means in the interests of the Kingdom of God that has resulted in the Antichrist's pre-empting of the field for his own purposes. A new effort should be made by the Christian forces to capture the field for God, for Christ. Berdyaev even daringly suggests that "the Christian creativity in the world shall be the work of monasticism," meaning thereby a new monasticism, an asceticism that surrenders itself, denies itself, for the sake of creating new aesthetic values of a distinctly Christian character.[28]

But it would be a misunderstanding to regard Berdyaev's concept of creativity as if it were something basically nonessential for ordinary living, something to be expected only of specially gifted people, or as an exclusively utilitarian matter of "being good for something." Berdyaev complains of being misrepresented in this regard.

> "My concept is altogether different, much deeper. I have never raised the question regarding the justification of creativity; I have raised the question regarding *justification by means of creativity.* Creativity needs no justification; on the contrary, it justifies man, it is anthropodicy. It has to do with man's relation to God, with man's response to God. The problem of its relation to human culture, to cultural values and products, is secondary and derivative." [29]

Man in his sins is justified by God's grace, and henceforth lives by that grace. This is the usual summary of the process of redemption. Berdyaev accepts it, but thinks that it does not go far enough. Does God expect nothing from the justified sinner? Is there nothing the justified sinner can contribute toward the process of his justification? Berdyaev insists that there is — in fact, that God expects the redeemed man to make such a contribution: it is the transformed man's duty to devote his now purified, consecrated gifts to the service of God. In this way he "works out" his salvation, he participates in the process that Berdyaev calls justification but that would more correctly be designated sanctification.

But since both the creative talents with which man is endowed and redemptive grace are the gifts of God, what can man contribute that is really his own? To make a correct response, one must remember Berdyaev's concept of freedom: for freedom is *uncreated,* it does not derive from God, but from the primal "meonic nothing." Accordingly, man actually has something that is his own which he can offer in the service of God: he does not merely return what is God's own gift, but makes his own voluntary offering to God. In that sense Berdyaev can speak of creativity as a means of justifying man, an anthropodicy.[30] Man's creativity is thus a "continuation of the creation of the world."

In another place Berdyaev further sharpens his concept of creativity by insisting that it deals only in a subordinate manner with cultural productivity.

"The creative experience reveals that 'I,' the subject, am more primary and higher than the 'not-I,' the object. And along with it, creativity is opposed to egocentrism, is the forgetting of oneself, and is the directing of oneself to that which is higher than I. . . . Creativity is least of all the pleasing of oneself; it is always a transcendence of oneself." [31]

Thus creativity has a liberating function and effect, not only releasing man from his own ordinary and customary immersion in the objective world, but also transforming him and the world.

Moreover, man's creativity is not only the fulfillment of the Creator's intention for man, and a response to God's grace; it also yields the highest satisfaction just because it fulfills man's destiny. Happiness can never become the goal of a noble life, for it is a result, not the goal, of moral or creative life. Accordingly, the ethic of creativity is not a utilitarian, eudaemonistic ethic. For only spiritual values may become the ends of life. "Therefore, the positive secret of life is hidden in love, in sacrificial giving, in creative love. All creativity, as we have already said, is love, and all love is creativity. If you wish to receive, give; if you wish to feel satisfaction, do not seek it, never think of it, yea, forget the very word. If you wish to increase power, manifest it and impart it to others." [32]

Although Berdyaev wrote a great deal about the concrete problems of politics, economics, and culture, it would be a mistake to regard him as a politician or an economist: he regards himself as "a moralist defending his idea of man in an epoch that is inimical to man." [33] Accordingly, his writings in the above-mentioned categories must be understood from an essentially eschatological point of view, namely, as human relations should ultimately be, rather than as they are. His proposals are therefore consciously provisional: he does not expect the realization of some perfect society within the near future (or within time, for that matter), whether it be in the form of a "classless society" or of the Kingdom of God. Applying the above-discussed ethical categories to a few concrete concepts, we may choose in the first place the all-important and oft-discussed problems of government, political life, war, and the Christian's relation to the State.

As has already been said, no government, by its nature, can be Christian. Christianity rejects all absolute pretensions of the State. The latter has no means of overcoming evil, and may itself easily become evil. As Vladimir Solovev wrote: "Government exists not for the purpose of converting the terrestrial life into a paradise, but of preventing it from converting that life into Hades. Sinful humanity cannot live without government, without the ontological principles of rule. It must be subjected to law; it must fulfill law." [34] This applies to all forms of government: monarchical, democratic, totalitarian. But it does not follow that there is no relative difference among the various types. A monarchy may be dominated, as far as that is consonant with its character, by a Christian or anti-Christian spirit, just as much as a democracy may. It depends on the spiritual, not the formal, character of the political body in question.

Accordingly, although all expectations that the good life can be brought about exclusively by the State are utopian and radically false, the State has a great relative value and a necessary and beneficial mission to perform: to create and preserve order in society; to preserve legal justice by restraining one individual or group in society from depriving others of their basic human rights; to protect itself and its citizens from outside attack and from inner armed strife; to promote common economic prosperity; to provide educational facilities; to create stable conditions for social life. This must be regarded as the "divine ordering" for a sinful society. But every State has a tendency to accumulate power for its own sake. It is subject to an almost overwhelming temptation to pervert the normal and socially beneficial use of power. As Lord Acton has warned: "All power corrupts, and absolute power corrupts absolutely." It is this tendency that inevitably leads to war. A powerful State always discovers in its "manifest destiny" an excuse for imperialistic policies of extending its might over weaker nations.

As has already been explained, Berdyaev shares the German-Russian philosophical repudiation of the Lockean democratic presuppositions of the Anglo-American cultures. The Lockean doctrine of the primacy of the rights of private property over other human values is unacceptable to him, not only because he was brought up in another philosophical tradition, but also because the Russian people have almost traditionally regarded private property as morally unjustifiable where its use conflicts with other human values. Marxism taught him that mere political democracy without economic democracy is a mockery and an illusion. Hence, his strictures upon Western democracy are severe; but he is condemning the failures of democracy, rather than its objectives and ideals. I believe that Berdyaev, too, is a democrat in the sense in which Lincoln defined democracy—as a society in which there are neither slaves nor masters. Nevertheless, it is in this respect that Anglo-American intellectuals are likely to experience the greatest difficulties in understanding, not to say sharing, Berdyaev's views: for his presuppositions are likely to appear to them unfamiliar and therefore unconvincing. One must resolutely hold to the guiding principle that Berdyaev judges all things from the point of view of the supreme value of human personality. Every political system, whether it be of Lockean or Hegelian or any other philosophical derivation, that places some other value—property, race, class—above human rights and values, is repudiated by him. Judging from this vantage point, he regards all modern forms of government, including the Western democratic one, as tending to subordinate the highest values to lesser ones. Such a judgment may indeed strike one as "abstract," "perfectionist"; nevertheless, in order to understand Berdyaev properly, it is essential to keep it in mind.

In the first place, therefore, Berdyaev criticizes the fundamental principle of Lockean democracy which asserts the rule "of the people, by the people, for the people." This implies, of course, that the majority of votes decides the policy. But the majority need not be right. The assumption that "fifty million Frenchmen cannot be wrong" may be an empty demagogic slogan.

The "*vox populi*" is rarely, if ever, the "*vox Dei.*" For the "natural" man is selfish; consequently his will cannot but be selfish too. No "Kingdom of God" (even if the modern secularist democracies aspired after it — which they do not!) can ever be attained by the method of accepting the declared will of selfish human beings as the highest norm of political life. Only by subjecting the political life to a higher spiritual criterion, God's will, can the basically selfish character of the democratic political structure be changed. But with the increasing secularization of the modern world, the masses have long ago lost faith in any divine standard. "Democracy is skeptical; it originated in a skeptical age, the age of unbelief, when people were losing the firm criterion of truth and were powerless to profess any kind of absolute truth. Democracy is extreme relativism, rejection of everything absolute . . . an acknowledgment of the quantitative principle of rule, bowing before the general election, which is possible only with unbelief in, or ignorance of, truth." [35] But this is by no means a crypto-Fascist or crypto-Communist argument against the rule of the majority. Communism, which at the present stage is the rule of a minority, the dictatorship of the proletariat, has nevertheless for its aim the same bourgeois ideals of material well-being as does capitalism.

However, in reality democracies are not so much governed by the will of the whole people as by a minority who control the votes, whether they be professional politicians or financial, labor, or other groups. Historically, democracies have favored the rise of the *bourgeoisie* to political power. "Democracies are bound up with middle-class domination and with the industrial-capitalistic system, and defend the interests of these classes by the organization of groups of professional politicians. The masses of the people are ordinarily indifferent to politics, and never have the strength to realize their will to rule." [36] Since the emergence of the political power of the professional proletarian and labor politicians in the Soviet Union and elsewhere, Berdyaev's statement lacks in comprehensiveness and accuracy.

Moreover, since democracies are basically individualistic, rather than collectivist, and since the individuals strive to assert their will rather than the will of God, democracies necessarily tend toward an atomistic disintegration. The lack of cohesion is implied in the Lockean philosophy, which defined man in terms of an autonomous individual. Consequently, political life represents the strife of individuals or parties for power and dominance, rather than for the highest common good. Communism has overcome this atomism, but in the wrong way: by the forcible and exceedingly cruel imposition of unification through the euphemistically called "dictatorship of the proletariat." Only a free community, bound by love, can rightly overcome atomistic individualism.

Furthermore, Berdyaev charges that much of political life deals with mere externals, superficialities, rather than with vital issues:

> "A great deal of political and social life of present-day humanity is not real, ontological, but fictional, illusory life. The struggle of the parties, parliaments, meetings, newspapers, programs and platforms, propaganda and demonstrations, the struggle for power — all that is not genuine life, has no relation to the content and goal of life; it is difficult to discern the ontological kernel in it all." [37]

Finally, democracy presupposes an extreme optimism in regard to human nature:

> "The optimistic presupposition of the natural goodness and kindness of human nature lies at the basis of democracy. The spiritual father of democracy was J. J. Rousseau, and his optimistic ideas concerning human nature have been passed on to the democratic ideology. Democracy does not want to acknowledge the radical evil of human nature. It does not seem to foresee that the will of the people may be directed toward evil, that the majority may stand for lie and injustice, and that truth and justice may be upheld by a small minority. There are no guarantees in democracy that the will of the people shall be directed toward good, that they shall desire freedom instead of destroying all freedom altogether." [38]

Such being the case, Berdyaev has but little hope that any radical improvement is possible. He certainly does not believe that by shuffling the political or economic organizations of modern society a millennium will be brought about. All such external expedients are not radical enough. The only really fundamental change, the spiritual transformation of the people, is not likely to be regarded by any government as "practical politics." It is not. But without it there can be no better government, no better world. Democracy is the self-assertion of the Renaissance man in the political sphere. But all self-assertion has led to self-destruction. Only a free theonomy, a voluntary subjection of the will of the people to the will of God, can overcome the dangers inherent in individualistic autonomy, which involves disintegration; the alternative is collectivism, which is tyranny. Only the Kingdom of God can be the true goal of political, as well as any other, life. But this is not, of course, a plea for the restoration of the pseudo theocracies of the past, whether Catholic, Eastern Orthodox, or Protestant. Berdyaev denounces them in explicit terms so often that he should not be suspected of some surreptitious propaganda of the current Roman Catholic type. "The old theocratic government cannot be restored; there is no return to it; for God's truth did not actually exist in it." [39] Nevertheless, he has been bitterly denounced as a reactionary. One of his Russian critics, the American-educated Methodist minister who became a Communist, Julius Hecker, charged him with advocating feudalism, a return to aristocracy, rank individualism, and other such absurdities.[40] It is certainly to be expected that many as capable and as honest thinkers as Berdyaev himself will resolutely repudiate Berdyaev's views on democracy; but, assuming good will, it is not possible to misunderstand Berdyaev's motive in his strictures upon democracy; he believes that the present forms of democracy preserve but inadequately the highest value in the world, the human personality. That is the real issue.

Finally, Berdyaev makes a very tentative and somewhat timid and disappointing suggestion as to the form of government he visualizes for the future. It still retains the essence of democracy, although in form it is radically changed. According to him it will be supremely and truly for the people, but not of the people. This latter phrase, however, is misleading — as we shall see. His conception takes the syndicalist form of a corporate state made up of representatives of professional, economic, and cultural associations — composed of both employers and workers — and defending the broad interests of their respective groups. This is essentially the form of co-operative society in which the class struggle is eliminated, since both the employers and the workers realize that their interests are basically identical, and one group is necessary to the other. Thus the policies will not be determined on the basis of political parties that are concerned chiefly with the seizure of power and with the perpetuation of themselves in office; or on the basis of compromises among the political parties which represent results of bargaining and not solutions of problems; but upon the real, vital interests of the actual, concrete corporate groups that make up society. The function of the Government, then, is to act as an umpire between the various professional associations, so that none would concentrate in its keeping tyrannous economic power, thus depriving other groups of their rights.

Unfortunately, the reorganization of society on the guild pattern suggested by Berdyaev is open to a good many of the criticisms that he levels against liberal democracies. A pattern similar to his (and to that officially propounded by the papacy since the days of Leo XIII) was tried in Italy under Mussolini, so that the objections are by no means purely theoretical. Of course, I do not mean to imply that Berdyaev was in the least tainted by Fascism; such a charge would be absurd. But the guild pattern has been utilized by Fascists for their purposes. The Italian production councils, representative of both owners and workers, and responsible to the Government, did not insure a fair treatment of the workers. In fact, the "corporate state," turned Fascist (i.e., by combining the interests of the employers and the Government against the workers), deprived labor of all effective power. For, after all, given the same "fallen" human nature that operates in liberal democracies, the success of the guild depends upon the right balance between the employers and the workers constituting the guild; upon the unbiased character of the Government, which is supposed to act in the interests of the common good; and upon the proper adjustment of the interests of the guilds and/or the Government toward the consumers. For the basic economic problem remains the same: it still consists of the bushel of wheat which the farmer wishes to sell as high as he can and which the consumer desires to buy as cheaply as he can. If the same selfish motives that operate in the democratic capitalistic society continue unchanged, will a mere reorganization of the social machinery cure the social ills? No one knows better than Berdyaev that such hope is a snare and a delusion. The unredeemed future corporate society will be subject to the same degenerative forces that operate at present.

Passing on to the subject of war, Berdyaev observes that it is because of the inherent character of every State that wars result. War is always a great evil, although not the greatest possible evil. But with the utter brutalization of modern wars, all moral distinctions tend to disappear completely. And yet, difficult though it may be, it is still possible to discern the broad distinction between wars of defense and liberation, and wars of conquest and aggression. From the Christian point of view, the moral problem in relation to war is among the most difficult, almost hopelessly involved in self-contradictions. Since wars have almost ceased to be governed by any moral considerations, and have become as foul as Vulcan's smithy, it is desperately difficult to continue to apply to them the traditional criteria of discrimination.

But, "if one should denounce war as a great evil and a great sin, one must beware not to fall into the opposite extreme of abandoning oneself to an abstract pacifism at any price." [41] There are greater evils than war: for instance, acceptance of slavery. "To condemn war from the point of view of absolute morality is easy enough, but this does not solve the painful problem. . . . From the absolute, normative point of view, war is evil; but from the relative point of view it may be the least evil, or even good, because absolute moral principles operate in dark and sinful spheres of life. . . . Pure and absolute good can appear only in the world which shall be beyond good and evil." [42]

What attitude, then, is a Christian to take toward war? The only positive truth that pacifism embodies is the will that wars should cease. All Christians, in fact, all men of good will, share that will. " But pacifism does not want to recognize the spiritual conditions for the cessation of wars; it rests in superficialities, in the sphere of unrealistic politics and legal formulas, unconscious of the irrational forces of history. Pacifism is rationalism. But the spiritual preaching of peace and the brotherhood of nations is a Christian task, and Christian ethics must dispute it with rationalistic pacifism." [43] The task is to do everything to prevent wars; " but once a war begins and it can no longer be stopped, a person cannot throw off its yoke, to walk away from the common responsibility, from the vicious circle; he must take upon himself the guilt of war in the name of higher goals, but must experience it tragically as a horror and a destiny. . . . War is a punishment. It must be accepted in an enlightened spirit, as all other trials of life." [44] Those who believe in God must live and act differently from those who do not. To think that wars can be eliminated by anything short of the transformation of humanity, in the terminology of Berdyaev, by God-manhood, is unrealistic.

Similarly, the whole attitude toward political life must be informed by the realization of its true nature. But the abandonment of political action to the forces of secularism and reaction is not the way of the cross, is not a truly redemptive action. Nevertheless, the Christian must not seek power for its own sake. To hold political office is a duty, an exceedingly difficult task, not a right or a privilege. If the motive of the politician is the lust of power, then it is as sinful as any other lust. A Christian has a positive duty to engage in political life, but with a redemptive purpose, and in a sacrificial spirit.

A related problem is that of nationalism and internationalism. Nationalism has become the latest of the idols: it substitutes for personality a biological, zoological concept of consanguinity. The nation becomes an absolute value which can do no wrong. All Fascist ideologies have substituted the nation for God and the State for the nation. The State has changed itself into a

State Church, claiming the right of ruling man body, soul, and spirit. Religion itself becomes a tool of the national totalitarian rule — a mystical adoration of blood and soil. Quite logically, therefore, Berdyaev denounced Nazism as early as 1931, when this movement was not generally recognized for what it was even by the German religious leaders: "Fascists and Hitlerites are enemies of Christianity, and pagans!" he then boldly wrote.[45]

Such are, undoubtedly, the dangers of nationalism. Nor is the terse description given above a product of exuberant imagination: no one with a memory of the Nazi and Italian Fascist ideologies can for a moment dispute it, unless on the ground that it understates the case. But is internationalism a cure for nationalism? Berdyaev decidedly denies that it is. For nationalism is at least concretely real: it deals with natural loyalties, the love of a human being for his native land, for his mother tongue, for his own people. It is only the demonic abuse of that which is good and real that makes nationalism such a source of danger. Denial of nationalism does not possess this concrete reality: a man is an American, an Englishman, a German, or a Russian. But he is not born an internationalist, for that is a mere abstraction. Genuine, natural loyalties cannot be aroused for or by an abstraction any more than one can worship the law of gravitation. The so-called Platonic love is not love. Masses of mankind will rise to defend their homes, their land, their families, but not "internationalism." An internationalist is a man without a country, a "displaced person."

Does that mean, then, that humankind is condemned to remain narrowly nationalistic? Not at all. But in order to transcend a concrete loyalty such as nationalism actually embodies, one must develop a higher loyalty at least as real as the one to be transcended. If man is not to worship exclusively the half-gods of nationalism, he must worship Him who is above all nations, the universal Father of all nations. War has plunged modern man into a problem that is insoluble except on the basis of religious faith. For in God alone can man establish spiritual communion with other human beings not of his race or nationality; acknowledgment and worship of one God and Father of mankind provides the only true means of transcending nationalism. The effective remedy for the evils of nationalism is not internationalism but ecumenicism—*sobornost*—which rests upon the concrete ground of religiously substantiated reality. And since ecumenicism, even though in an imperfect form, exists only in the Christian Church, the Church is again underscored as being essential to the solving of this world problem.

But it is interesting to note in this connection the exceedingly strong nationalism of Berdyaev himself. He was a Russian through and through. He did not regard his native land and his people realistically, but idealized them. He was as much of a *narodnik*—a populist—as Dostoevsky and Tolstoy were. He loved his country, but forgot that love is blind, or that it sees in the loved object what other people cannot see. Perhaps it was his long exile that contributed to Berdyaev's nostalgic longing for and idealization of Russia, which is obvious to others, although he did not seem to be aware of it. He persisted in believing in "Holy Russia," in the messianic mission of Russia to the end of his life: his *Russian Idea* is wholly devoted to this theme. Shortly before his death he wrote:

> "The historic destiny of the Russian people is to create a social order more just and more human than that of the West. It has to realize the brotherhood of men and of peoples, for that *is* the Russian Idea. The Russian people must create a new world which will be neither bourgeois nor capitalistic." [46]

This was indeed a faith that overcame the difficulties of the concrete situation then prevailing in Russia, the fact of the Soviet regime. Berdyaev simply ignored the fact, treated it as nonexistent, in order to affirm his indomitable faith in the messianic mission of his beloved Russia. May God grant that Berdyaev's magnificent faith be justified!

Let us now consider Berdyaev's social ethics, particularly in the economic and industrial spheres. In the former realm, the self-assertion of the Renaissance man takes the form of capitalism.

For Berdyaev, "free enterprise" is just that. Man's economic activity is conceived in terms of unrestrained, competitive struggle. State interference or regulation is particularly resented, for they are looked upon as a restraint of the strong from utilizing their natural advantage in relation to the weak. In the true spirit of the Lockean concept, that Government is best which governs least. The so-called freedoms in the economic sphere are illusory. But any civilization that regards life as consisting in the possession of things, of a "high standard of living," is essentially bourgeois, not Christian. To be sure, in this primitive form, laissez-faire capitalism no longer exists. Berdyaev's attack upon it is misleading, because he ignores the very considerable modifications and limitations that have been imposed upon modern capitalism — the limitations imposed by the Government, by organized labor, and by the changing structure of the capitalistic form of economy.

Nevertheless, for Christianity the chief criterion is how much a given civilization contributes toward the development of the highest spiritual values. "For the economic order is for man's benefit, not man for the benefit of the economic order." "The social problem is likewise a religious, Christian problem, particularly in relation to labor." For it is a problem of the spiritual basis of society. "Man is above all a spiritual, not a political, being; and his absolute and unalienable rights are rooted in the spiritual, not in the changeable, impermanent, transient, civic-political world." Therefore, it is the duty of the Christian Church to pass judgment upon any theory defining the relation of one man toward another, in the economic sphere as well as in any other: "For the Christian conscience the turning of a man into a thing, of his labor into a commodity, and the heartless egoism of competition, should not be allowable." [47] Likewise, it is only in Christianity that the class conflict can be transcended. "The true Church of Christ is not corrupted by worldly interests, knows no classes. When a man enters the Church and seeks salvation and spiritual nurture therein, he ceases to be wellborn or a plebeian, a bourgeois, or a proletarian." [48]

Furthermore, Berdyaev holds that the economic order of the future society belongs to the spiritual aristocracy. The aristocracy of the future has nothing to do with the feudal or money aristocracy of the past, which claims pre-eminence by reason of birth, special privileges, or inherited wealth. If such groups should survive at all, they should be deprived of their privileged status. The true aristocracy of the future is composed of those who are endowed by God with special gifts and talents, and use them in the service of society. Thus, the "charismatic" order of early Christianity is reasserted in a new form. For the "spiritual aristocracy" receives its talents from above. It consists of "prophets, religious teachers, religious and social reformers, philosophers, the learned, inventors, poets, artists, musicians—they belong to the spiritual aristocracy and cannot be thrust into any scheme of class division that is based upon the economic order." [49] They are not "bourgeois" either. For genius recognizes no class.

The manual worker too must be recognized not as a mere tender of machines, but as a creator of necessary values upon which the life and well-being of society depend. His labor must cease to be drudgery and must become creative. He is not merely earning a living, but is also developing his special talent and endowment, in which he can make a free contribution toward the enrichment of society. In other words, economic wage-earning must partake of the character of creativity. This presupposes a hierarchy of different gifts, organized professionally on the order of guilds, not, however, for the exploitation of society, but for its benefit. Berdyaev speaks of such workers as the "true aristocracy" of talent and accomplishment, which should displace the privileged classes of capitalism or Communism.[50]

Under such conditions class struggle would cease. In this matter, Berdyaev regards Marx as having been in the right. "If we Christians part from Marx in our evaluation, it is certainly not for the reason that we are ready to side with the bourgeois class and capitalism in the class struggle; certainly not that!" [51] The reason for "parting from Marx" is that his system has no more consideration for the human spirit as the highest value than has capitalism. "The proletarian who strives to become a bourgeois and to possess the land is spiritually identical with the bourgeois; he has merely put on a new dress." [52] "The Socialist-Communist ideal of man is the bourgeois ideal of the economic man, altogether depersonalized and soulless, assuming the image of a mechanical collective, and devoted exclusively to the economic and technical kind of life." [53]

This is his judgment as regards the essential nature of both capitalism and Communism: the former has long ago ceased to be individualistic and has become collectivist, the control of its mechanism passing over to the managerial class; while the latter, which has abandoned real Marxian Communism and has become State capitalism, has created privileged classes which exploit the workers as much as capitalism does. Moreover, both are filled with the same bourgeois desire for the "good life," consisting of an abundance of things, and both deny the supreme human values.

The type of economic organization that Berdyaev himself advocates is a personalist socialism of the syndicalist type. "The realistic power capable of restraining the rule of capitalism and of transforming the web of the bourgeois society appears to be, in the final analysis, not a parliamentary struggle of socialist parties, but syndicates of workers. Only socialism of the syndicalist type is real." "Russian Communism has nothing in common with syndicalism, and in the Soviet life there exists no class war because the workers are powerless before the Government. Communism is a form of State capitalism." [54] But after the close of the Second World War, perhaps under the influence of a temporary enthusiasm and pride in the heroic role that the Red Army and the Russian people played in the struggle, Berdyaev expressed rather extremely favorable views in regard to Communism, insisting that the Soviet Government is socialist rather than Communist.[55] Nevertheless, in his autobiography, which one may be justified in regarding as representing his final views, he wrote:

"I would be willing to accept Communism socially, as an economic and political organization, but I would not be willing to accept it spiritually. Spiritually, religiously, and philosophically, I am a convinced and determined anticollectivist. That does not mean that I am an antisocialist. I am a partisan of socialism, but my socialism is personalist, not authoritarian; it does not admit the primacy of society over personality. . . . I am an anticollectivist in so far as I do not admit the exteriorization of personal conscience, or its transfer to the collective." [56]

9

The End of Time and the Kingdom of God

Among the basic concerns of Berdyaev's thought was a preoccupation with the beginning and the end of time, and with the aeon of the Holy Spirit which will ultimately supervene. Accordingly, he regarded himself primarily as a metahistorian. "The philosophy I wish to expound is a dramatic philosophy of destiny, of existence in time which loses itself in eternity, and of time which precipitates itself toward an end which is not death but transformation. . . . The philosophy of history cannot but be prophetic, revealing the secrets of the future." [1]

Thus the concept of time is of great importance for human destiny. For Berdyaev, "time has an ontological significance, for in it is revealed meaning. So thinks Christianity, and therein is to be found the dynamism of history." [2] Berdyaev distinguishes different kinds of time: there is cosmic time which governs all nature and which is cyclical in character; there is historical time in which human life on earth transpires; and there is finally existential time — eternity — occasionally breaking through into the historical time. For the Christian, the historical time provides the needed opportunity for the transforming experience that eventuates in God-manhood. Since human personality is the highest value in the world, the significance of the world must be conceived in personal terms. One is reminded of Origen, for whom the world was the abode of fallen spirits, each undergoing a discipline, a remedial treatment. Since the spirit had, in its pre-existent state, chosen disease rather than health, self-assertion rather than communion with God, the great Physician in his undefeatable love could do no better than to provide an opportunity for cure. The world is, for Origen, not a place of punishment but an opportunity for regaining health.[3] Berdyaev agrees with this idea of the significance of the created world; moreover, he also agrees with Origen's concept that this is not the only chance that human spirits possess for the regaining of their original status. There will be other opportunities open to those souls who have not utilized their present chance, although these opportunities will not be offered to them on the terrestrial plane.

More than that: human history not only emerges from eternity but is itself broken into by events of an eternal order. These are the moments of existential reality. At such moments, time gives way to eternity. Berdyaev speaks of these occasions as metahistorical. The revelation of God in Jesus Christ was such an irruption of eternity, of existential time—which Paul Tillich calls *kairos*—into historical time. Jesus Christ cannot be accounted for as the sum total of the natural, hereditary forces, nor as the product of Judaism. We too have moments when the scales fall off our eyes and we perceive a glimpse of eternity. Such is the experience of mystical ecstasy that Plotinus enjoyed but a few times during his lifetime.

Consequently, the world has a noumenal meaning which has nothing to do with a concept of automatically, externally determined and inevitable "progress." The idea of progress is of Christian origin. The Greeks thought of history in terms of cycles, so that history had no goal. The nineteenth century secularized, naturalized, the Jewish-Christian idea of history by conceiving of it as having a goal, but connected the process with natural evolution. The latter, however, is a deterministic concept without any true teleology. Whatever truth the evolutionary theory possesses, it is not to be identified with the Christian eschatological concept of which Berdyaev speaks. Any naturalistic, positivist theory of progress can have no meaning because it has no goal; accordingly, all such theories necessarily must posit blind, natural forces as the moving elements—evolution, *élan vital,* economic determinism. They all lack true teleology—a goal, a purpose, the far-off event toward which all creation tends.

Without God, a goal of history is impossible, for a goal must be consciously conceived. No impersonal force, no natural law, can act purposefully; all mechanical forces are blind, determined, bound to the necessary relation of cause and effect. From the scientific point of view, the world process is meaningless. There is no teleology in a machine: for the function of the machine was built into it by some human being who was not a machine, but a conscious, purposive being.

History must have an end for the very reason that an endless progression, even if it were from worse to better — and it is not always that — would be meaningless unless it reached a goal. Endless progress is unthinkable, it must be directed toward a consummation. "The end is the triumph of meaning." In vain would one seek meaning in history if he limited himself to the past alone, for the meaning is given only in terms of the final consummation of history; consequently, the secularist philosophies of history are usually incoherent. For history cannot be understood except from the point of view of the end, that is, eschatologically. This type of philosophy of history was basic to Berdyaev: he devoted to its exposition his books *The Meaning of History* and *An Essay on Eschatological Metaphysics,* and referred to it repeatedly in many other books. For him, Christianity is the religion of the future, of the end, of the aeon of the Holy Spirit. Philosophically expressed, the end of the world is identical with the triumph of the existential type of life over all objectification: instead of self-alienation, hatred, injustice, war, men shall live in the existential relations of their true selves toward other true personalities in "the communion of saints."

Thus the meaningfulness of the world is possible only for those who believe in God. Progress presupposes freedom, free will. It is potentiality, not law, not necessity. But by postulating a God-given goal it is easy to think of the relation of all creation — human beings included — as necessarily, inexorably, determined thereby. Some classical theologians have so conceived of the process: Augustine, Luther, and Calvin did. For that matter, some classical philosophers — Hegel, Marx, and Nietzsche — by secularizing the messianic hope were likewise prophets of an externally determined "messianism." There is much truth in the views of these theologians, truth that is often intentionally or unintentionally perverted into absurd or unworthy dogmas ascribing to God unethical motivation. The supreme confidence of Calvinism that despite man's folly or malice God's will shall ultimately conquer expresses the great and comforting truth that only good is existentially real and evil is self-destructive. But this truth is sometimes so presented as to deny man's freedom in the process.

It is the perversion of the correct formulation of the concept that Berdyaev strenuously opposes. He is painfully aware of the antinomy involved in the relation between God's will and each individual human will. He protests against every theory that solves the problem by sacrificing the human to the divine—which is to him the essence of the Monophysite heresy. The only true solution is in Dyophysitism, in the doctrine of two natures, divine and human, and in the free union of the two natures. That is why he stresses so persistently the concept of God-manhood. But if at the heart of the relation between God and man is freedom, there is likewise a possibility that the fallen man will not choose to return to God. He can, and often does, reject God's gracious offer of salvation and persists in spurning the proffered reconciliation. Incredible though it may appear, the puny human being—a creature that literally depends for his very breath upon Him who made him and sustains him—that creature can and does deny and reject his Creator. And since it is inadmissible to suppose that God at any future time would change his mind and *force* man into a loving relationship with himself—such an idea being spiritually impossible—one must conclude that man may continue to deny God to the bitter end, whatever it may be.

Because this is a "fallen" world and man is a "fallen" creature who prefers to live in proud self-assertion and autonomy, alienated from God, rather than living in communion with God, there exists fate. Not all events that happen in the world are

God's will; in fact, the majority of them are not. Human society, with its injustice and wrong, is man-made: it is the result of man's objectification, his evil imagination. And yet these evils are as real to the men who are crushed by them as if they had been crushed by a juggernaut. The natural man, in the grip of passions, or suffering the many forms of social injustice, his life a mere pawn in time of war and often in time of peace, is a slave of fate. Fate, chance, operate " when the world abandons God or God abandons the world."

Christianity is an eschatological, messianic religion because it expects a transformation of the present world into the Kingdom of God. But to realize the absolute will of God in all relations as depicted in the Sermon on the Mount is obviously impossible as long as men continue to hate, covet, kill — in short, as long as they remain spiritually untransformed. Any uncompromisingly absolute ideal is impossible in this " fallen " world; but anything less than the uncompromising ideal is unthinkable in the Kingdom of God. The pitiful " watering down " of the uncompromising ideal, such as is often done by maximalist Christian sects which think of themselves as realizing the ideals of the Sermon on the Mount, must be excused, if excused it be, on the ground of mental confusion or spiritual myopia.

Consequently, an expectation of an earthly Kingdom of God in its fully realized form, as the will of God reigning supreme over all men, is utopian. Man has always looked forward to the time when the conditions of the world which lies in evil would be transcended, and ideal relationships among men themselves, and men and nature, would supervene. This is the essence of the Jewish messianic hopes; and the Jewish dream was inherited by early Christians who, although obviously mistakenly, looked toward the appearance of the Kingdom within the lifetime of the first generation of believers. These same messianic, apocalyptic, hopes, in their utterly secularized form, have inspired even the utopia of a " classless society " of such atheistic world views as the Marxist.

The Kingdom of God, then, cannot be realized within time.

Such an unavoidable conclusion, however, does not preclude the admission of a partial realization of the will of God in the lives of men, but only where man willingly and freely submits to God's will. Transformed lives of individual believers, and a society of such transformed individuals, the ecumenical Church, are not only possible but are the very reason for the redemptive sacrificial work of Christ. Where love prevails, where reigns the will of God, there is the Kingdom. But such a realization is to be expected, not in society in general, but only within the "beloved community" of the ecumenical Church which is *sobornost*. But it is a basic error, committed by Augustine and persisted in by the Roman Catholic and every other authoritarian Church, to identify the human institution of the Church with the perfect society, with the Kingdom of God. Where the Spirit of Christ is, there is the Church. It is this that binds the Spirit-filled Christians into one ecumenical fellowship, no matter what communion they belong to. No Church, as such, has an exclusive possession of the Spirit. To bind the gift of grace, the presence of the Spirit, to any external symbol whatsoever, is magic, not a sacrament. "The wind blows where it wills, and you hear the sound of it, but you do not know whence it comes or whither it goes; so it is with every one who is born of the Spirit."[4] The only true bond of ecumenicity is the communion of the Holy Spirit; and "where the Spirit . . . is, there is liberty."

The Church is then to be identified with the divine society only to the extent to which it realizes the Lord's petition, "Thy will be done in earth, as it is in heaven." The Kingdom of God, however, not only is to be expected in the future, but also is partially present in the hearts of those who have submitted to the divine will. Nevertheless, historical Christian Churches have often woefully failed in the task of realizing God's will on earth, and not infrequently have been used as means of human self-assertion, whether it be of papal, imperial, or some other equally reprehensible form. They have failed to heed the warning, "Be not conformed to this world: but be ye transformed." Alas! how often the Church thinks in purely worldly fashion! It seeks to be rich, powerful, respected, held in honor, comfortable. Its message comes suspiciously near to "All this, and Heaven too!" It forgets what Kierkegaard perceived with such uncanny clarity, and proclaimed with such uncompromising stubbornness, that the day when the Church becomes glorious on earth is the day it shall be lost. The Church is in the world but not of the world in so far as it consciously strives to realize the divine will — love. So far as love is realized in the transformed, theanthropic humanity, the rule of God, the Kingdom of God, has come.

But Berdyaev's eschatological faith soars infinitely higher than the concept of human co-operation in the partial realization of the Kingdom of God on earth. The Christian has the positive duty to bring about the end of time, the consummation of history which will usher in the new aeon of the Holy Spirit. A passive waiting for the end is more likely to bring about God's judgment upon the world than the inauguration of the Kingdom of God. The new aeon will not descend upon us like the rain from heaven. Christians have an active part to play in bringing it about. For the cosmos, that is, an ordered universe, does not yet exist; "divine harmony" does not yet prevail; they must be created. We are living in the "eighth day of creation," and have a part in the creative task. Accordingly, Berdyaev's eschatology is active, creative, positive. Only when man ceases to treat himself and others as objects, as things, and begins to live in the depths of his own true being as a real person among persons, in intimate communion with God and man, the end of the objectified human society will come. Then "this world" will become "the other world." Time, the historical time of objectified human history, will be no more. The new aeon of the Holy Spirit will begin.

Furthermore, Berdyaev's eschatological views led him to a consideration of death and immortality. Death is a natural event in the physical realm. Since man belongs to both the natural and the spiritual realms, that which is dust shall return to dust. That which is of the earth, earthy, cannot inherit the Kingdom of God. Physical death reigns, therefore, only in the world of time and space; it has no sway in the spiritual world.

But natural death does not terminate the human spirit's destiny. For the spirit's existence reaches back before the world was, to pre-existence, and under certain conditions continues into eternity. The infinitesimally short span of human life — the threescore years and ten of the psalmist — is but a brief moment in human destiny. As for the Eternal, "a thousand years in thy sight are but as yesterday when it is past," because time does not exist for him; similarly, the human spirit may live eternal life in the midst of time. It is its quality which makes it eternal.

Accordingly, the terrestrial existence of the human spirit, so fleeting and short, cannot decide man's eternal destiny. And although Berdyaev rejects the idea of a new "incarnation" of the human spirit on earth, he affirms that there may be an existence "on another plane." [5]

Nevertheless, it does not follow that every spirit is *ipso facto* immortal and shall be, after repeated redemptive opportunities, whether on the earthly or another plane of existence, ultimately saved. This was the supremely optimistic faith of Origen; but it did not find acceptance in the historic Christian Church. In fact, it was condemned as a heresy. Nor does Berdyaev accept it. But his reasons for rejection are different. He feels that universalism does not take human free will seriously enough. Man "has a right to hell, as it were." [6]

Man does not possess immortality as an endowment. It is acquired, attained, although not earned, since salvation is by grace.[7] Its source is God, not nature. Immortality has to be won; it involves a struggle for personality. Only the spirit that consciously and freely chooses to unite itself with Christ, who has conquered death and is the Life eternal, attains immortality. In Christ man becomes a new creature, is born to a higher life in the spiritual birth of the New Adam. That life is eternal which possesses a new quality — is transformed into the divine-human.[8] "What is eternal and immortal in man is not the psychical or the physical elements as such, but the spiritual element which, acting in the other two, the psychical and the physical, effects personality and realizes the image and likeness of God. Man is immortal and eternal as a spiritual being belonging to the incorruptible world, but he is not a spiritual being by nature; he is a spiritual being when he realizes himself as such, when the spirit in him gains victory over his natural elements. . . . Immortality has to be won by the person and is a struggle for personality." [9]

The view that immortality is an attainment does not appear wholly consistent with Berdyaev's conception of the spirit's pre-existence, or at least leaves uncertain what becomes of those spirits that do not attain it. For is not attainment of immortality identical with the attainment of existence? And if so, did not the human spirit possess existence before? Or is this perhaps equivalent to an assertion that a human spirit which indeed possessed a real being ever since its creation in the preterrestrial existence, having failed to measure up to the demands of the terrestrial or other phases of existence, loses being, i.e., returns into the nothingness whence it came? In other words, does nonattainment of immortality imply annihilation?

To return once more to Berdyaev's treatment of the subject, his concept of immortality does not exclude or deny that of resurrection, as is often the case with liberal thought. The Greek idea of immortality, the freeing of the spirit from the prison of the flesh, implied a decisive rejection of the idea of resurrection of the body. Plato's teaching regarding immortality applies, not to the individual, but to the universal soul. The traditional doctrine of the Church affirmed the resurrection of the flesh. Berdyaev agrees with neither the liberal nor the Greek nor the traditional concepts; he formulates his ideas in essentially Pauline terms. The immortal spirit is not a "ghost," i.e., a disembodied spirit. Nor is the actual, physical body, when decomposed into its constituent elements, brought back to life. The whole body-soul-spirit entity, with the exception of the bodily corruption consequent upon sin, is transfigured or spiritualized, transformed into a "spiritual body." This is the persistent concept of the Eastern Fathers (although by the time of John of Damascus it was already coarsened into the idea of the resurrection of flesh, despite the explicit Pauline assertion that "flesh and blood cannot inherit the kingdom of God").[10] For them immortality is integral, involving the whole personality. For that matter, there is no other kind of personality.

The tremendous conclusion that attainment of personality implies immortality and resurrection in the sense of a transformed "spiritual" body, while the natural man is subjected in death to dissolution, only underscores Berdyaev's central thesis, the theme of all his thought, that among all God's creation human personality is the highest hierarchical value in time as well as in eternity. What, then, becomes of such spirits as refuse the proffered chance and obstinately persist in their self-affirmation which is the way of negation? This leads Berdyaev to the consideration of the concept of hell as it is often formulated in popular Christianity. Philosophically, it is the objectification of natural man's sadism. Berdyaev finds such a concept utterly perverse from both the moral and the spiritual point of view. Hell is chiefly the creation of the Western Church, beginning with Saint Augustine, and firmly incorporated in the thought of Saint Thomas Aquinas. But Dante did not hold it. Over the gate of the Inferno is written, "Primal Love . . . made me." It is the best God can do for those who will have none of him. Not that Berdyaev agrees with Dante that God made hell. God did not send anyone to hell; men chose to go. But there is something sadistic in the gloating of those "good" men who consign "bad" men to such a place of never-dying torment. Evil men need to be transformed, not destroyed.

The only hell there is, then, is of our own creation, is our own objectification. Hell, evil, belong to this world. God never created them.

Purgatory, paradise, and hell are all foreign to the Christian religion.[11] There can be no "eternal" hell, since it is a creation of time, a phenomenal—not a noumenal—entity. But nonetheless its torments are real. Man, the fallen man, has a range of possibilities that go far beyond the bestial on the lower scale, and all the way to the divine-human at the upper end of the scale.

Man-made hell is very real and terrible — ask any survivor of the concentration camps! Dostoevsky and Ibsen took over the idea of hell from the theologians who had thrown it out of the window, and depicted the reality of hell in the human soul with unforgettable and wholly convincing realism. Freud has also described it: he believes in a scientific hell, from which there is no escape, and in no heaven whatever.

But if hell be not eternal, what becomes of the spirits who, in their pride, remain unyielding to all that the divine grace can do to win them back? Are they annihilated? Do they migrate into another body? Do they receive another opportunity, or never-endingly repeated opportunities? Does the divine Fashioner, as Ibsen suggested in *Peer Gynt,* cast the human soul into the mold to make a new button of it? Berdyaev did not reach a final conclusion about these important questions of eschatology. Logically, judging from the premises of his system, he ought to have said that once a human spirit has shown itself incorrigibly opposed to God, it annihilates itself. Even that would be an act of divine mercy, for evil entails suffering. Annihilation, under certain conditions, would be a blessing. The God of love, who desires not the death of a sinner, who inflicts no torture, would still remain a God of love even if he allowed evil to take its natural course — that of self-destruction. Berdyaev, to the best of my knowledge, does not specifically affirm such a conclusion. He definitely rejects any thought of metempsychosis on the earthly plane as well as Origen's notion of the ultimate redemption of all men.[12] Nevertheless, he passionately asserts as an article of his "larger faith" that "the final victory of God over the forces of hell cannot be a division into two kingdoms — divine and diabolic, the saved and the damned to eternal torments — it must be only one kingdom. The juridical division of the world and humankind is a this-worldly, not the otherworldly, concept. Christian eschatology was accommodated to the categories of this world, to the time and history of this world; it did not pass over into the other aeon. Such is my faith."[13]

Finally, does the redeemed man who has attained immortality

return to the condition that he had lost by his revolt in his pre-existent state? Or, in other words, is redemption a mere restoration of the *status quo ante?* By no means, answers Berdyaev. The human spirit that has performed the unimaginably long journey from the original state, through the Fall and the painful earthly existence, and has learned the lesson that separation, alienation from God, has taught him, returns to the divine Spirit immeasurably enriched by that experience. There is a difference in the quality of the two sons in the parable of the Prodigal Son — between the elder son, who never left the father's house, and the younger, who lived among the swine and who came to himself. The experience of the younger son could not be learned otherwise than the hard way; but it added to his life a quality of insight and of wisdom that the elder brother never attained. The glorified life of the redeemed spirit attains to a higher state of illumination and of understanding than is possible to the "innocent" spirit which has not gone this way of redemption. As Bloy was fond of saying, "Suffering passes; but the sense of having suffered never passes."

10

Berdyaev's Final Faith

We have reached the stage in our study of Berdyaev's spiritual pilgrimage where it is possible to summarize his final faith. For there are a few basic concepts that are fundamental to everything else in his thought. He himself drew up a "*confessio fidei*" in his autobiography, in which he frankly evaluates the results of his lifelong labors. But the summary of his thought is sketchy, and leaves out many important concepts altogether. Although it is not possible to restate the main articles of his faith without a certain amount of repetition and duplication, the value of it will, let us hope, outweigh the cost.

Above all else, and from the very beginning, Berdyaev identifies himself and all his thinking with the concepts of freedom and of the supreme value of human personality. These two concepts merge into one, for freedom exists only in persons—whether human or divine—and the development of personality and the attainment of God-manhood are impossible without freedom. Berdyaev's dualism is not so much ontological (the antithesis of the spiritual and the material) as it is metaphysical and moral (the antithesis between freedom and slavery of the human spirit). His existential philosophy is but an elaboration of this basic postulate of the primacy of freedom over every sort of necessity. To be a real person, to be "saved," redeemed, transformed, is to be free from all external compulsion, to live in the depths of one's own inner life; the opposite condition is that of slavery to external elements—natural, social, individual—in which man is alienated from his real personality, from his fellows, and from God. To be free is the supreme task and obligation of every human being; a failure in this duty is the ultimate failure. Man ought to be free, because he ought to be a real person.

It is obvious, however, that the vast majority of men are not free: they are slaves to their own passions and whims, or at least to their wills; they are mere biochemical organisms driven by natural impulses; they are slaves to the conditions under which they must make a living, to the amassing of wealth, to the ambition for power, to social fashions and pressures, to public opinion, to bourgeois standards of success, to the prevailing cultural patterns, to the effects of the mechanization of life, to the dehumanization and depersonalization inherent in a decadent civilization; they become mere pawns to be exploited and manipulated by governments or other organized forces of racial, class, or other ideological patterns. They subject themselves to natural forces and "laws" as if these were dominant over personal values; they are swayed by a vast variety of false opinions regarding nature, social conditions, and religious and philosophical systems. There is nothing more tragic in the world than the fact of human slavery.

Berdyaev cannot be understood apart from his revolt against the forces that enslave human beings. He was a rebel against the world in which necessity reigns. From his youth onward he ever felt himself a stranger in the world. Truly he had no abiding place in it, but ever sought for "a city . . . whose builder and maker is God." He never felt "at home in the universe," if by the universe one means the material world. "World harmony" and "an ordered cosmos" did not exist for him; they still have to be created. "Many delight in asserting that they are in love with life; I could never say that."[1] In this sense he was a born Platonist.

But if, along with Plato, Berdyaev regarded the sense-perceived world as not the primary, real world, and spoke of it as "fallen," he followed Kant rather than Plato in the philosophical exposition of this concept. For Plato, only the world of ideas was truly intelligible; for Kant, on the contrary, only the world of appearances, i.e., the world of nature, of things, could be scientifically known. The real, the noumenal, world is not knowable in the same way as is the phenomenal world. And although Kant himself failed to draw adequate and correct conclusions from his own premises, he nevertheless provided the ground upon which others built a philosophy of the primacy of the spiritual over the material, of the " existential " over the external. Among them was Berdyaev who, starting from Kant's premises, developed an existential philosophy that identified the real world with the spiritual, noumenal realm, and made human personality, not the world of things, primary.

Having established the starting point, Berdyaev proceeded to develop his own system. Among the concepts peculiarly his own — although not original in the absolute sense — he counted the process of objectification, the relation between the person who alone is the existential subject and the external world of nature, of things, and of society. For the external world, instead being the only " objective reality," is on the contrary derived, dependent upon the thinker for whatever rationality and meaning he imparts to it. For things as such possess no meanings in themselves; only the subject perceives meanings and ascribes them to the object. Accordingly, only in the existential subject is reality known, not in nature, or in a thing.

To understand the process of objectification in the simplest terms — even at the risk of oversimplification — we may reduce the process to its lowest common denominator, that of treating a person as a thing. Objectification is literally what the term implies — the mental creation of an object. In the realm of personal and social relations, where this concept primarily applies, one is said to " objectify " when he treats another man as if he were merely a labor commodity; when he regards a businessman as living solely to make profit, or a technical expert as using his knowledge merely to conquer nature by mechanical means, or an artist whose creativity subserves exclusively commercial or utilitarian purposes; or when he treats a woman or a child as a plaything, a doll, an object of pleasure; in short, when he treats other human beings in a thousand different ways as means rather than an end in themselves, as things rather than persons. To be sure, men and women must serve in society as workers, businessmen, technicians, artists, and in countless other occupations. But such relations, basically sociological, are secondary, subordinate. In themselves, human beings are more than economic or sociological factors. They are, potentially or actually, persons of spiritual worth. They represent the highest hierarchical value in the world.

To a less degree, a similar process of objectification applies to nature, although in that relation the term signifies an abuse of a thing or an object, rather than converting a person into a thing. To see in nature only an object of commercial exploitation, to use it exclusively for enrichment, is to abuse its true purpose. Human life does not consist in the abundance of things one possesses, and to devote one's life exclusively to "the conquest of nature" to get great wealth is to become a slave to the process, to make an idol of the thing. "Thou shalt have no other gods before me"! To worship the half-gods made of gold is the great temptation of the bourgeois civilization, particularly in its capitalistic form, although the Communist society is by no means free from it.

Objectification, then, is the process whereby the utilitarian rather than the spiritual criterion is applied to men and things. Human beings are treated as if they were things; things are treated not as legitimate means whereby human life is sustained — as food and materials necessary for a worthy standard of living — but as commodities for producing wealth or as means of power. If, then, the whole intricate fabric of society is woven out of such warp and woof, let us not forget that we are its creators; it is the product of our own "objectification."

But this very concept affords a solution of the problem: if the evils of society are of our own making, the remedy is at hand. We must cease to deal with men as if they were things and must establish relations with them worthy of our own and their spiritual natures. The only proper relation between human beings is communion. For this term connotes the relation of man with his fellows on the spiritual level. There can be no *community* — a society knit together by a common spirit — without communion.

Accordingly, the only truly radical method of improving, transforming the world is by transforming human beings. But what are they to be transformed into, and by what means? To the first question Berdyaev replied that men are to be transformed from human into divine-human beings. In fact, he held that they are not truly human unless they are divine-human. They were created in God's image. Jesus Christ revealed the true man as well as true God. He was divine-human, a God-man; we are to be like him. But how is this transforming process to be accomplished? By the restoration of communion between God and man, by the restoration of the self-alienated man to primal unity with God. For the "fallen" man is alienated from God. His "fall" consisted in the act of self-assertion whereby he cut himself off from God, isolated himself in his "autonomy." This is the "original sin," which consists not so much in disobedience toward God as in self-alienation, self-isolation, in the loss of one's true self which is divine-human. The remedy for this "fallen" state is a return to God, resumption of the loving, intimate communion with God and consequently with other human beings. This is Berdyaev's ideal of God-manhood. Nothing short of the transforming experience of God-manhood is adequate, because nothing short of it goes deep enough. Only transformed men can transform society.

Consequently Berdyaev stressed the duty of creativity as the way whereby men who themselves had been freed from slavery to the objectified world devote their purified and consecrated energies to the building of the Kingdom of God. But although this Kingdom is partially realized in the lives of such redeemed men, the complete realization of it cannot take place in "this world," but only in eternity. For unless this world of objectification first pass away, the new era of ideal relations between God and men cannot come. In other words, the "objectified" world and human history must come to an end before the Kingdom of

God, the reign of the true existential communion of men with God and with each other, can be established. This, then, is Berdyaev's concept of eschatology. The Kingdom of God, the "other world," cannot be realized within human history, within "historical time," for the Kingdom is not the product of the historical process. Only when time is no more can the eternal order begin.

History, then, has meaning only because it has an end. Berdyaev scornfully rejected superficial metaphysical evolutionism, the naturalistic concept of automatic "progress" which is imbedded in the Marxist notion of "classless society." All such concepts he deemed naïve and philosophically self-contradictory. Logically, every such notion is a *non sequitur.* The natural order of cause and effect can possess no conscious goal toward which it is moving. Therefore, it represents no "progress," for in reality it is not going anywhere. Only a teleological, eschatological view of history, e.g., the Christian view, imparts meaning to the historical process.

But Berdyaev's eschatology has nothing to do with fatalistic apocalypticism. It is not an event with which we, as human beings, have no concern. In fact, it is a divine-human concern. Our attitude toward this event should not be one of merely passive expectancy, a resignation; it should be active, dynamic, a conscious straining toward the goal of bringing about "the end of time."

For the end of the world—of the present aeon—is in reality the end of historical time, and along with it the end of objectification which is the chief characteristic of our life in time. Since objectification—conversion of a spiritual reality into a thing—is the product of our own mental activity, the assiduous, sustained elimination of objectification is the way of bringing about "the end of time." This is the creative, dynamic understanding of Christian eschatology. A passive expectation of the end is more likely to bring about God's terrible judgment than the Kingdom of God. Berdyaev, who is often criticized for his "sterile perfectionism," and his consequent indifference toward the immediate, short-term implementation of the long-term goals of Christianity, is in reality intensely concerned about the intervening period between the present and "the end of time." He is perhaps unique in his emphasis upon the creative, dynamic interpretation of eschatology.

> "I dare go so far as to affirm that the eschatological morality is alone the true morality. In every moral act — an act of love, compassion, sacrifice — begins the end of this world in which reign hatred, cruelty, and avarice. In every creative act begins the end of this world in which reign necessity, inertia, and limitation and arises a new world, the 'other' world. Man who persistently performs acts of an eschatological character brings about the end of this world, leaves it behind and enters into the 'other' world. The 'other' world is therefore another mode of life, a victory over the objectification that characterizes the present world." [2]

Thereupon will follow the aeon of the Holy Spirit in which human spirits, immeasurably enriched by their experience of the terrestrial or of any further existence, shall live eternally in communion with God, the great Father of spirits, and in love with one another.

Such is Berdyaev's final faith.

NOTES

SELECTED BIBLIOGRAPHY

INDEX

NOTES

Chapter 1

1. The best source of biographical material concerning Berdyaev is found in his posthumously published "philosophical autobiography" entitled *Samopoznanie* (*Self-knowledge*). Cf. particularly pp. 14 ff.
2. *O rabstvye i svobodye chelovyeka,* p. 11; tr. *Slavery and Freedom,* p. 8.
3. *Filosofiya svobody,* p. 34.
4. *Samopoznanie,* p. 60.
5. *Sub specie aeternitatis,* pp. 199–200.
6. *O rabstvye i svobodye chelovyeka,* p. 14; tr. *Slavery and Freedom,* p. 13.
7. *Ibid.,* p. 15.
8. *Subyektivismus i individualismus v obshchestvennoi filosofii* (St. Petersburg, 1901).
9. *Ibid.,* pp. 195–196, footnote.
10. *Ibid.,* p. 266.
11. *Khristianstvo i klassovaya borba,* pp. 16–17; tr. *Christianity and Class War.*
12. *Samopoznanie,* p. 132.
13. *Put'* (No. 11, June, 1928), p. 82.
14. *Khristianstvo i klassovaya borba,* p. 20.

Chapter 2

1. *Sub specie aeternitatis,* pp. 2, 4.
2. *Ibid.,* pp. 135–136.
3. *Filosofiya svobodnago dukha,* I, pp. 8–9; tr. *Freedom and the Spirit,* pp. ix–x.
4. *Samopoznanie,* p. 158.
5. "O novom religioznom soznanii," in *Voprosy zhizni,* pp. 151–152.
6. *Ibid.,* p. 157.
7. *Ibid.,* p. 158.
8. *Sub specie aeternitatis,* pp. 409–411.
9. From a private letter of Berdyaev written to the author.
10. *Mirosozertsanie Dostoevskago;* the English translation, *Dostoievsky,* by Donald Attwater.
11. F. M. Dostoevsky, *Bratya Karamazovy* (Berlin, 1924), I, pp. 385 ff.
12. *Samopoznanie,* p. 193.

13. "Critique of Historical Materialism," in *Sub specie aeternitatis,* p. 101.
14. *Sub specie aeternitatis,* pp. 429–431, 434.
15. *Dukhovny krizis inteligentsii,* p. 10.
16. *Samopoznanie,* pp. 144–145.
17. *Ibid.,* p. 174.
18. S. L. Frank, *Krushenie kumirov,* p. 16.
19. "The Philosophical Truth and the Truth of the Intelligentsia," in *Dukhovny krizis inteligentsii,* pp. 171 ff.
20. *Put'* (October, 1928), pp. 23–24; also cf. *Samopoznanie,* p. 201.
21. "Nihilism on Religious Soil," in *Dukhovny krizis inteligentsii,* pp. 201–203, 205.
22. This was an extremely reactionary organization of ignorant and brutal elements of the population, largely under the direction of some churchmen and hierarchs. Many Jewish pogroms were ascribed to the activity of this group.
23. It was originally published in the *Moscow Weekly* for August 15, 1909, and reprinted in *Dukhovny krizis inteligentsii,* pp. 299 ff.
24. An untranslatable word, connoting a different concept of ecumenicity or catholicity than the prevailing Western sense of those terms. A short definition of it may be expressed by the sentence, "Where the Spirit of Christ is, there is the ecumenical Church."
25. "Conflict of Church and State in Russia," in *Dukhovny krizis inteligentsii,* p. 221.
26. *Dukhovny krizis inteligentsii,* p. 223.
27. *Ibid.,* pp. 45–46.
28. "Sick Russia," in *Dukhovny krizis inteligentsii,* pp. 84–85.
29. *Ibid.,* p. 86.
30. *Dukhovny krizis inteligentsii,* p. 9.
31. *Ibid.,* p. 44.
32. *Ibid.,* p. 43.
33. *Ibid.,* p. 52.
34. *Ibid.,* pp. 93–94.
35. *Ibid.,* p. 208.

Chapter 3

1. *Samopoznanie,* p. 203.
2. *Filosofiya svobody.* Published by a firm called *Put'* (*The Way*), which was organized by an adherent of the new movement; it was intended to publish the literary productions of this group. Berdyaev served as its director. But Bulgakov was likewise a member of the firm.
3. *Smysl tvorchestva.* (Moscow, 1916.) The date on the inside of the front page is given as 1915. Either one of these dates is a typographical error, or the process of publishing lasted from one year to the other. It must be remembered that these were the war years. Cf. also *Samopoznanie,* pp. 229 f.
4. *Samopoznanie,* p. 229.
5. *Ibid.,* p. 231.

6. *Smysl tvorchestva,* p. 288.
7. *Ibid.,* p. 273.
8. *Ibid.,* p. 276.
9. *Ibid.,* pp. 287–288.
10. *Samopoznanie,* p. 219.
11. *Sudba Rossii,* p. iii.
12. *Ibid.*
13. *Samopoznanie,* p. 247.
14. *Ibid.,* p. 264.
15. *Ibid.,* p. 161.
16. *Filosofiya neravenstva. Pisma k nedrugam po sotsialnoi filosofii.*
17. *Ibid.,* pp. 6–7.
18. *Ibid.,* pp. 8–9.
19. *Ibid.,* p. 12.
20. *Ibid.,* p. 42.
21. *Ibid.,* p. 41.
22. *Ibid.,* p. 44.
23. *Ibid.,* p. 45.
24. *Sudba Rossii.*
25. *Filosofiya neravenstva,* pp. 244, 245–246.
26. *Novoe srednovyekovie.* The book was translated by Donald Attwater and published under the title *The End of Our Time* (Sheed & Ward, Inc., 1933). I am quoting from the original Russian edition, because there are some differences between the original text and the translation. Mr. Attwater based his translation on the French version which, according to him, was approved by Berdyaev.
27. *Ibid.,* p. 59.
28. *Ibid.,* p. 60.
29. *Ibid.,* p. 65.
30. *Ibid.,* p. 71.
31. *Ibid.,* pp. 84, 77.
32. *Ibid.,* p. 67.
33. *Ibid.,* p. 105.
34. *Samopoznanie,* p. 253.
35. *Ibid.,* p. 253, reported by Berdyaev's sister-in-law.
36. *Mirosozertsanie Dostoevskago;* tr. *Dostoievsky.*
37. *Samopoznanie,* p. 255.
38. *Ibid.,* p. 263.
39. *Ibid.,* pp. 266–267.

Chapter 4

1. "Illyuzii i realnosti v psikhologii imigrantskoi molodyezhi," in *Put'* (December, 1928), p. 9.
2. G. W. F. Hegel, *The Philosophy of History* (Willey Book Co., 1944), p. 38.
3. *The Fate of Man in the Modern World,* p. 2.
4. *Ibid.,* p. 4.

5. *The End of Our Time*, p. 70.
6. *Opyt eskhatologicheskoi metafiziki*, p. 20; tr. *Essai de metaphysique eschatologique*, p. 20.
7. *Filosofiya svobody*, p. 176.
8. *The End of Our Time*, p. 25.
9. *Ibid.*, p. 20.
10. *Ibid.*
11. *Ibid.*, p. 25.
12. *Filosofiya svobody*, p. 181; cf. *Freedom and the Spirit*, pp. 354–355.
13. *The Fate of Man in the Modern World*, p. 29.
14. *Filosofiya svobody*, p. 23.
15. *Sub specie aeternitatis*, pp. 267, 291.
16. *Filosofiya svobody*, p. 23.
17. *Opyt eskhatologicheskoi metafiziki*, pp. 15 fl.; tr. *Essai de metaphysique eschatologique*, pp. 13 ff.
18. *Ibid.*, p. 15; tr. *ibid.*, p. 13.
19. *O naznachenii chelovyeka*, pp. 13–14; tr. *The Destiny of Man*, pp. 15–16. Cf. also *The Divine and the Human*, pp. 32–33.
20. *Thus Spake Zarathustra*, pp. lxxiii, 3.
21. "The End of Renaissance," in *Slavonic Review* (London, June, 1925), p. 16.
22. *The Fate of Man in the Modern World*, p. 31.
23. *Opyt eskhatologicheskoi metafiziki*, p. 39; tr. *Essai de metaphysique eschatologique*, p. 44.
24. *The Fate of Man in the Modern World*, p. 31.
25. *Ibid.*, p. 32.
26. *The Bourgeois Mind and Other Essays.*
27. *Ibid.*, p. 14.
28. *Ibid.*, p. 15.
29. *Ibid.*, p. 22.
30. *The Fate of Man in the Modern World*, p. 18.
31. *Ibid.*, pp. 80–81.
32. *The Bourgeois Mind*, p. 31.
33. *Samopoznanie*, p. 281.
34. *Ibid.*, p. 284.
35. Hélène Iswolsky, *Au temps de la lumière* (Montreal, Quebec: Éditions de l'Arbre, 1945).
36. *Ibid.*, p. 102.
37. *The Divine and the Human*, p. 151.
38. Hélène Iswolsky, *op. cit.*, pp. 115–116.
39. *Samopoznanie*, p. 364.
40. The French edition is entitled *Dialectique existentielle du divin et de l'humain.*
41. *Samopoznanie*, p. 364.
42. *Ibid.*, p. 371.
43. *Ibid.*, p. 372.

CHAPTER 5

1. *Ya i mir obyektov*, p. 5; tr. *Solitude and Society*, p. 30.
2. F. S. C. Northrop, *The Meeting of East and West* (The Macmillan Company, 1946), p. 115.
3. G. W. F. Hegel, *The Philosophy of History*, pp. 38–39.
4. *Filosofiya svobody*, pp. 7, 9.
5. *Opyt eskhatologicheskoi metafiziki*, p. 15; tr. *Essai de metaphysique eschatologique*, p. 13.
6. *Ya i mir obyektov*, p. 25; cf. *Slavery and Freedom*, p. 76. In his *Essai de metaphysique eschatologique*, Berdyaev draws up a similar series of contrasts, in which he adds the category of eschatological philosophy to the previous list.
7. *Filosofiya svobody*, p. 47.
8. *Ya i mir obyektov*, pp. 46–47.
9. *Samopoznanie*, p. 297.
10. *Toward a New Epoch* (Geoffrey Bles, Ltd., London, 1949), p. 11, footnote.
11. *O naznachenii chelovyeka*, p. 14; tr. *The Destiny of Man*, p. 16.
12. *Samopoznanie*, p. 50.
13. *Ibid.*, p. 46.
14. *O naznachenii chelovyeka*, p. 17; tr. *The Destiny of Man*, p. 19.
15. *Ibid.*, p. 4; tr. *ibid.*, p. 4.
16. *Ibid.*, p. 15; tr. *ibid.*, p. 18.
17. Rudolf Otto, *Mysticism East and West* (The Macmillan Company, 1932), p. 141.
18. *Smysl tvorchestva*, p. 291.
19. *Ibid.*, p. 296.
20. *The Divine and the Human*, pp. 26–27.
21. *Ibid.*, p. 27. For Eckhart's "Defense," see Raymond B. Blakney, tr., *Meister Eckhart* (Harper & Brothers, 1941), pp. 258 ff. The whole question of Eckhart's "pantheism" has been subjected to an exhaustive and close scrutiny by Rudolf Otto in his *Mysticism East and West*. He calls any identification of Eckhart with pantheism "sheer folly" (p. 197). But there is plenty of ground for misunderstanding of Eckhart!
22. *Samopoznanie*, pp. 194–195.
23. *Ibid.*
24. Hebrews 11:9 (Revised Standard Version).
25. *Samopoznanie*, p. 197.
26. *Ibid.*, p. 61.
27. Jacob Boehme, *Mysterium Magnum*, 10:46.
28. *The World as Will and Idea*, Book II, par. 21, pp. 72–73 (The Modern Library, New York, 1928).
29. *Samopoznanie*, p. 61.
30. *Opyt eskhatologicheskoi metafiziki*, p. 121; tr. *Essai de metaphysique eschatologique*, p. 153.

CHAPTER 6

1. *Samopoznanie,* p. 187.
2. *Ibid.*
3. *Ibid.,* p. 188.
4. *Sub specie aeternitatis,* p. 436. In a footnote to this passage, Berdyaev adds: "Such was the view of John Scotus Erigena, very daring in the ninth century which was blinded by authority. The gnosis of Origen is very near to my views; such Eastern theologian-philosophers as Saint Dionysius the Areopagite and Saint Maximus the Confessor are likewise congenial to me."
5. *Filosofiya svobodnago dukha,* I, p. 36; tr. *Freedom and the Spirit,* p. 11.
6. *Ibid.,* p. 86; tr. *ibid.,* pp. 49–50.
7. *Samopoznanie,* p. 182.
8. *Ibid.,* p. 199.
9. V. V. Rozanov, *Legenda o velikom Inkvizitorye.*
10. *O naznachenii chelovyeka,* p. 28; tr. *The Destiny of Man,* p. 33.
11. This subject is treated with greater detail in my article, "Origen and Berdyaev: a Comparison," in *Church History* (March, 1947), pp. 3 ff.
12. The fullest statement of Berdyaev's interpretation of Boehme appears in two articles: "Iz etyudov o Yakovye Bemye," in *Put'* (February and April, 1930); but it may conveniently be found also in *The Destiny of Man,* pp. 32–35, 39–40, 46–47, 52, 55, 190, 377; also in *Smysl tvorchestva,* pp. 12, 15; *Spirit and Reality,* pp. 38, 56, 77, 111, 114–115, 144–145; *The Divine and the Human,* p. 31.
13. *Smysl tvorchestva,* p. 60.
14. There is an excellent treatment of Boehme's views in Howard H. Brinton's *The Mystic Will* (The Macmillan Company, 1930), upon which I rely in many respects. Also cf. Alexandre Koyré, *La philosophie de Jacob Boehme* (Paris, 1929); Hans L. Martensen, *Jacob Boehme* (Harper & Brothers, 1949).
15. *Ibid.,* p. 104.
16. *Put'* (September, 1929), p. 120; cf. also *Samopoznanie,* pp. 189 f.
17. *Smysl tvorchestva,* pp. 143–144.
18. *Smysl istorii,* p. 68; tr. *The Meaning of History,* p. 55.
19. *The Destiny of Man,* p. 163.
20. *Put',* I, p. 61.
21. *Samopoznanie,* p. 239.
22. Donald Attwater, ed., *Modern Christian Revolutionaries,* p. 346, footnote 4.
23. *O naznachenii chelovyeka,* p. 136; tr. *The Destiny of Man,* p. 163.
24. *Put'* (February, 1930), p. 60.
25. *Filosofiya svobodnago dukha,* I, p. 237; tr. *Freedom and the Spirit,* p. 163.
26. *Ibid.,* p. 241; tr. *ibid.,* p. 166.
27. *O rabstvye i svobodye chelovyeka,* pp. 75–77; tr. *Slavery and Freedom,* pp. 88–89.
28. *Samopoznanie,* p. 190.

29. *Ibid.*
30. *The Destiny of Man,* p. 69.
31. Raymond B. Blakney, tr., *Meister Eckhart,* p. 62.
32. "*Ich weiss, dass ohne mich Gott nicht ein Nu kann leben;*
Wäre ich zu Nichts, er muss von Noth den Geist aufgeben."
33. *Slavery and Freedom,* p. 140.
34. *Ibid.,* p. 139.
35. Reinhold Niebuhr, *The Nature and Destiny of Man* (Charles Scribner's Sons, 1943), I, pp. 268–269.
36. See my article in *Church History* (March, 1947), pp. 7, 9; also *The Destiny of Man,* p. 79.
37. S. L. Frank, *God with Us,* p. 49.
38. *O naznachenii chelovyeka,* p. 67; tr. *The Destiny of Man,* p. 79. Cf. also pp. 86, 324, 328, and *The Meaning of History,* pp. 39–41, 44–45.
39. But the legend is obviously alluded to in II Peter 2:4, although no names are mentioned.
40. *Filosofiya svobodnago dukha,* I, p. 235; tr. *Freedom and the Spirit,* p. 161.
41. Martin Luther, *Commentary on Genesis,* quoted in Hugh Thomson Kerr, Jr., ed., *A Compend of Luther's Theology* (The Westminster Press, 1943), pp. 80–83.
42. Karl Barth, "No!," in *Natural Theology* (London, 1946), p. 88.
43. *O naznachenii chelovyeka,* p. 159; tr. *The Destiny of Man,* p. 189.
44. *Filosofiya svobodnago dukha,* I, p. 192; tr. *Freedom and the Spirit,* p. 131; cf. also p. 208.
45. *O naznachenii chelovyeka,* p. 159; tr. *The Destiny of Man,* p. 189.

Chapter 7

1. *Smysl istorii,* p. 95; tr. *The Meaning of History,* p. 77.
2. *Filosofiya svobodnago dukha,* I, p. 63; tr. *Freedom and the Spirit,* p. 32.
3. *O naznachenii chelovyeka,* p. 116; tr. *The Destiny of Man,* p. 140.
4. *Smysl tvorchestva,* p. 250.
5. *Filosofiya svobody,* pp. 154–155.
6. *O naznachenii chelovyeka,* p. 39; tr. *The Destiny of Man,* p. 46.
7. *Filosofiya svobodnago dukha,* I, p. 9; tr. *Freedom and the Spirit,* p. x.
8. *Novoe religioznoe soznanie i obshchestvennost,* p. 229.
9. *Filosofiya svobodnago dukha,* I, p. 249; tr. *Freedom and the Spirit,* p. 172.
10. *O naznachenii chelovyeka,* p. 117; tr. *The Destiny of Man,* p. 140.
11. My treatment of Berdyaev's concept of God is based on his *Slavery and Freedom,* pp. 82 ff.
12. See the preceding chapter.
13. *Ya i mir obyektov,* p. 90.
14. *Samopoznanie,* p. 191.
15. *The Destiny of Man,* p. 72; also *Slavery and Freedom,* p. 27.
16. *Sub specie aeternitatis,* p. 17; also *Ya i mir obyektov,* p. 148.
17. *Ya i mir obyektov,* p. 168; cf. also *Slavery and Freedom,* p. 28.

18. "Chelovyecheskaya lichnost i sverkhlichnaya tsennosti," in *Personalizm*, pp. 331–332.
19. *O naznachenii chelovyeka*, p. 60; tr. *The Destiny of Man*, p. 71. Also *Ya i mir obyektov*, p. 146.
20. *Ibid.*, p. 61.
21. *Ya i mir obyektov*, p. 149.
22. *O rabstvye i svobodye chelovyeka*, p. 28; tr. *Slavery and Freedom*, p. 31.
23. *Ibid.*, p. 41; tr. *ibid.*, p. 47.
24. *Ibid.*, p. 42; tr. *ibid.*, p. 48.
25. *Ya i mir obyektov*, p. 182.
26. *Ibid.*
27. *O rabstvye i svobodye chelovyeka*, p. 53; tr. *Slavery and Freedom*, p. 63.
28. *Samopoznanie*, p. 195.
29. *Ibid.*, p. 227.
30. *O naznachenii chelovyeka*, p. 318; tr. *The Destiny of Man*, p. 377.
31. *Smysl tvorchestva*, pp. 125–126.
32. *O rabstvye i svobodye chelovyeka*, p. 39; tr. *Slavery and Freedom*, p. 45.
33. *Dukh i realnost*, p. 129; tr. *Spirit and Reality*, p. 149.
34. *O naznachenii chelovyeka*, p. 261; tr. *The Destiny of Man*, p. 307.
35. *Smysl tvorchestva*, p. 100.
36. *Ibid.*, p. 105.
37. *Ibid.*, p. 138.
38. *Ibid.*, p. 153.
39. *Ibid.*, p. 143.
40. *Ibid.*, pp. 136–137.
41. *O naznachenii chelovyeka*, p. 159; tr. *The Destiny of Man*, p. 189.
42. *Smysl tvorchestva*, p. 132.
43. Hebrews 11:39 (Revised Standard Version).

Chapter 8

1. *Put'* (April, 1936), p. 34.
2. *O naznachenii chelovyeka*, p. 122; tr. *The Destiny of Man*, p. 147.
3. *Ibid.*, p. 314; tr. *ibid.*, pp. 372–373.
4. *Smysl tvorchestva*, p. 260.
5. Romans 8:21 (Revised Standard Version).
6. *Smysl istorii*, p. 72; tr. *The Meaning of History*, p. 58.
7. *Filosofiya svobody*, p. 150.
8. This is a very common charge; cf., e.g., Emery Reves, *The Anatomy of Peace* (Harper & Brothers, 1945), pp. 76 ff.
9. *Khristianstvo i aktivnost chelovyeka*, p. 3; tr. "Christianity and Human Activity," in *The Bourgeois Mind*.
10. *O dostoinstvye Khristianstva i nedostoinstvye Khristian;* tr. "The Worth of Christianity and the Unworthiness of Christians," in *The Bourgeois Mind*.

11. Cf. my article, "Peter Chelčický, the Spiritual Father of the Unitas Fratrum," in *Church History,* XII (1943), pp. 271–291.
12. *O dostoinstvye Khristianstva,* pp. 9–10.
13. "Tserkovnaya smuta i svoboda sovyesti," in *Put'* (October–November, 1926), p. 43.
14. *Ibid.,* p. 45.
15. *Ibid.*
16. *Smysl tvorchestva,* pp. 246–247.
17. Lev N. Tolstoy, *My Religion* (New York, 1885), p. 242; cf. also "What Is Religion," in Tolstoy's *Letters and Essays* (Boston, 1905), pp. 77–128.
18. *O dostoinstvye Khristianstva,* pp. 22–23.
19. "Koshmar zlogo dobra," in *Put'* (June–July, 1926), p. 106.
20. *O naznachenii chelovyeka,* pp. 131–132; tr. *The Destiny of Man,* pp. 158–159.
21. The entire discussion of the three types of ethics is based primarily on *The Destiny of Man,* pp. 109–196.
22. Romans 13:1–3 (Revised Standard Version).
23. *O naznachenii chelovyeka,* pp. 108–109; tr. *The Destiny of Man,* p. 130.
24. *Ya i mir obyektov,* p. 70.
25. *O naznachenii chelovyeka,* pp. 132–133; tr. *The Destiny of Man,* pp. 159–160.
26. *Ibid.,* p. 141; tr. *ibid.,* p. 169.
27. *Put'* (April, 1926), p. 42.
28. *Ibid.,* p. 43.
29. *Samopoznanie,* p. 225.
30. *Ibid.,* p. 232.
31. *Ibid.,* pp. 228–229.
32. *O naznachenii chelovyeka,* p. 151; tr. *The Destiny of Man,* pp. 180–181.
33. *Samopoznanie,* p. 237.
34. *Filosofiya neravenstva,* p. 55.
35. *Novoe srednovyekovie,* p. 108; tr. *The End of Our Time.*
36. *Ibid.,* pp. 51–52; tr. *ibid.,* p. 113.
37. *Ibid.,* p. 140.
38. *Ibid.,* pp. 109–110; cf. also *The Destiny of Man,* p. 282.
39. *Ibid.,* p. 135.
40. *The Origin of Russian Communism,* p. 218.
41. *Dialectique existentielle,* p. 129.
42. *O naznachenii chelovyeka,* p. 215; tr. *The Destiny of Man,* pp. 253–254.
43. *Ibid.,* pp. 217–218; tr. *ibid.,* pp. 256–257.
44. *Ibid.,* p. 216; tr. *ibid.,* p. 255.
45. *Khristianstvo i klassovaya borba,* p. 134.
46. *Toward a New Epoch,* p. 67.
47. *Khristianstvo i klassovaya borba,* p. 54.
48. *Ibid.,* p. 128.
49. *Ibid.,* pp. 101–102.
50. *Ibid.,* pp. 75–76.
51. *Ibid.,* p. 77.

52. *Khristianstvo i klassovaya borba,* p. 81.
53. *Ibid.,* p. 117.
54. *Ibid.,* p. 84.
55. *Toward a New Epoch,* pp. 46–47.
56. *Samopoznanie,* p. 265.

Chapter 9

1. *The Divine and the Human,* pp. v–vi.
2. *Ya i mir obyektov,* p. 120.
3. G. W. Butterworth, tr., *Origen on the First Principles* (London, 1936), pp. 78, 89, 126, 209, 237 ff., 249; cf. my article, "Origen and Berdyaev," in *Church History* (March, 1947), pp. 3 ff.
4. John 3:8 (Revised Standard Version).
5. *Samopoznanie,* p. 321.
6. *Filosofiya svobodnago dukha,* II, p. 186; tr. *Freedom and the Spirit,* p. 324.
7. *Ibid.,* p. 187.
8. *Ibid.,* I, p. 73.
9. *O naznachenii chelovyeka,* p. 275; tr. *The Destiny of Man,* pp. 324–335. Cf. *Filosofiya svobodnago dukha,* I, p. 73; tr. *Freedom and the Spirit,* p. 40.
10. *Freedom and the Spirit,* pp. 40–41; *Slavery and Freedom,* pp. 54–55; *The Destiny of Man,* pp. 328–329.
11. *The Divine and the Human,* p. 11.
12. Cf. *Freedom and the Spirit,* pp. 323–324.
13. *Samopoznanie,* p. 329.

Chapter 10

1. *Samopoznanie,* p. 57.
2. *Ibid.,* p. 327.

SELECTED BIBLIOGRAPHY

I. Berdyaev's Own Writings

1. *Books*

1901. *Subyektivismus i individualismus v obshchestvennoi filosofii* (St. Petersburg, 1901).
1907. *Sub specie aeternitatis* (St. Petersburg, 1907).
1907. *Novoe religioznoe soznanie i obshchestvennost* (St. Petersburg, 1907).
1911. *Filosofiya svobody* (Moscow, 1911).
1911. *Dukhovny krizis inteligentsii* (St. Petersburg, 1911).
1912. *Aleksei S. Khomyakov* (Moscow, 1912).
1916. *Smysl tvorchestva* (Moscow, 1916); tr. *Der Sinn des Schaffens* (Berlin).
1918. *Sudba Rossii* (Moscow, 1918).
1923. *Smysl istorii* (Obelisk, Berlin; 1923); tr. *The Meaning of History* (Charles Scribner's Sons, 1936).
1923. *Filosofiya neravenstva. Pisma k nedrugam po sotsialnoi filosofii* (Berlin, 1923).
1923. *Mirosozertsanie Dostoevskago* (Y.M.C.A. Press, Prague, 1923); tr. *Dostoievsky* (Sheed & Ward, Inc., 1934).
1924. *Novoe srednovyekovie* (Berlin, 1924); the first essay under that title, published in 1919, before the complete work was published, was included in *The End of Our Time* (Sheed & Ward, Inc., 1933); tr. *Un nouveau moyen âge* (Paris, 1930).
1924. *Problemy russkago religioznago soznaniya* (Y.M.C.A. Press, Paris, 1924); tr. "L'idée religieuse russe," in *Cahiers de la nouvelle journée* (No. 8).
1926. *Konstantin Leontyev* (Y.M.C.A. Press, Paris, 1926); tr. *Leontiev* (London, 1940); tr. *Const. Leontieff* (Paris, 1938).
1927. *Filosofiya svobodnago dukha,* 2 vols. (Y.M.C.A. Press, Paris, 1927); tr. *Freedom and the Spirit* (Charles Scribner's Sons, 1935).
1928. *O dostoinstvye Khristianstva i nedostoinstvye Khristian* (War-

saw, 1928); tr. "The Worth of Christianity and the Unworthiness of Christians," in *The Bourgeois Mind and Other Essays* (Sheed & Ward, Inc., 1934).

1929. *Marksizm i religiya* (Warsaw, 1929).

1929. *Khristianstvo i aktivnost chelovyeka* (Y.M.C.A. Press, Paris, 1929); tr. "Christianity and Human Activity," in *The Bourgeois Mind and Other Essays* (Sheed & Ward, Inc., 1934).

1931. *The Russian Revolution* (Sheed & Ward, Inc., London, 1931).

1931. *O naznachenii chelovyeka* (Y.M.C.A. Press, Paris, 1931); tr. *The Destiny of Man* (Charles Scribner's Sons, 1937).

1931. *O samoubiistvye* (Y.M.C.A. Press, Paris, 1931).

1931. *Russkaya religioznaya psikhologiya i kommunistichesky ateizm* (Y.M.C.A. Press, Paris, 1931); tr. in Carl Schmitt *et al., Vital Realities* (Sheed & Ward, Inc., 1932), as "Russian Religious Psychology and the Communistic Atheism"; tr. *Wahrheit und Lüge des Kommunismus* (Luzern, 1934).

1931. *Khristianstvo i klassovaya borba* (Y.M.C.A. Press, Paris, 1931); tr. *Christianity and Class War* (Sheed & Ward, Inc., 1933).

1933. *Chelovyek i mashina* (Y.M.C.A. Press, Paris, 1933); tr. "Man and the Machine," in *The Bourgeois Mind.*

1934. *Sudba chelovyeka v sovremennom mire* (Y.M.C.A. Press, Paris, 1934); tr. *The Fate of Man in the Modern World* (Morehouse-Gorham Company, Inc., 1935); tr. *Destin de l'homme dans le monde actuel* (Paris).

1934. *Ya i mir obyektov* (Y.M.C.A. Press, Paris, n. d.); tr. *Solitude and Society* (Charles Scribner's Sons, 1937); tr. *Cinq méditations sur l'existence* (Paris, 1936).

1937. *Dukh i realnost* (Y.M.C.A. Press, Paris, 1937); tr. *Spirit and Reality* (Charles Scribner's Sons, 1939).

1937. *The Origin of Russian Communism* (Charles Scribner's Sons, 1937).

1939. *O rabstvye i svobodye chelovyeka* (Y.M.C.A. Press, Paris, n. d.); tr. *Slavery and Freedom* (Charles Scribner's Sons, 1944); tr. *De l'esclavage et de la liberté* (Paris, n. d.).

1946. *Russkaya ideya* (Y.M.C.A. Press, Paris, 1946); tr. *The Russian Idea* (The Macmillan Company, 1948).

1946. *Opyt eskhatologicheskoi metafiziki* (Y.M.C.A. Press, Paris, 1947); tr. *Essai de metaphysique eschatologique* (Paris, 1946).

1947. *Dialectique existentielle du divin et de l'humain* (J. B. Jarrin, Paris, 1947); tr. *The Divine and the Human* (The Macmillan Company, London, 1949).

1948. *Au seuil de la nouvelle époque* (Delachaux & Niestlé S.A.,

Neuchâtel, 1948); tr. *Toward a New Epoch* (Geoffrey Bles, Ltd., London, 1949).

1949. *Samopoznanie* (Y.M.C.A. Press, Paris, 1949).

2. *Articles*

"A. Lange i kriticheskaya filosofiya," in *Mīr Bozhii* (July, 1900).

"O novom religioznom soznanii," in *Voprosy zhizni* (St. Petersburg, 1905).

"'Russkii soblazn.' Po povodu Serebryannago golubya A. Belago," in *Russkaya Mysl* (1910).

"A. S. Khomyakov," in *Put'* (1911).

"Stilizovannoe pravoslavie," in *Russkaya Mysl* (1914).

"Religiya monizma," in *Voprosy filosofii i psikhologii* (1914).

"Stavrogin," in *Russkaya Mysl* (1914).

"Religiya voskresheniya, Filosofiya Obshchago Dyela N. F. Fedorova," in *Russkaya Mysl* (1915).

"Tipy religioznoi mysli v Rossii; Novoe Khristianstvo," in *Russkaya Mysl* (1916).

"Dva tipa mirosozertsaniya," in *Voprosy filosofii i psikhologii* (1916).

"Povest o nebesnom rodye," in *Russkaya Mysl* (1916).

"Khomyakov i svyashchenik P. A. Florenski," in *Russkaya Mysl* (1917).

"Dusha Rossii," reprinted in *Sudba Rossii* (Moscow, 1918).

An article in *Osval'd Shpengler i zakat Evropy* (Moscow, 1922).

"Konets Rennesansa," in *Sofiya* (Berlin, 1923, pp. 21–46; tr. "The End of Renaissance," in *The Slavonic Review* (London), Part I, June, 1925; Part II, December, 1925. Also in *The End of Our Time* (London, 1933).

"'Zhivaya Tserkov' i religioznoe vozrozhdenie v Rossii," in *Sofiya* (Berlin, 1923).

"Tsarstvo Bozhie i tsarstvo kesara," in *Put'* (September, 1925).

"Tserkovnaya smuta i svoboda sovyesti," in *Put'* (October–November, 1926).

"Spasenie i tvorchestvo," in *Put'* (January, 1926).

"O dukhovnoi burzhoaznosti," in *Put'* (March–April, 1926).

"Koshmar zlogo dobra," in *Put'* (June–July, 1926).

"Dnevnik filosofa," in *Put'* (June–July, 1926).

"Nauka o religii i khristianskaya apologetika," in *Put'* (January, 1927).

"Iz razmyshlenii o teoditseye," in *Put'* (April, 1927).

"Problem khristianskago gosudarstva," in *Sovremennyya zapiski* (xxxi, 1927, pp. 280–305).

"Katolichestvo i Action Française," in *Put'* (April, 1928).

"Obskurantizm," in *Put'* (October, 1928).
"Svoboda i tvorchestvo," in *Put'* (1928).
"Pravomyslie i svobodomyslie," in *Sovremennyya zapiski* (1928).
"Tri yubileya — L. Tolstoy, Gen. Ibsen, N. Fedotov," in *Put'* (June, 1928).
"Illyuzii i realnosti v psikhologii emigrantskoi molodyezhi," in *Put'* (December, 1928).
"Drevo zhizni i drevo poznaniya," in *Put'* (September, 1929).
"Iz etyudov o Ya. Bemye." Etyud I, in *Put'* (February, 1930); Etyud II, *ibid.* (April, 1930).
"Paradoksi svobody v sotsialnoi zhizni," in *Novy Grad* (Paris, 1931, No. 1).
"O gordosti smirennykh," in *Put'* (December, 1931).
"Khristianstvo pered sovremennoi sotsialnoi deistvitel'nostyu," in *Put'* (February, 1932).
"General'naya liniya sovyetskoi filosofii i voinstvuyushchi ateism," in *Put'* (July, 1932); tr. "The General Line of Soviet Philosophy," in *The End of Our Time* (London, 1933).
"Uchenie o percvoploshchenii i problema chelovyeka," in *Pereselenie dush* (Paris, 1935).
"Neogumanism, Marksizm, i dukhovnyya tsennosti," in *Sovremennyya zapiski* (1936).
"Chelovyecheskaya lichnost i sverkhlichnaya tsennosti," in *Personalizm* (Paris, 1937).
"The Crisis of Christianity," in *Christendom* (Spring, 1937).
"O fanatizmye, ortodoksii, i istinye," in *Russkiya zapiski* (1937).
"O sovremennom natsionalismye," in *Russkiya zapiski* (1938).
"Pravomyslie i svobodomyslie," in *Sovremennyya zapiski* (1938).
"War and the Christian Conscience" (1938).
"Le Christianisme et l'antisémitisme" (1940).
"The Crisis of European Consciousness," in *The Living Church* (February 15, 1948).

II. Secondary Works About Berdyaev

Aubrey, E. E., "The Philosophy of Nicolai Berdyaev," in *Theology Today* (January, 1948).
Bourke, Vernon J., "The Gnosticism of N. Berdyaev," in *Thought* (1936).
Lampert, Evgeny, "Nicolas Berdyaev," in *Modern Christian Revolutionaries,* Donald Attwater, ed. (The Devin-Adair Company, 1947. $4.00).

Lundberg, Ye. G., "Tvorchestvo kak spasenie," in *Mysl i slovo* (1917).

Reymond, Arnold, "Les caractères de la philosophie russe d'après Nicolas Berdiaeff," in *Revue de Théologie et de Philosophie* (April–June, 1946).

Schultze, Bernard, "Die Schau der Kirche bei Nicholas Berdiajew," in *Orientalia Christiana analecta* (Rome, 1938).

Shestov, L., "Nikolai Berdyaev," in *Sovremennyya zapiski* (1938).

Shpakovsky, Anatoly, *Razreshenie sudby chelovyekovskoi* (Novy Sad, Yugoslavia, 1924).

Spinka, Matthew, "Origen and Berdyaev: a Comparison," in *Church History* (March, 1947).

——, "Berdyaev's Critique of Communism," in *The International Review of Missions* (London, July, 1948).

III. General Works on the Modern Religious Situation

Anderson, Paul B., *People, Church and State in Modern Russia* (The Macmillan Company, 1944).

Casey, Robert P., *Religion in Russia* (Harper & Brothers, 1946).

Fedotov, G. P., *I yest i budyet* (Paris, 1932).

Florovski, G., *Puti russkago bogosloviya* (Paris, 1937).

Iswolsky, Hélène, *Soul of Russia* (Sheed & Ward, Inc., 1943).

Jakovenko, Boris, *Dejiny ruské filosofie* (Prague, 1939).

Miliukov, Paul (ed. Michael Karpovich), *Outlines of Russian Culture,* I: Religion and the State (University of Pennsylvania Press, 1942).

Reyburn, H. Y., *The Story of the Russian Church* (London, New York, 1924).

Spinka, Matthew, *The Church and the Russian Revolution* (The Macmillan Company, 1927).

——, *Christianity Confronts Communism* (Harper & Brothers, 1937).

Timasheff, N. S., *Religion in Soviet Russia, 1917–1942* (Sheed & Ward, Inc., 1942).

Zernov, N., *The Church of the Eastern Christians* (The Macmillan Company, 1944).

Zernov, N., *Three Russian Prophets* (The Macmillan Company, 1944).

Zyenkovsky, V. V., *Russkie mysliteli i Evropa* (Paris, n. d.).

IV. Some Russian Religious Thinkers

Arseniev, Nicolas

Arseniev, Nicolas, *Mysticism and the Eastern Church* (London, 1926).

——, *Pravoslavie, Katolichestvo, Protestantizm* (Paris, 1930).

——, *We Beheld His Glory* (London, 1937).

Bulgakov, Sergius

Bulgakov, Sergius, *Na piru bogov* (Sofia, Bulgaria, 1920).

——, *Lestvitsa Iakovlya* (Paris, 1929).

——, *Ikona i ikonopochitanie* (Paris, 1931).

——, *Agnets Bozhii. O bogochelovyechestvye,* I (Paris, 1933).

——, *Social Teaching in Modern Orthodox Theology* (Evanston, 1934).

——, *The Orthodox Church* (London, New York, Milwaukee, 1935).

——, *Utyeshitel. O bogochelovyechestvye,* II (Paris, 1936).

——, *The Wisdom of God* (New York, 1937).

——, *Nevyesta Agntsa. O bogochelovyechestvye,* III (Paris, 1945).

——, *Avtobiograficheskiya zamyetki* (Paris, 1946).

Zander, L. A., *Bog i mir,* 2 vols. (Paris, 1949).

Dostoevsky, F. M.

Dostoevsky, F. M., *Complete Works,* any edition. Particularly, *Brothers Karamazov, The Idiot, Crime and Punishment,* and *The Possessed.*

Losski, N. O., *Dostojevskij a jeho kresťanský svetonáhľad* (Liptovský sv. Mikuláš, Slovakia, 1946).

Metropolitan Antony, *Slovar k tvoreniyam Dostoevskago* (Sofia, Bulgaria, 1921).

Rozanov, V. V., *Legenda o velikom Inkvizitorye* (St. Petersburg, 1906).

Skobtsova, E., *Dostoevsky i sovremennost* (Paris, 1929).

Zander, L. A., *Dostoevsky* (London, 1948).

Frank, S. L.

Frank, S. L., *Krushenie kumirov* (Berlin, 1924).

——, *Smysl zhizni* (Paris, 1925).

——, *Dukhovnyya osnovy obshchestva* (Paris, 1930).

——, *God with Us* (New Haven, Conn., 1946).

Khomyakov, A. S.

Polnoe sobranie sochinenii A. S. Khomyakova, 8 vols. (Moscow, 1900).

Gratieux, A., *A. S. Khomiakov et le Mouvement Slavophile,* 2 vols. (Paris, 1939).

Zernov, N., "Khomyakov," in *Three Russian Prophets* (New York, 1944).
Kiryeevsky, I. V.
Koshelev, A. I., ed., *Polnoe sobranie sochinenii I. V. Kiryeevskago,* 2 vols. (Moscow, 1861).
Losski, N.
Losski, N. *Tipy mirosozertsanii* (Paris, 1931).
——, *Tsyennost i bytie* (Paris, 1931).
——, *Dialekticheski materialism v SSSR* (Paris, 1934).
——, *Chuvstvennaya, intellektual'naya, i misticheskaya intuitsiya* (Paris, 1938).
Solovev, Vladimir S.
Mochulsky, C., *Vladimir Solovev, Zhizn i uchenie* (Paris, 1936).
Sobranie sochinenii V. S. Soloveva, 10 vols. (St. Petersburg, 1901).
Solovev, V., *God, Man and the Church* (Milwaukee, n. d.).
——, *Rossiya i vselenskaya tserkov* (Moscow, 1911).
——, *War and Christianity* (New York, 1915).
——, *The Justification of the Good* (New York, 1918).
——, *La Russie et l'Église universelle* (Paris, 1922, 5th ed.).
——, *On Godmanhood* (New York, 1944).
Strémooukhoff, D., *Vladimir Soloviev et son œuvre messianique* (Paris, 1935).
Trubetskoi, Prince Evgeny, *Mirosozertsanie Vl. S. Soloveva,* 2 vols. (Moscow, n. d.).
Zernov, Nicolas, "Soloviev," in *Three Russian Prophets* (New York, 1944).
Trubetskoi, Prince E. N., *Vospominaniya* (Sofia, Bulgaria, 1922).
——, *Smysl zhizni* (Berlin, 1922).
Trubetskoi, Prince Gregory, *Krasnaya Rossiya i svyataya Rus* (Paris, 1931).

INDEX